North 40

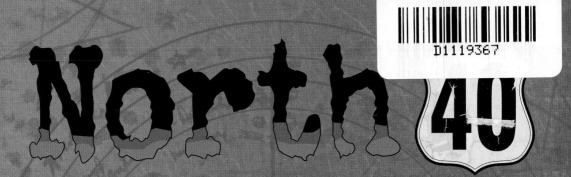

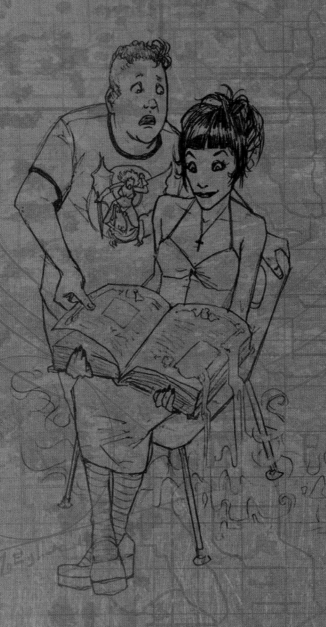

AARON WILLIAMS
WRITER

FIONA STAPLES
ARTIST

ROB LEIGH
LETTERER

Scott Peterson	Editor
Kristy Quinn	Assistant Editor
Ed Roeder	Art Director
Diane Nelson	President
Dan DiDio and Jim Lee	Co-Publishers
Geoff Johns	Chief Creative Officer
John Rood	Executive Vice President– Sales, Marketing and Business Development
Patrick Caldon	Executive Vice President– Finance and Administration
Amy Genkins	Senior VP–Business and Legal Affairs
Steve Rotterdam	Senior VP–Sales and Marketing
John Cunningham	VP–Marketing
Terri Cunningham	VP–Managing Editor
Alison Gill	VP–Manufacturing
David Hyde	VP–Publicity
Hank Kanalz	VP–General Manager, WildStorm
Sue Pohja	VP–Book Trade Sales
Alysse Soll	VP–Advertising and Custom Publishing
Bob Wayne	VP–Sales
Mark Chiarello	Art Director

SUSTAINABLE FORESTRY INITIATIVE
Certified Chain of Custody
Promoting Sustainable
Forest Management
www.sfiprogram.org

NORTH 40, published by WildStorm Productions. 888 Prospect St. #240, La Jolla, CA 92037. Compilation and design sketches copyright © 2010 WildStorm Productions, an imprint of DC Comics. All Rights Reserved. Originally published in single magazine form as NORTH 40 © 2009-2010.

WildStorm and logo, NORTH 40, all characters, the distinctive likenesses thereof and all related elements are trademarks of DC Comics. The stories, characters, and incidents mentioned in this magazine are entirely fictional. Printed on recyclable paper. WildStorm does not read or accept unsolicited submissions of ideas, stories or artwork. Printed by Quad/Graphics, Dubuque, IA, USA. 10/13/10.

DC Comics, a Warner Bros. Entertainment Company

ISBN: 978-1-4012-2849-1

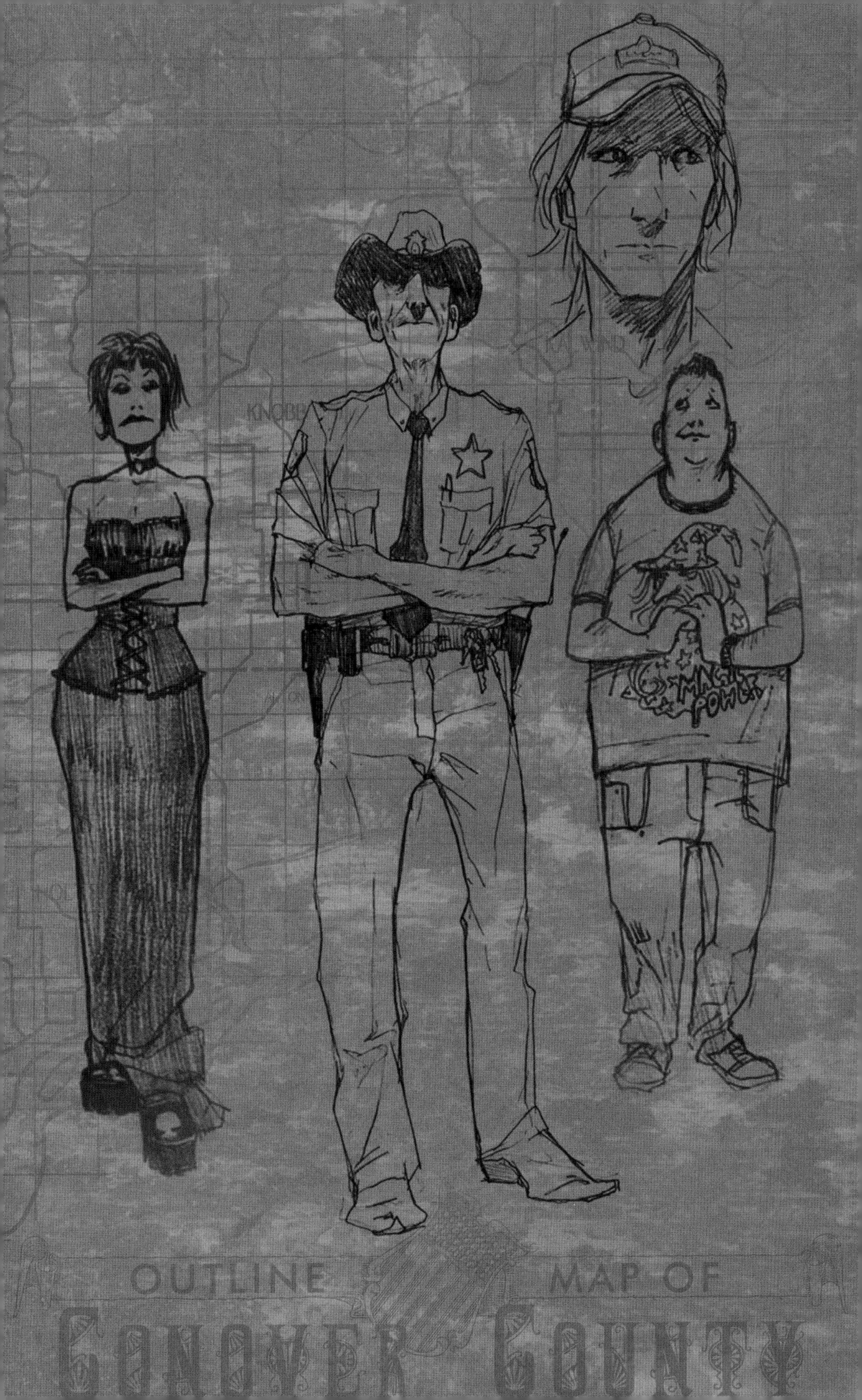
OUTLINE MAP OF
CONOVER COUNTY

CHAPTER ONE
NOW ENTERING CONOVER COUNTY

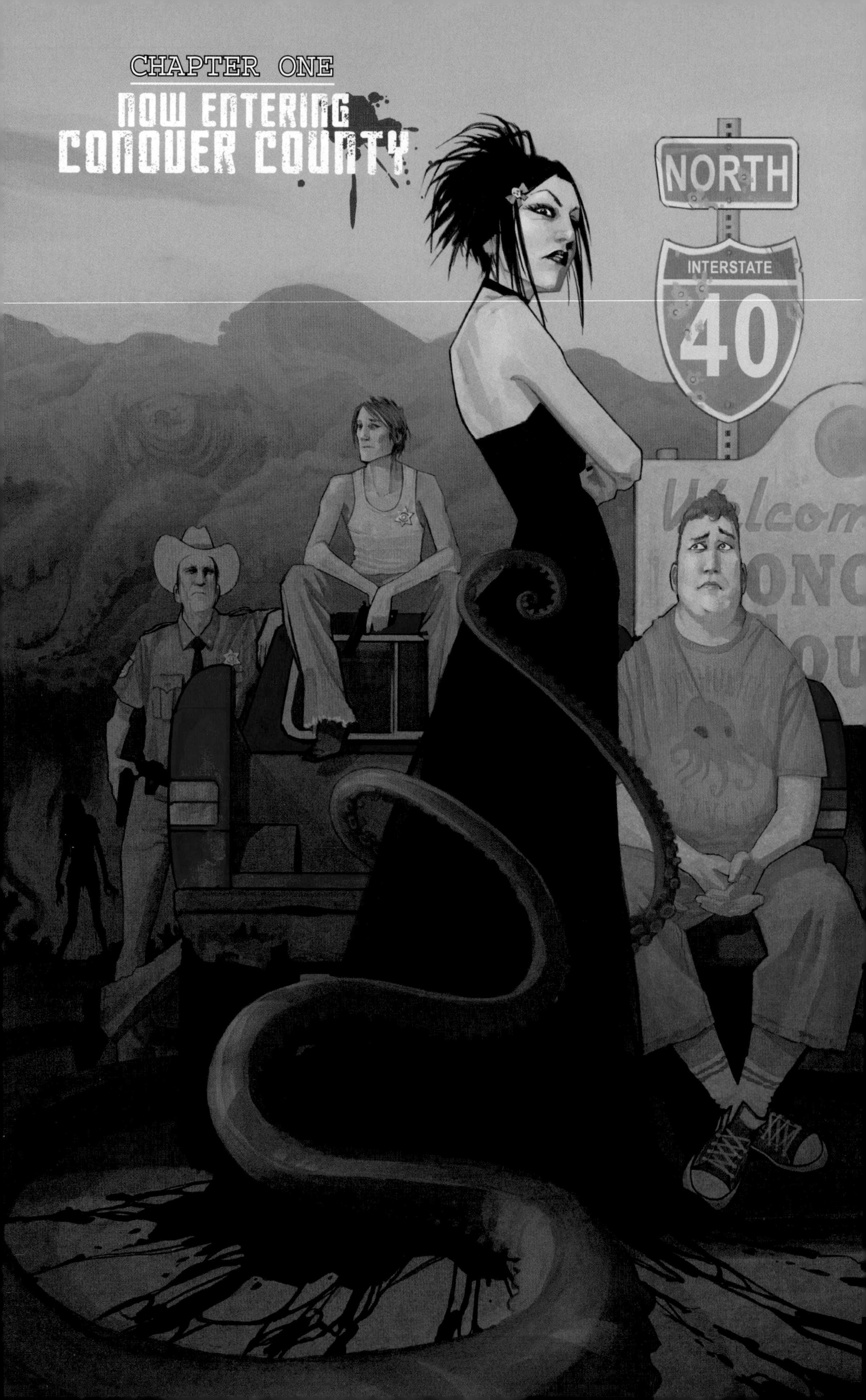
NORTH
INTERSTATE
40

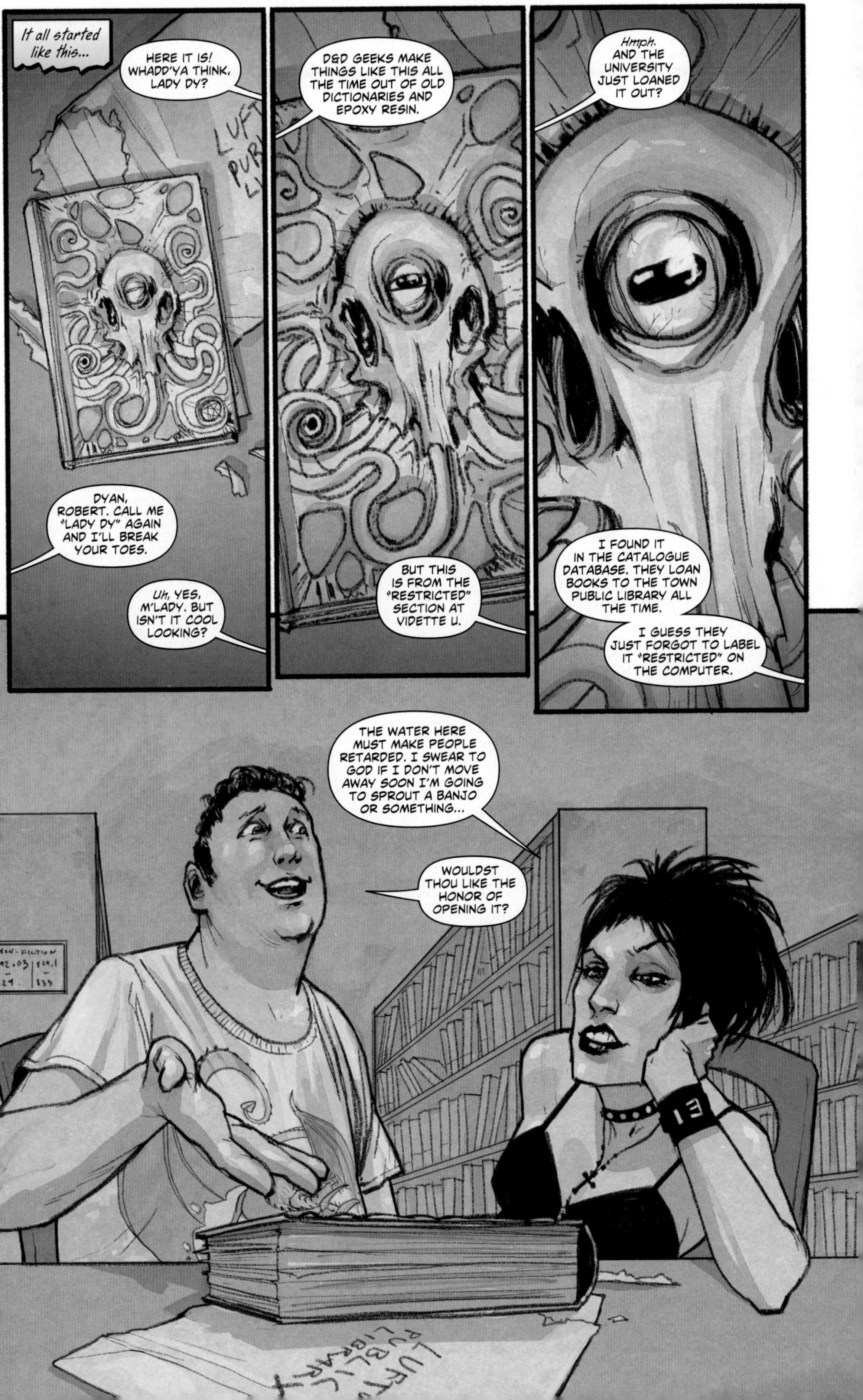
It all started like this...
HERE IT IS! WHADD'YA THINK, LADY DY?
DYAN, ROBERT. CALL ME "LADY DY" AGAIN AND I'LL BREAK YOUR TOES.
Uh, YES, M'LADY. BUT ISN'T IT COOL LOOKING?
D&D GEEKS MAKE THINGS LIKE THIS ALL THE TIME OUT OF OLD DICTIONARIES AND EPOXY RESIN.
BUT THIS IS FROM THE "RESTRICTED" SECTION AT VIDETTE U.
Hmph. AND THE UNIVERSITY JUST LOANED IT OUT?
I FOUND IT IN THE CATALOGUE DATABASE. THEY LOAN BOOKS TO THE TOWN PUBLIC LIBRARY ALL THE TIME.
I GUESS THEY JUST FORGOT TO LABEL IT "RESTRICTED" ON THE COMPUTER.
THE WATER HERE MUST MAKE PEOPLE RETARDED. I SWEAR TO GOD IF I DON'T MOVE AWAY SOON I'M GOING TO SPROUT A BANJO OR SOMETHING...
WOULDST THOU LIKE THE HONOR OF OPENING IT?
NON-FICTION

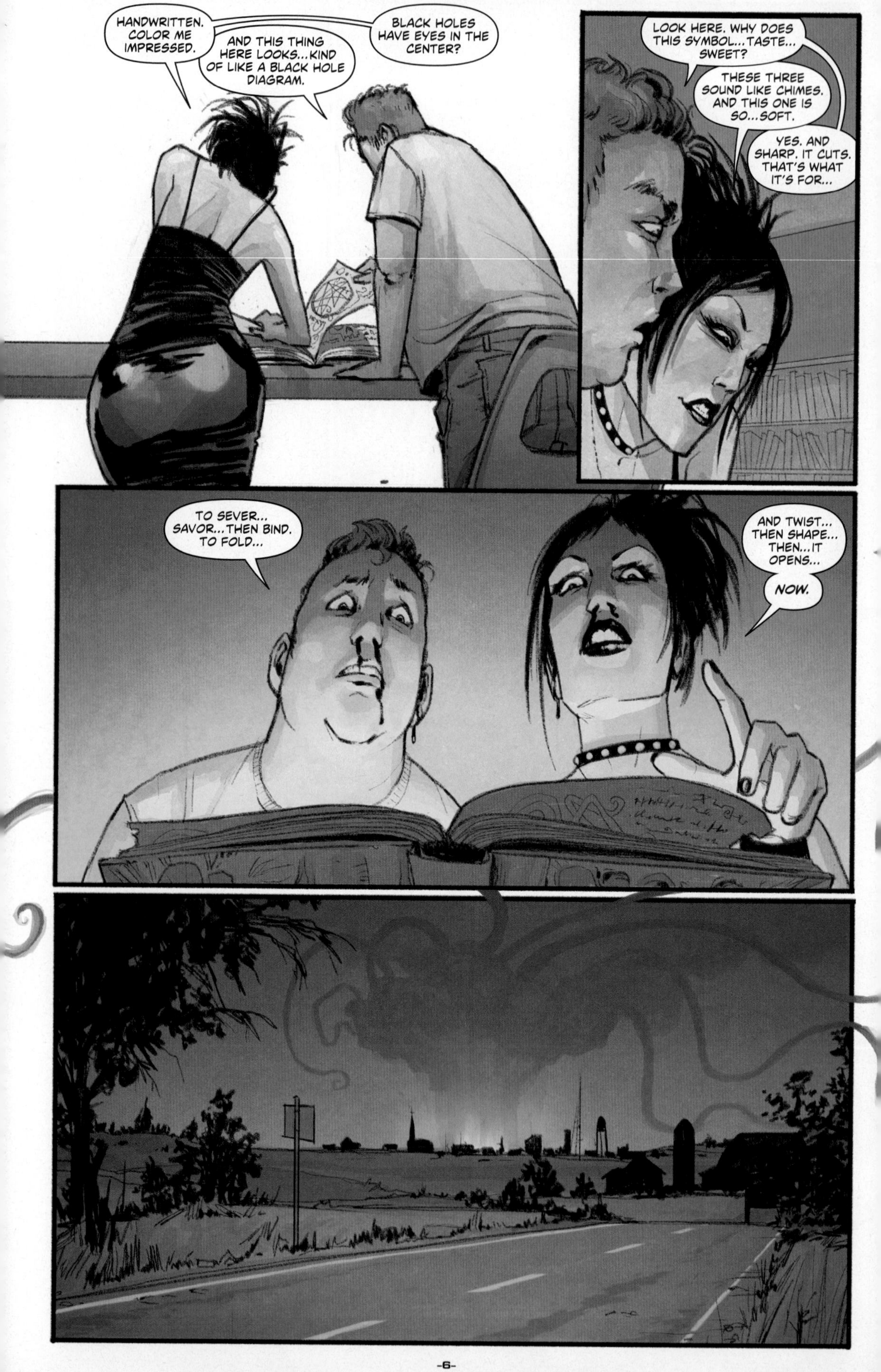
HANDWRITTEN. COLOR ME IMPRESSED.
AND THIS THING HERE LOOKS...KIND OF LIKE A BLACK HOLE DIAGRAM.
BLACK HOLES HAVE EYES IN THE CENTER?
LOOK HERE. WHY DOES THIS SYMBOL...TASTE... SWEET?
THESE THREE SOUND LIKE CHIMES. AND THIS ONE IS SO...SOFT.
YES. AND SHARP. IT CUTS. THAT'S WHAT IT'S FOR...
TO SEVER... SAVOR...THEN BIND. TO FOLD...
AND TWIST... THEN SHAPE... THEN...IT OPENS...
NOW.

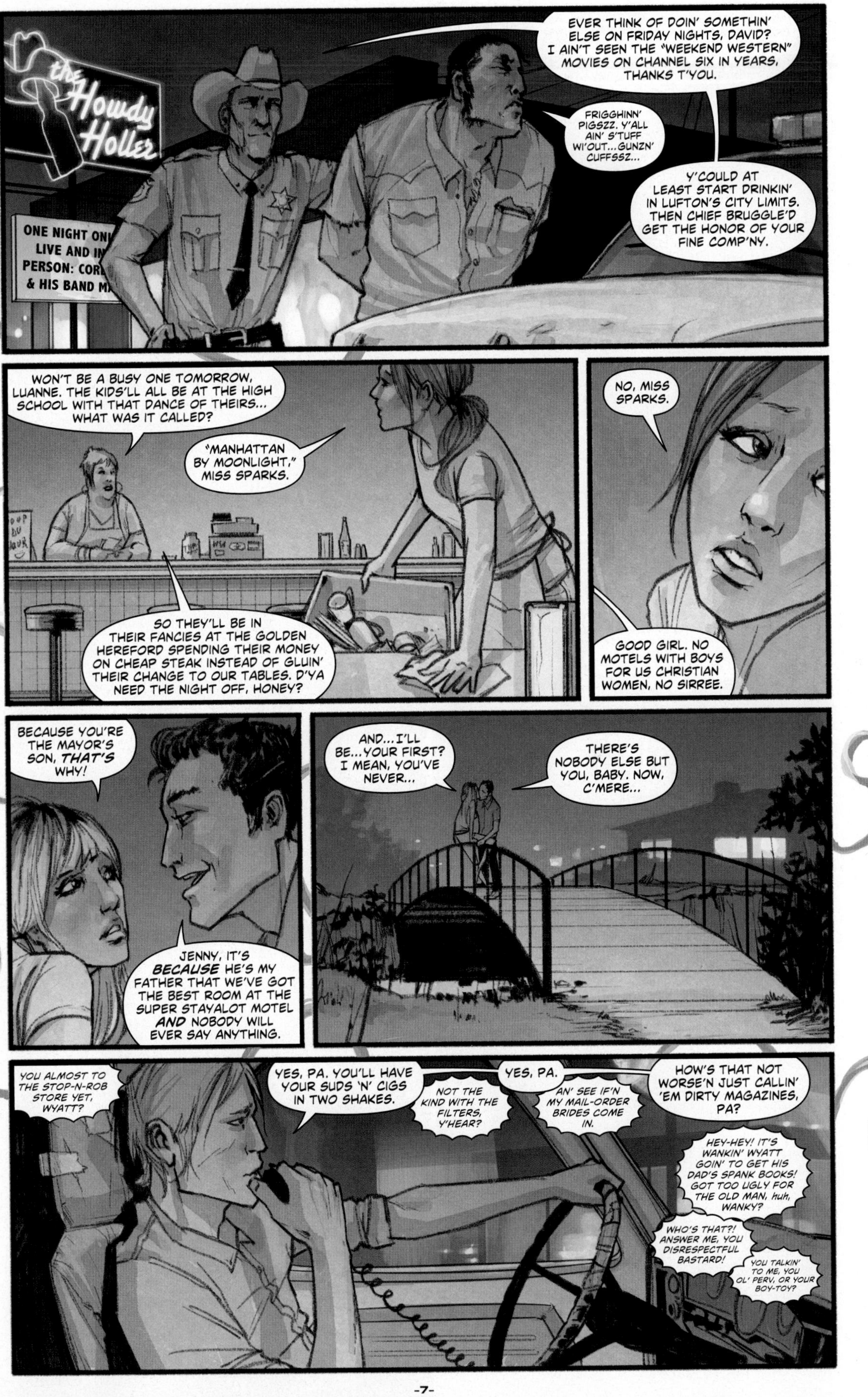
the Howdy Holler
ONE NIGHT ONL LIVE AND IN PERSON: CORD & HIS BAND MA
EVER THINK OF DOIN' SOMETHIN' ELSE ON FRIDAY NIGHTS, DAVID? I AIN'T SEEN THE "WEEKEND WESTERN" MOVIES ON CHANNEL SIX IN YEARS, THANKS T'YOU.
FRIGGHINN' PIGSZZ. Y'ALL AIN' S'TUFF WI'OUT...GUNZN' CUFFSSZ...
Y'COULD AT LEAST START DRINKIN' IN LUFTON'S CITY LIMITS. THEN CHIEF BRUGGLE'D GET THE HONOR OF YOUR FINE COMP'NY.
WON'T BE A BUSY ONE TOMORROW, LUANNE. THE KIDS'LL ALL BE AT THE HIGH SCHOOL WITH THAT DANCE OF THEIRS... WHAT WAS IT CALLED?
"MANHATTAN BY MOONLIGHT," MISS SPARKS.
SO THEY'LL BE IN THEIR FANCIES AT THE GOLDEN HEREFORD SPENDING THEIR MONEY ON CHEAP STEAK INSTEAD OF GLUIN' THEIR CHANGE TO OUR TABLES. D'YA NEED THE NIGHT OFF, HONEY?
NO, MISS SPARKS.
GOOD GIRL. NO MOTELS WITH BOYS FOR US CHRISTIAN WOMEN, NO SIRREE.
BECAUSE YOU'RE THE MAYOR'S SON, *THAT'S* WHY!
JENNY, IT'S *BECAUSE* HE'S MY FATHER THAT WE'VE GOT THE BEST ROOM AT THE SUPER STAYALOT MOTEL *AND* NOBODY WILL EVER SAY ANYTHING.
AND...I'LL BE...YOUR FIRST? I MEAN, YOU'VE NEVER...
THERE'S NOBODY ELSE BUT YOU, BABY. NOW, C'MERE...
YOU ALMOST TO THE STOP-N-ROB STORE YET, WYATT?
YES, PA. YOU'LL HAVE YOUR SUDS 'N' CIGS IN TWO SHAKES.
NOT THE KIND WITH THE FILTERS, Y'HEAR?
YES, PA.
AN' SEE IF'N MY MAIL-ORDER BRIDES COME IN.
HOW'S THAT NOT WORSE'N JUST CALLIN' 'EM DIRTY MAGAZINES, PA?
HEY-HEY! IT'S WANKIN' WYATT GOIN' TO GET HIS DAD'S SPANK BOOKS! GOT TOO UGLY FOR THE OLD MAN, huh, WANKY?
WHO'S THAT?! ANSWER ME, YOU DISRESPECTFUL BASTARD!
YOU TALKIN' TO ME, YOU OL' PERV, OR YOUR BOY-TOY?

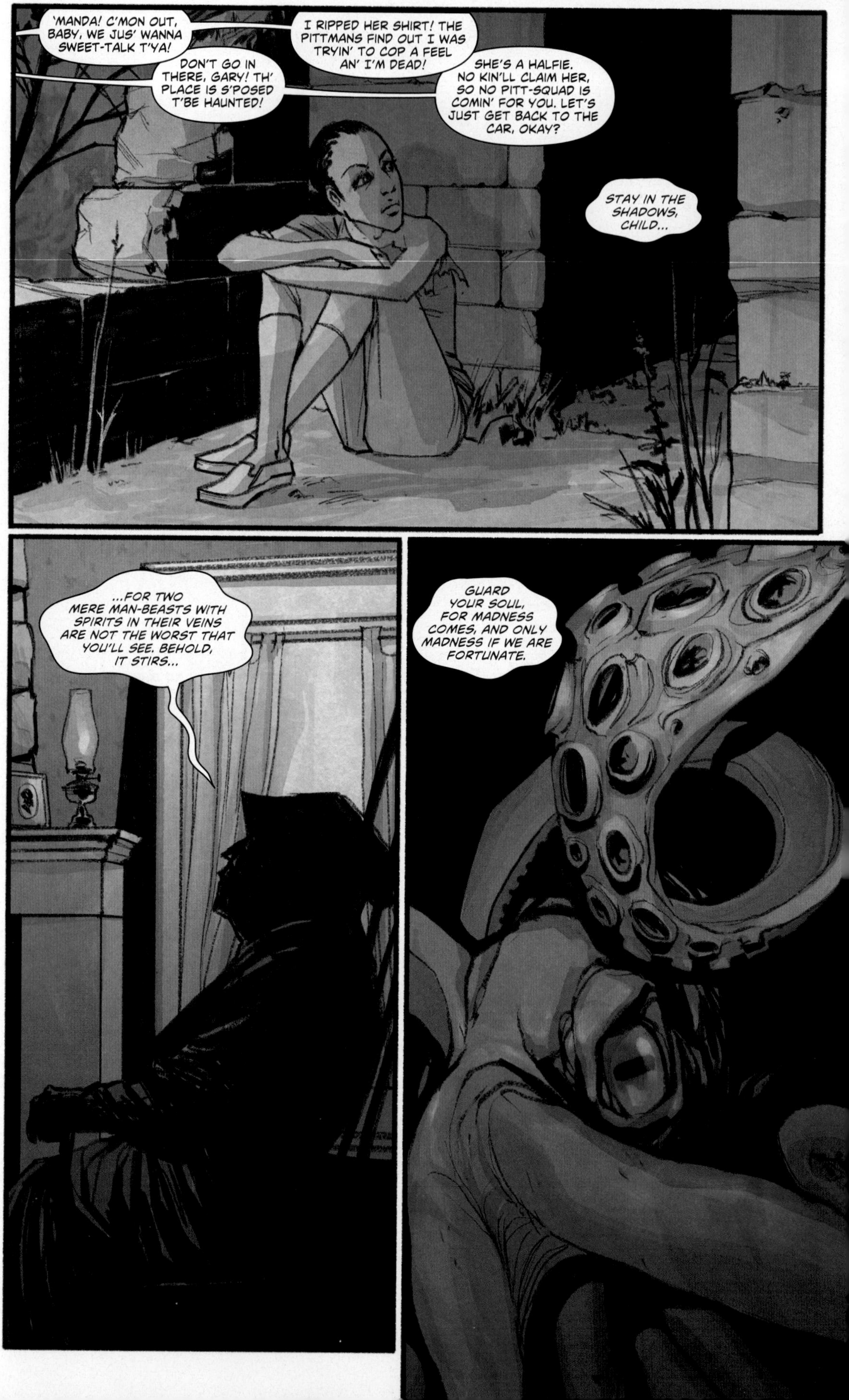
'MANDA! C'MON OUT, BABY, WE JUS' WANNA SWEET-TALK T'YA!
DON'T GO IN THERE, GARY! TH' PLACE IS S'POSED T'BE HAUNTED!
I RIPPED HER SHIRT! THE PITTMANS FIND OUT I WAS TRYIN' TO COP A FEEL AN' I'M DEAD!
SHE'S A HALFIE. NO KIN'LL CLAIM HER, SO NO PITT-SQUAD IS COMIN' FOR YOU. LET'S JUST GET BACK TO THE CAR, OKAY?
STAY IN THE SHADOWS, CHILD...
...FOR TWO MERE MAN-BEASTS WITH SPIRITS IN THEIR VEINS ARE NOT THE WORST THAT YOU'LL SEE. BEHOLD, IT STIRS...
GUARD YOUR SOUL, FOR MADNESS COMES, AND ONLY MADNESS IF WE ARE FORTUNATE.

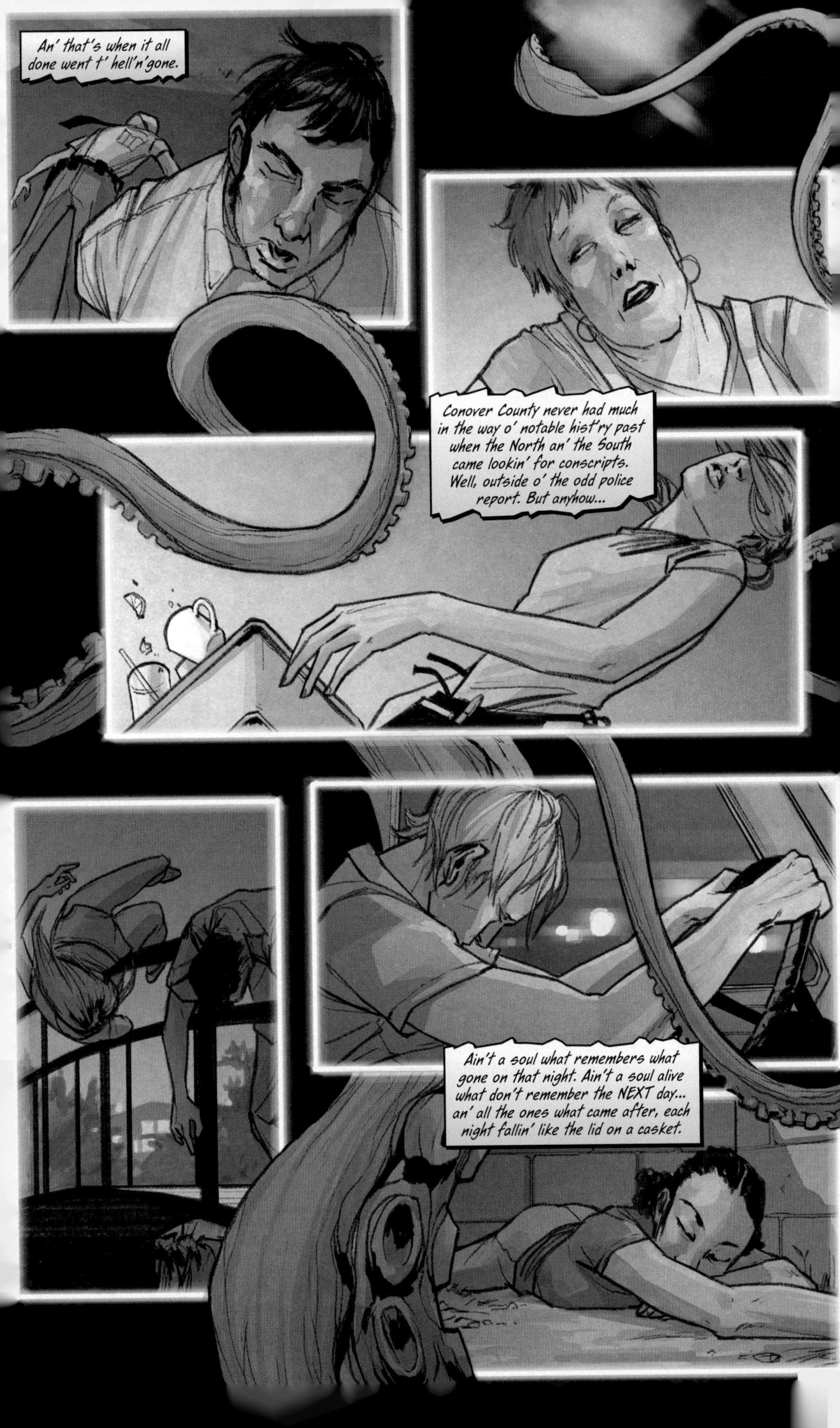
An' that's when it all done went t' hell'n'gone.
Conover County never had much in the way o' notable hist'ry past when the North an' the South came lookin' for conscripts. Well, outside o' the odd police report. But anyhow...
Ain't a soul what remembers what gone on that night. Ain't a soul alive what don't remember the NEXT day... an' all the ones what came after, each night fallin' like the lid on a casket.

It done picked up the next day at exactly 6:33 in the A.M.

LUFTON PUBLIC LIBRARY

NOBODY BETTER BE BRAGGIN' THEY HIT ME FROM BEHIND...

WHAT THE--?

the Howdy Holler

ONE NIGHT ON
LIVE AND I
PERSON: C
& HIS BA

DAVE AIN'T *THAT* STRONG, EVEN LIT UP LIKE--

AAIEEEEEE!

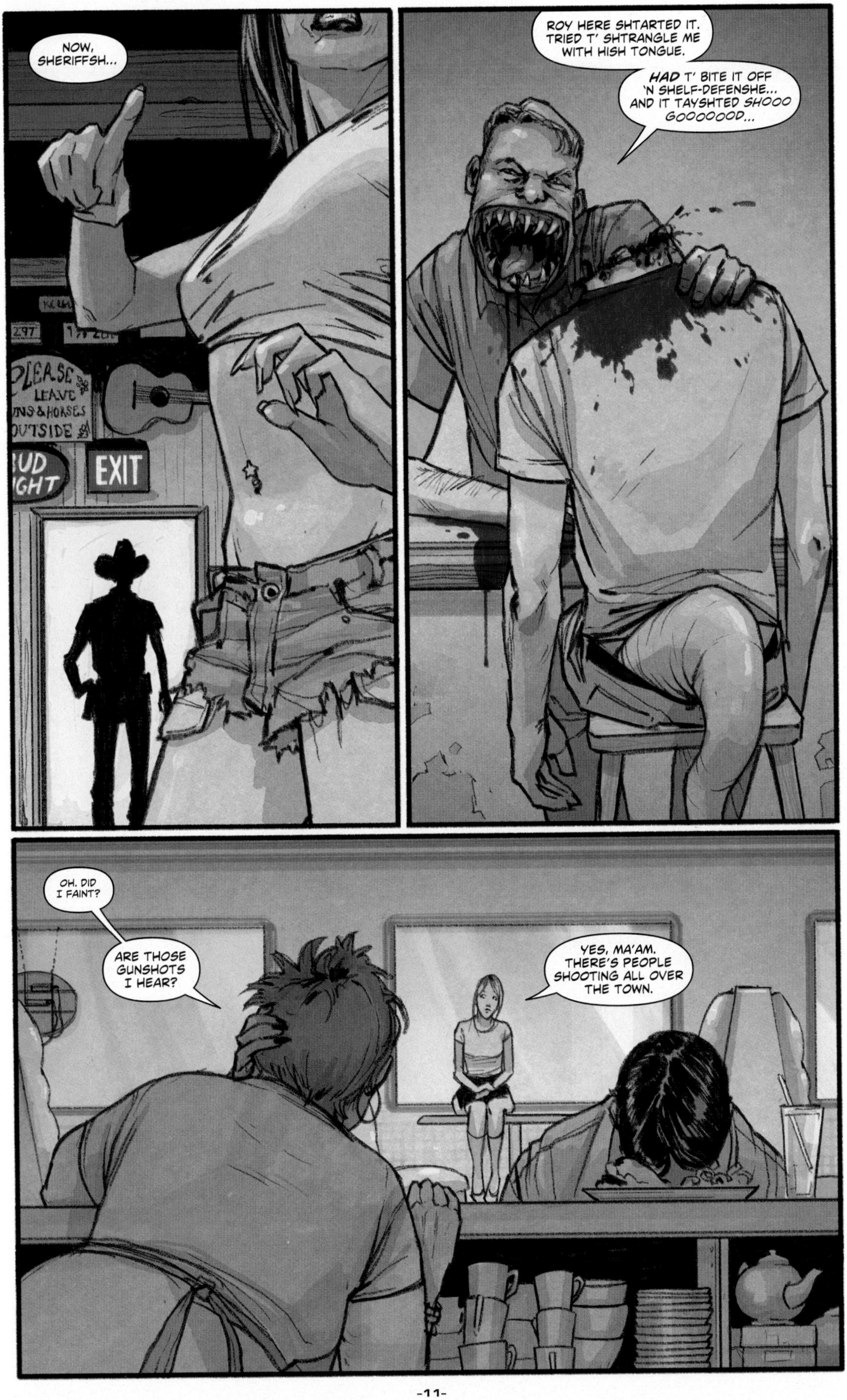
NOW, SHERIFFSH...
PLEASE LEAVE GUNS & HORSES OUTSIDE
EXIT
ROY HERE SHTARTED IT. TRIED T' SHTRANGLE ME WITH HISH TONGUE.
HAD T' BITE IT OFF 'N SHELF-DEFENSHE... AND IT TAYSHTED SHOOO GOOOOOOD...
OH. DID I FAINT?
ARE THOSE GUNSHOTS I HEAR?
YES, MA'AM. THERE'S PEOPLE SHOOTING ALL OVER THE TOWN.

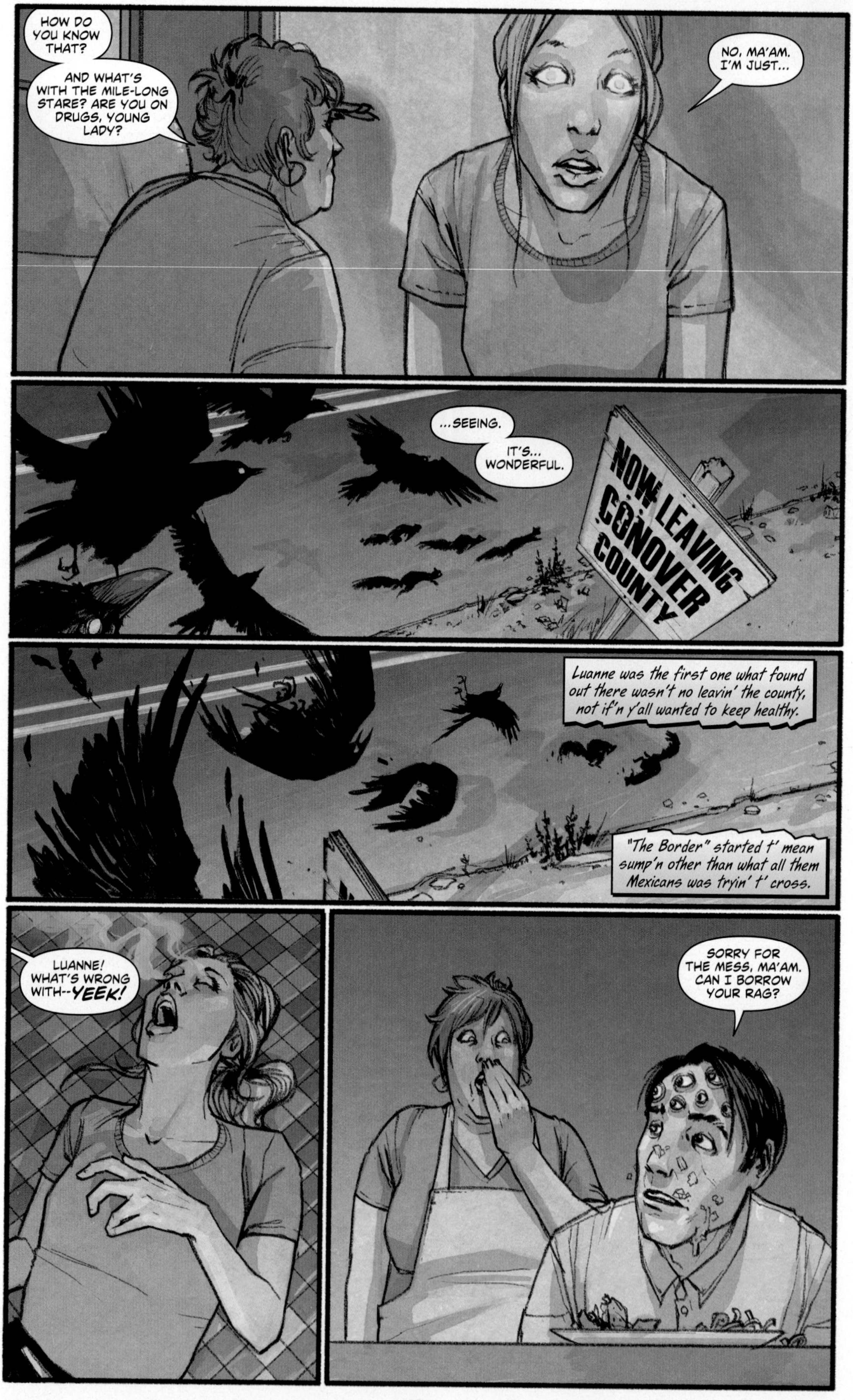
HOW DO YOU KNOW THAT?
AND WHAT'S WITH THE MILE-LONG STARE? ARE YOU ON DRUGS, YOUNG LADY?
NO, MA'AM. I'M JUST...
...SEEING.
IT'S... WONDERFUL.
NOW LEAVING CONOVER COUNTY
Luanne was the first one what found out there wasn't no leavin' the county, not if'n y'all wanted to keep healthy.
"The Border" started t' mean sump'n other than what all them Mexicans was tryin' t' cross.
LUANNE! WHAT'S WRONG WITH--YEEK!
SORRY FOR THE MESS, MA'AM. CAN I BORROW YOUR RAG?

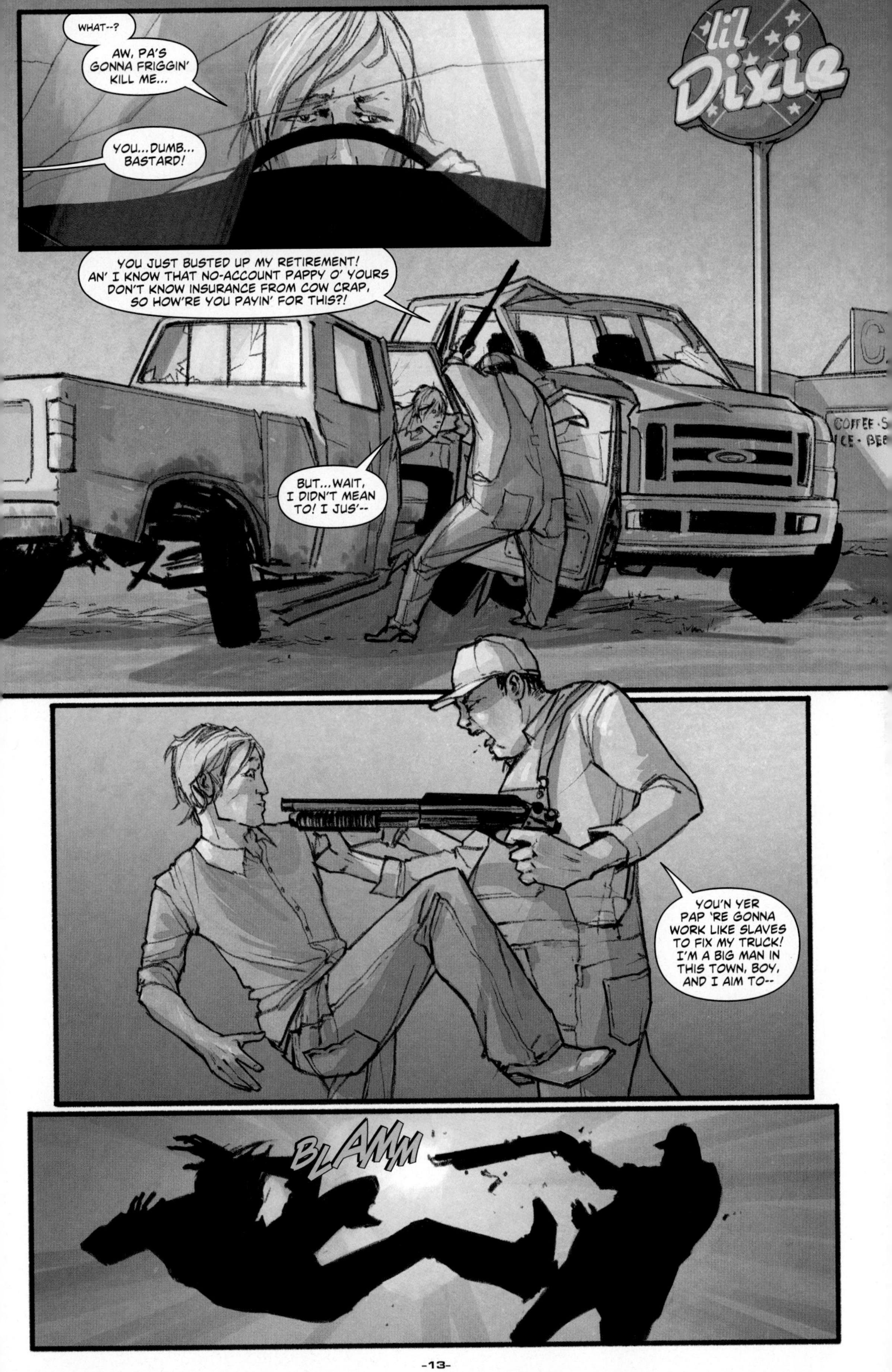
WHAT--?
AW, PA'S GONNA FRIGGIN' KILL ME...
YOU...DUMB... BASTARD!
li'l Dixie
YOU JUST BUSTED UP MY RETIREMENT! AN' I KNOW THAT NO-ACCOUNT PAPPY O' YOURS DON'T KNOW INSURANCE FROM COW CRAP, SO HOW'RE YOU PAYIN' FOR THIS?!
BUT...WAIT, I DIDN'T MEAN TO! I JUS'--
YOU'N YER PAP 'RE GONNA WORK LIKE SLAVES TO FIX MY TRUCK! I'M A BIG MAN IN THIS TOWN, BOY, AND I AIM TO--
BLAMM

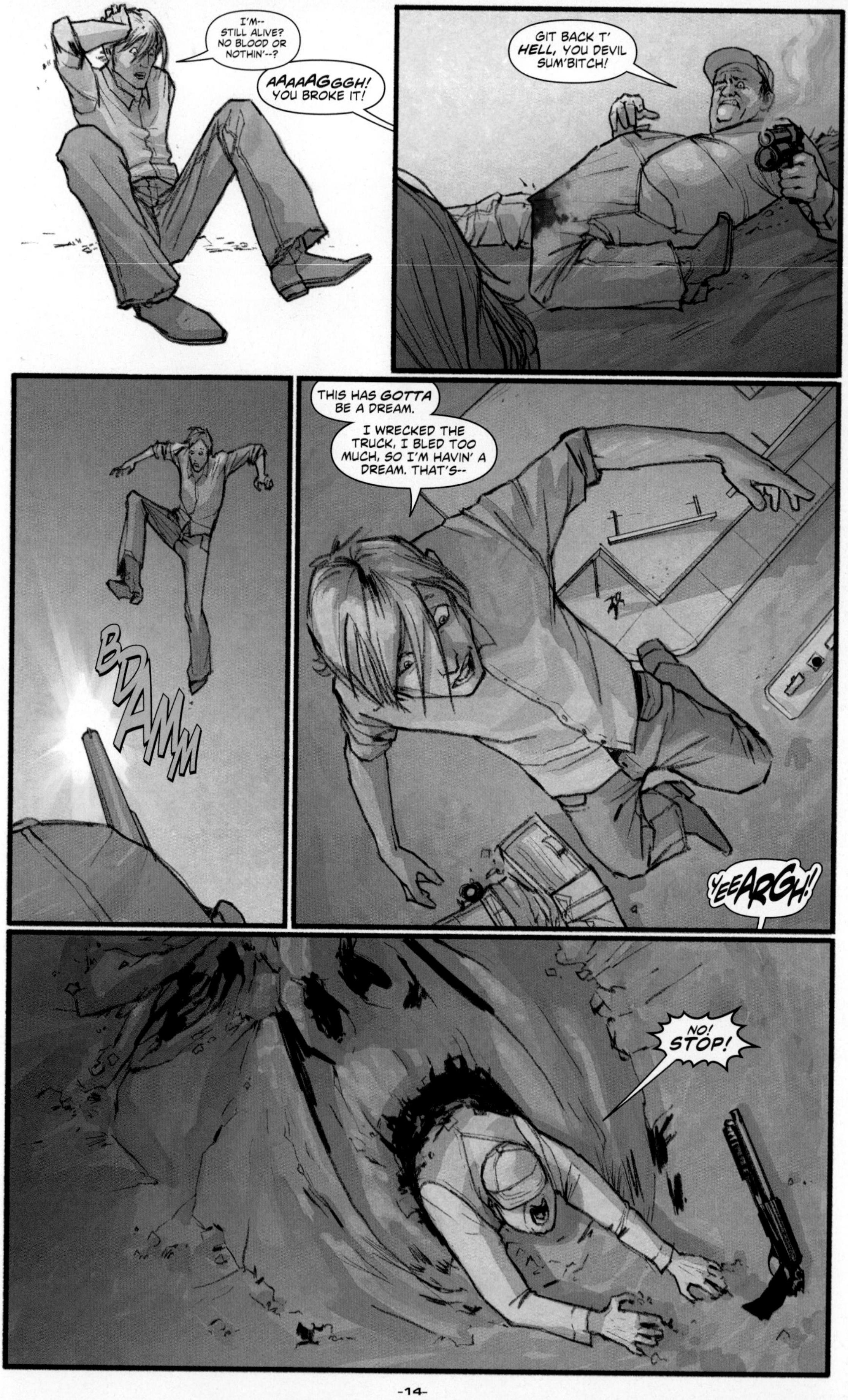
I'M-- STILL ALIVE? NO BLOOD OR NOTHIN'--?
AAAAAGGGH! YOU BROKE IT!
GIT BACK T' HELL, YOU DEVIL SUM'BITCH!
BDAMM
THIS HAS GOTTA BE A DREAM.
I WRECKED THE TRUCK, I BLED TOO MUCH, SO I'M HAVIN' A DREAM. THAT'S--
YEEARGH!
NO! STOP!

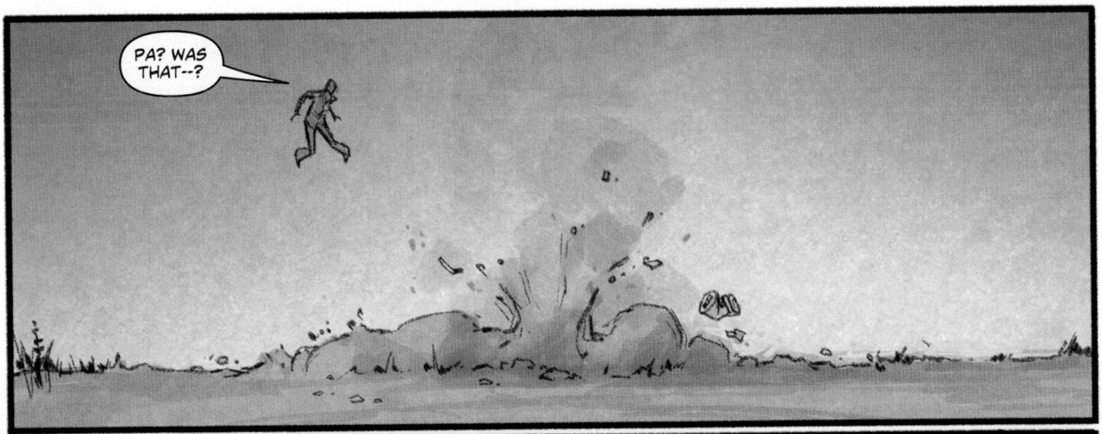
PA? WAS THAT--?

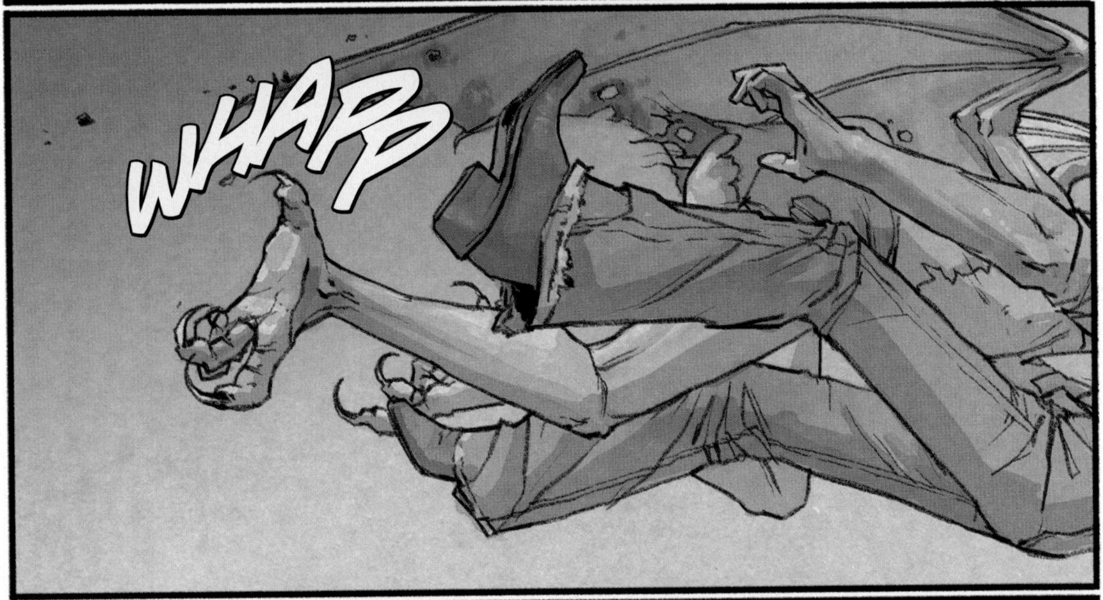
WHAPP

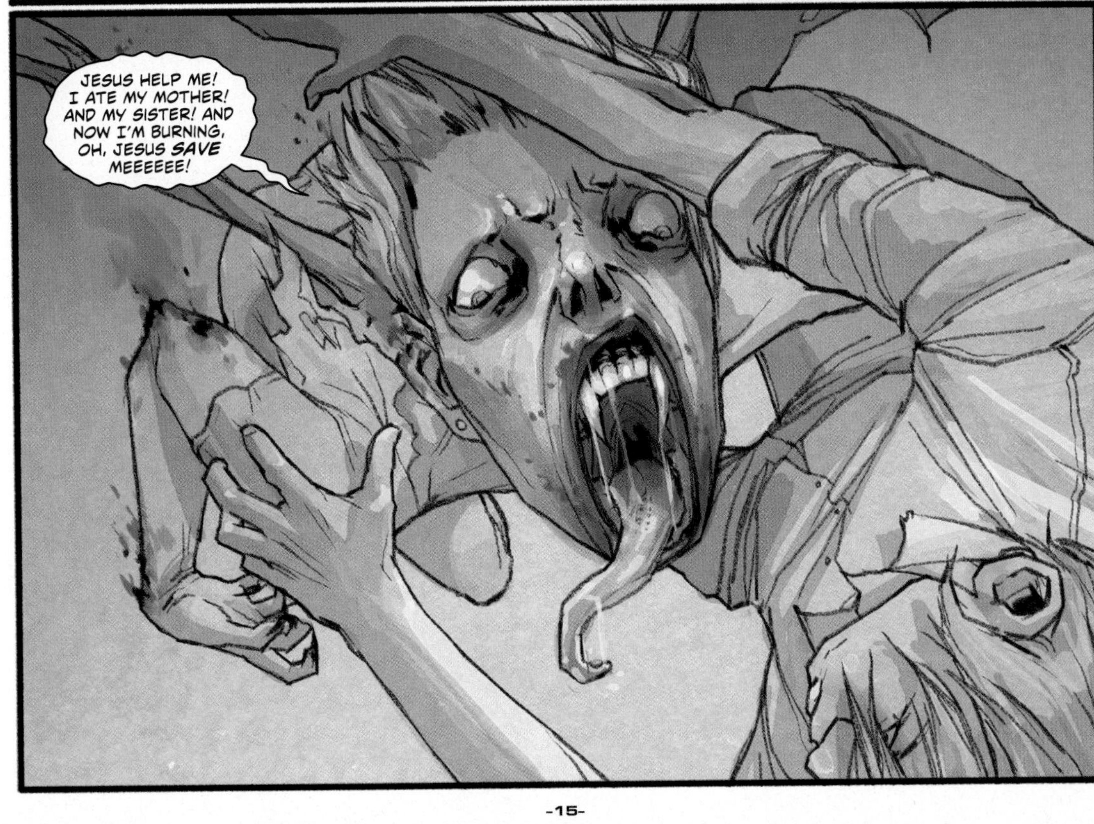
JESUS HELP ME! I ATE MY MOTHER! AND MY SISTER! AND NOW I'M BURNING, OH, JESUS *SAVE* MEEEEEE!

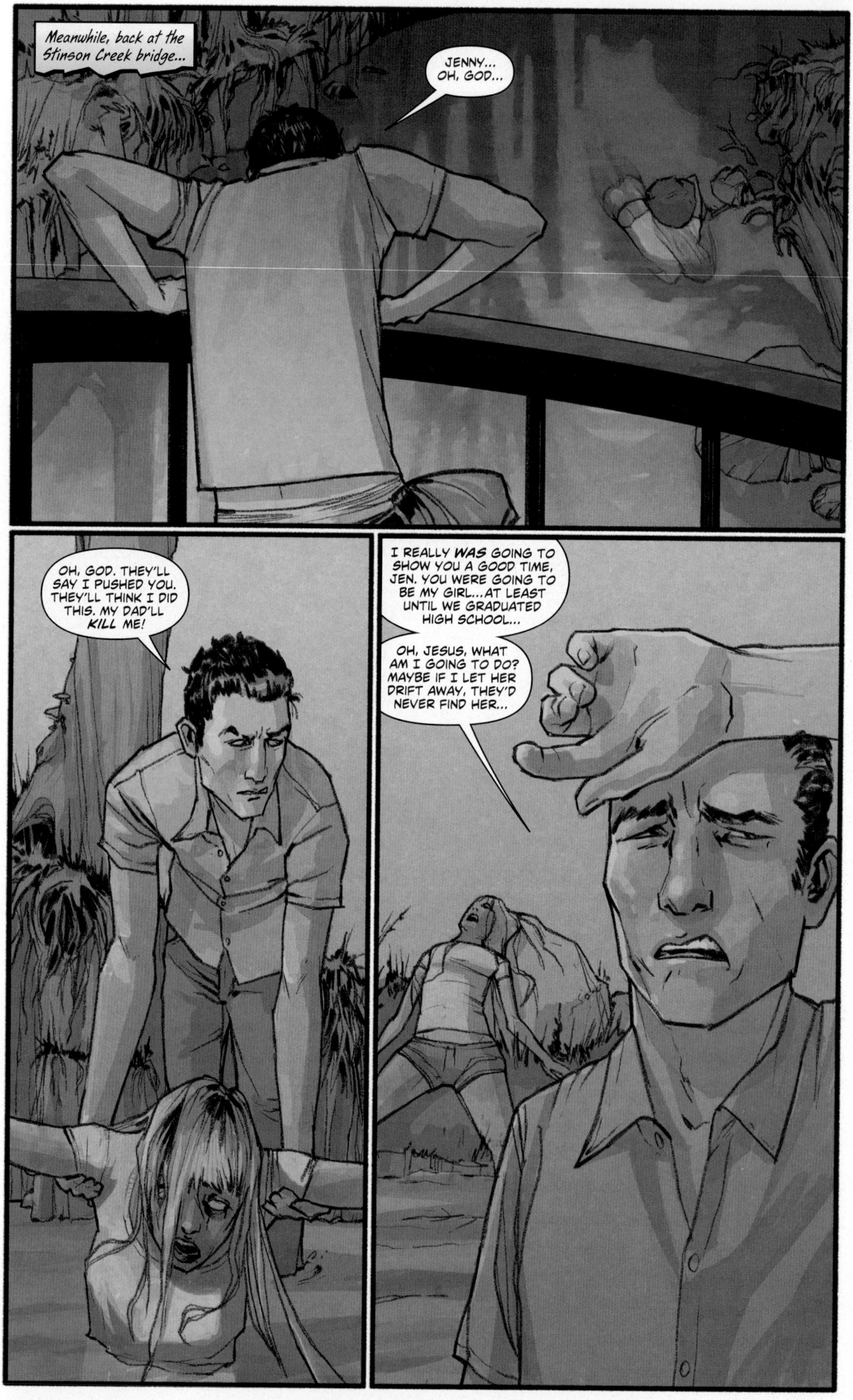
Meanwhile, back at the Stinson Creek bridge...
JENNY... OH, GOD...
OH, GOD. THEY'LL SAY I PUSHED YOU. THEY'LL THINK I DID THIS. MY DAD'LL KILL ME!
I REALLY WAS GOING TO SHOW YOU A GOOD TIME, JEN. YOU WERE GOING TO BE MY GIRL...AT LEAST UNTIL WE GRADUATED HIGH SCHOOL...
OH, JESUS, WHAT AM I GOING TO DO? MAYBE IF I LET HER DRIFT AWAY, THEY'D NEVER FIND HER...

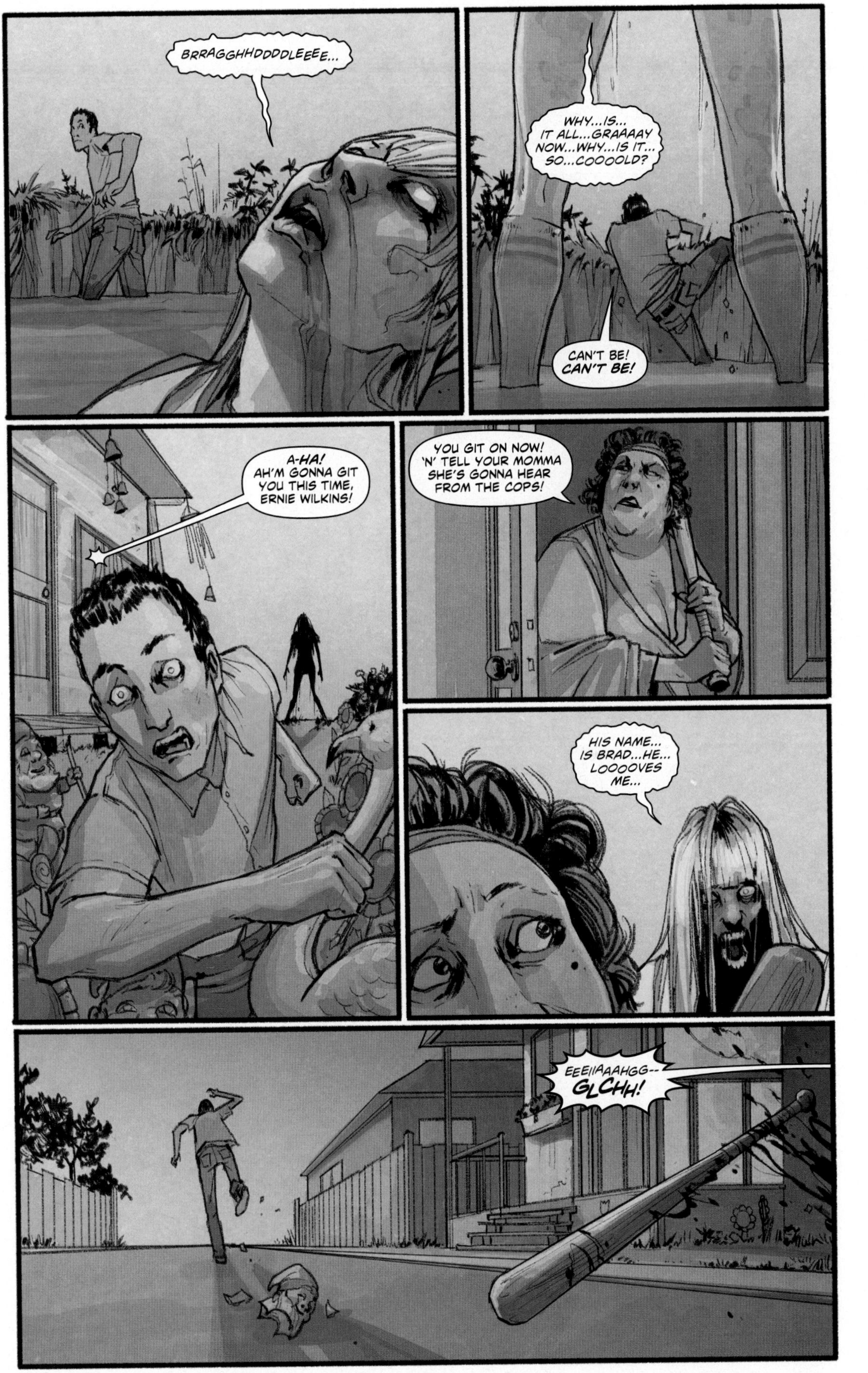
BRRAGGHHDDDDLEEEE...
WHY...IS... IT ALL...GRAAAAY NOW...WHY...IS IT... SO...COOOOLD?
CAN'T BE! CAN'T BE!
A-HA! AH'M GONNA GIT YOU THIS TIME, ERNIE WILKINS!
YOU GIT ON NOW! 'N' TELL YOUR MOMMA SHE'S GONNA HEAR FROM THE COPS!
HIS NAME... IS BRAD...HE... LOOOOVES ME...
EEEIIAAAHGG-- GLCHH!

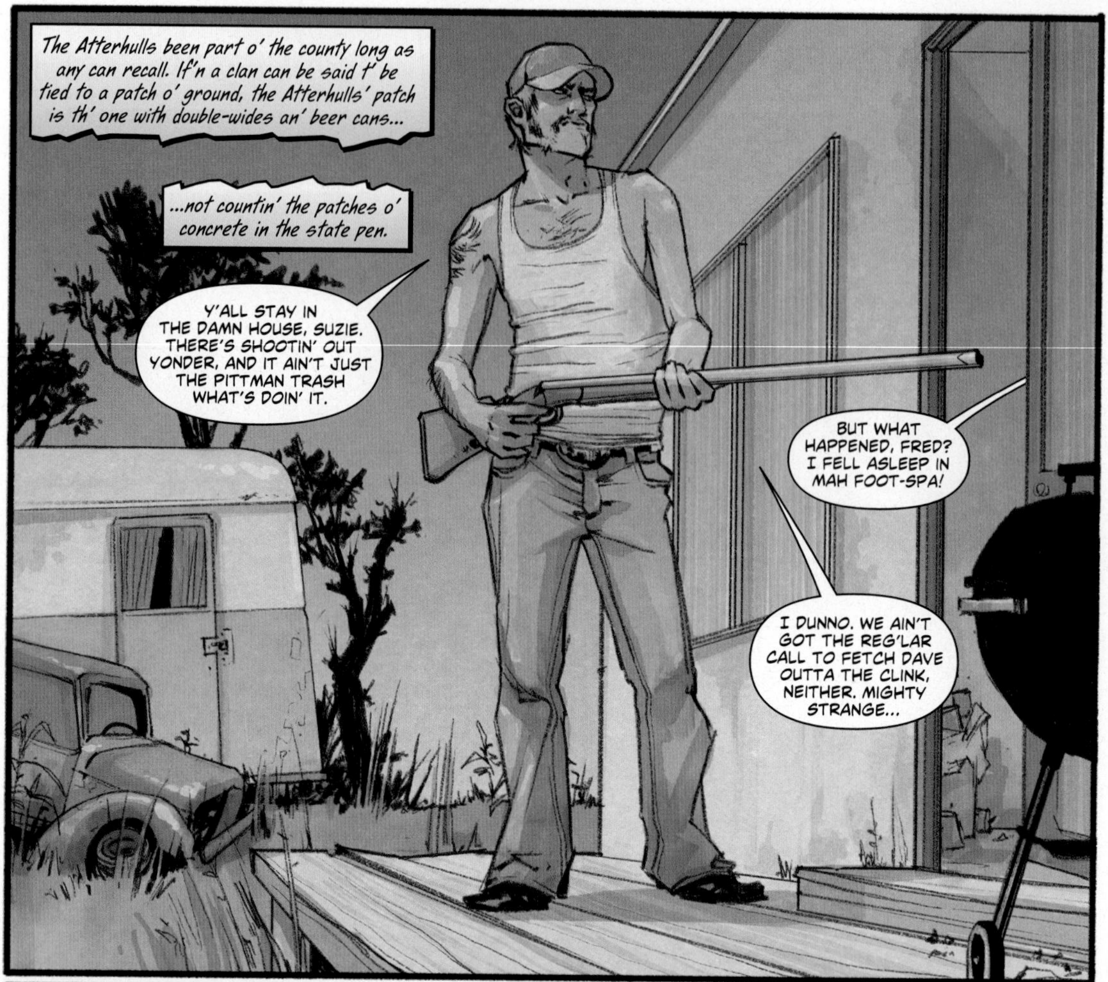
The Atterhulls been part o' the county long as any can recall. If'n a clan can be said t' be tied to a patch o' ground, the Atterhulls' patch is th' one with double-wides an' beer cans...
...not countin' the patches o' concrete in the state pen.
Y'ALL STAY IN THE DAMN HOUSE, SUZIE. THERE'S SHOOTIN' OUT YONDER, AND IT AIN'T JUST THE PITTMAN TRASH WHAT'S DOIN' IT.
BUT WHAT HAPPENED, FRED? I FELL ASLEEP IN MAH FOOT-SPA!
I DUNNO. WE AIN'T GOT THE REG'LAR CALL TO FETCH DAVE OUTTA THE CLINK, NEITHER. MIGHTY STRANGE...

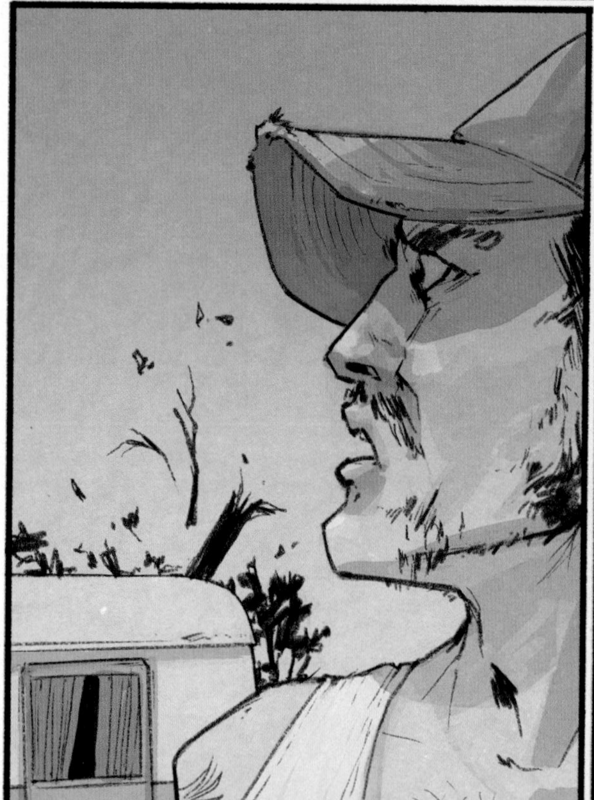

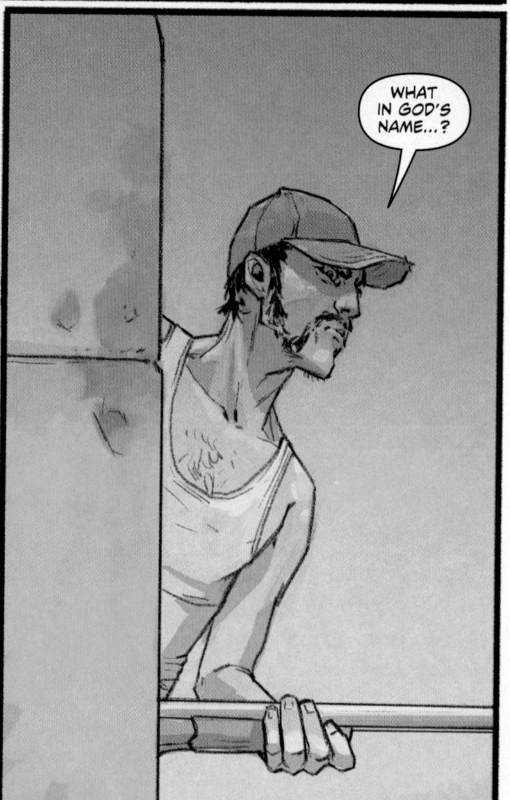
WHAT IN GOD'S NAME...?

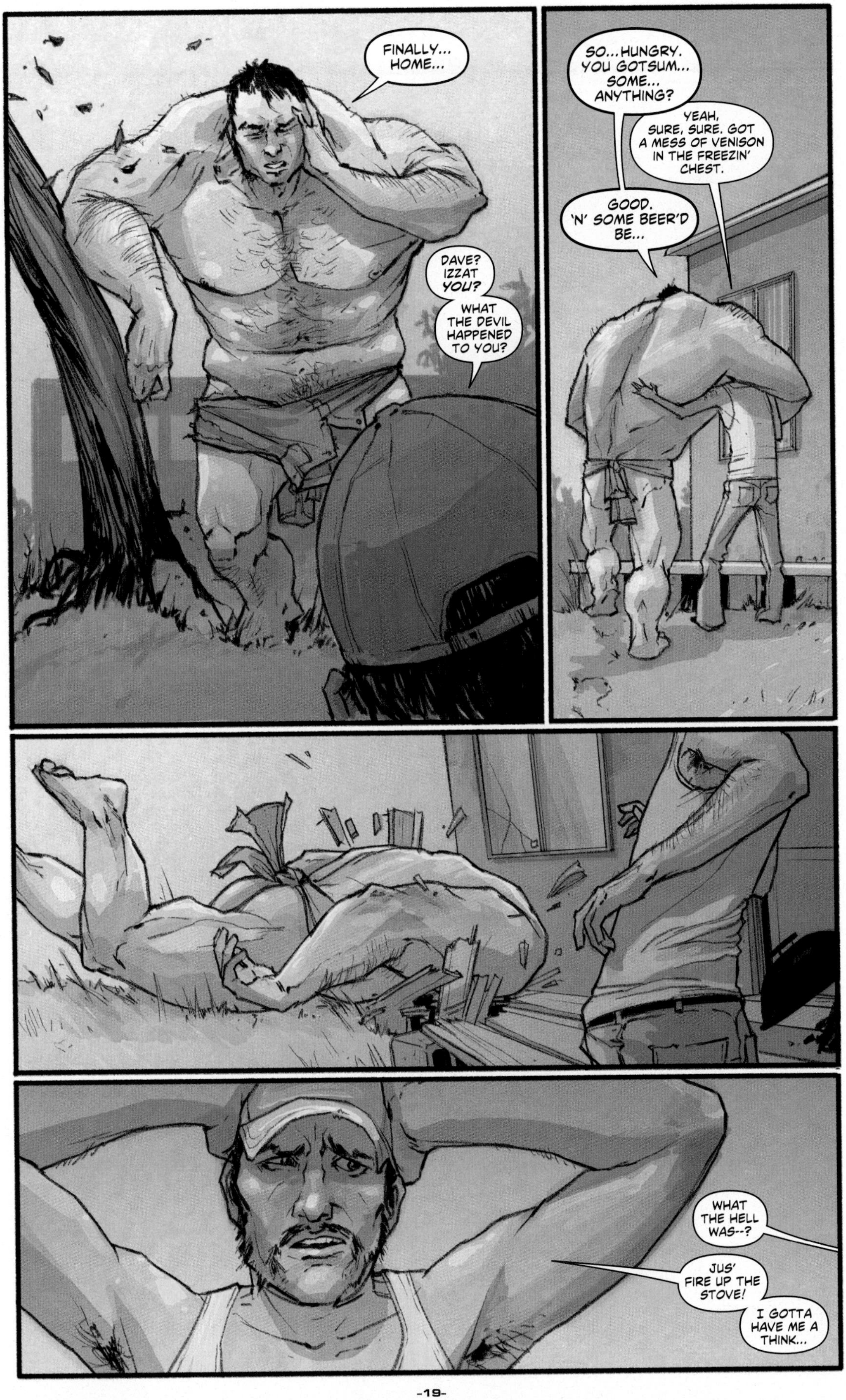
FINALLY... HOME...
DAVE? IZZAT YOU?
WHAT THE DEVIL HAPPENED TO YOU?
SO... HUNGRY. YOU GOTSUM... SOME... ANYTHING?
YEAH, SURE, SURE. GOT A MESS OF VENISON IN THE FREEZIN' CHEST.
GOOD. 'N' SOME BEER'D BE...
WHAT THE HELL WAS--?
JUS' FIRE UP THE STOVE!
I GOTTA HAVE ME A THINK...

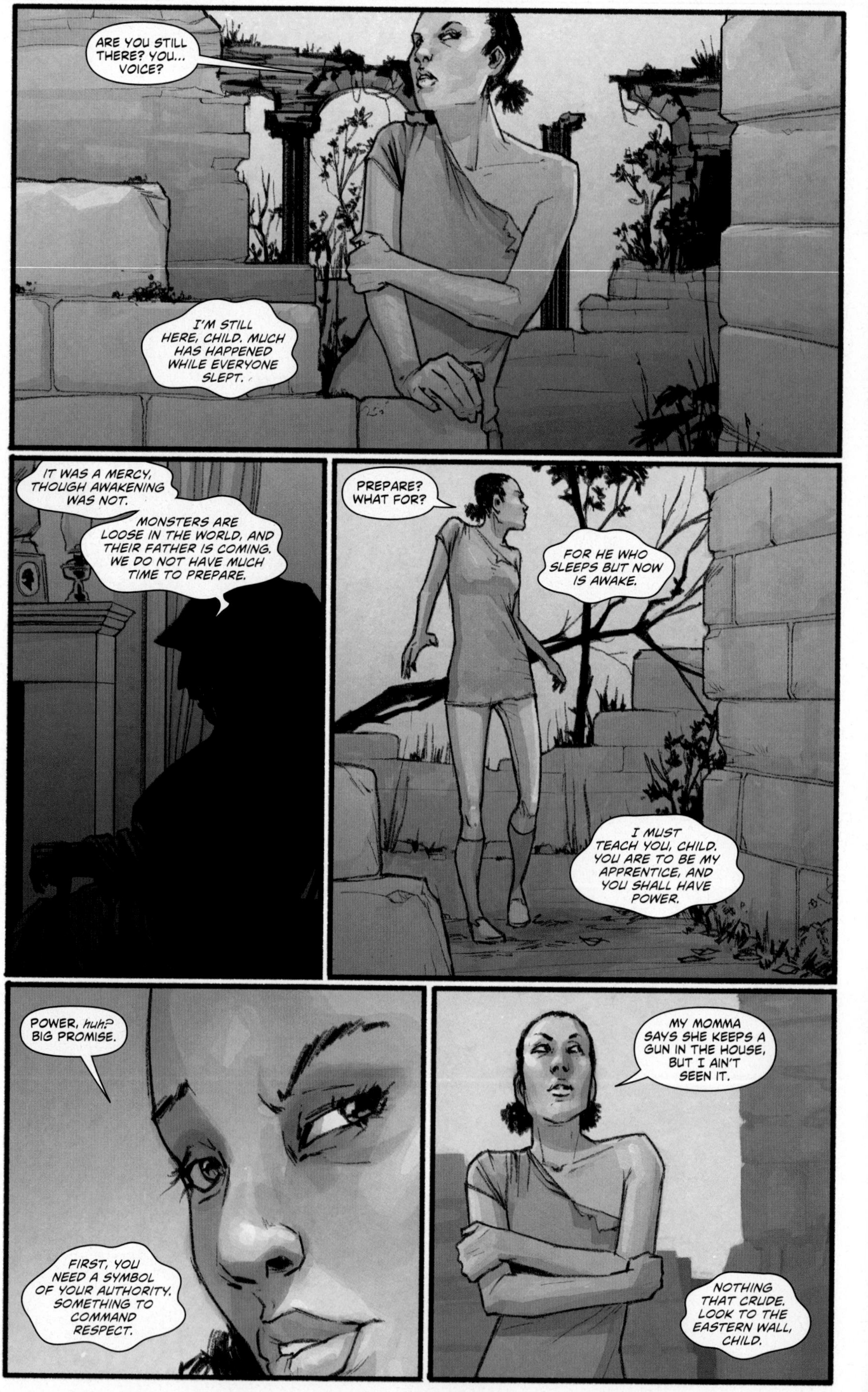
ARE YOU STILL THERE? YOU... VOICE?
I'M STILL HERE, CHILD. MUCH HAS HAPPENED WHILE EVERYONE SLEPT.
IT WAS A MERCY, THOUGH AWAKENING WAS NOT.
MONSTERS ARE LOOSE IN THE WORLD, AND THEIR FATHER IS COMING. WE DO NOT HAVE MUCH TIME TO PREPARE.
PREPARE? WHAT FOR?
FOR HE WHO SLEEPS BUT NOW IS AWAKE.
I MUST TEACH YOU, CHILD. YOU ARE TO BE MY APPRENTICE, AND YOU SHALL HAVE POWER.
POWER, *huh?* BIG PROMISE.
FIRST, YOU NEED A SYMBOL OF YOUR AUTHORITY. SOMETHING TO COMMAND RESPECT.
MY MOMMA SAYS SHE KEEPS A GUN IN THE HOUSE, BUT I AIN'T SEEN IT.
NOTHING THAT CRUDE. LOOK TO THE EASTERN WALL, CHILD.

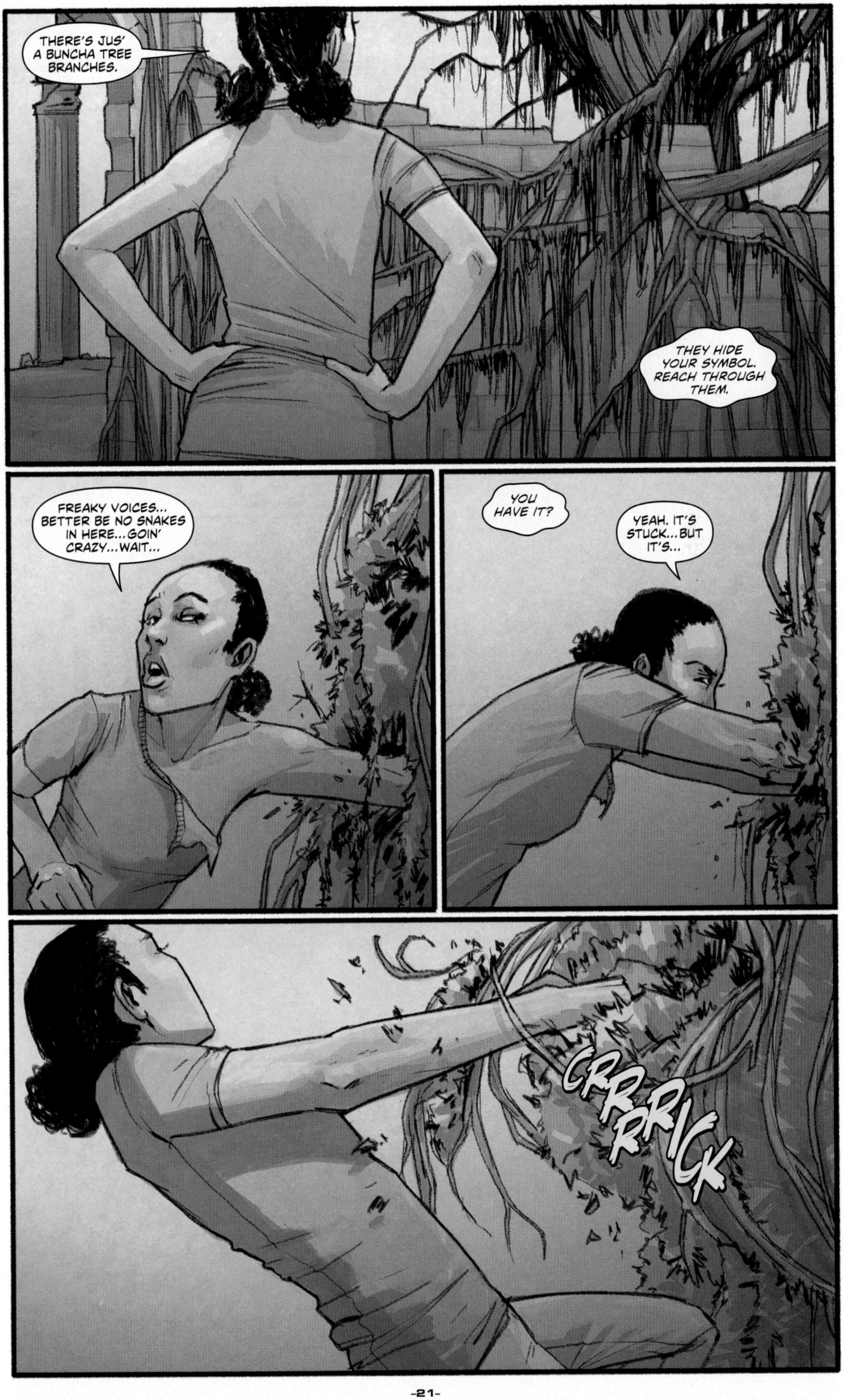
THERE'S JUS' A BUNCHA TREE BRANCHES.
THEY HIDE YOUR SYMBOL. REACH THROUGH THEM.
FREAKY VOICES... BETTER BE NO SNAKES IN HERE...GOIN' CRAZY...WAIT...
YOU HAVE IT?
YEAH. IT'S STUCK...BUT IT'S...
CRRRRICK

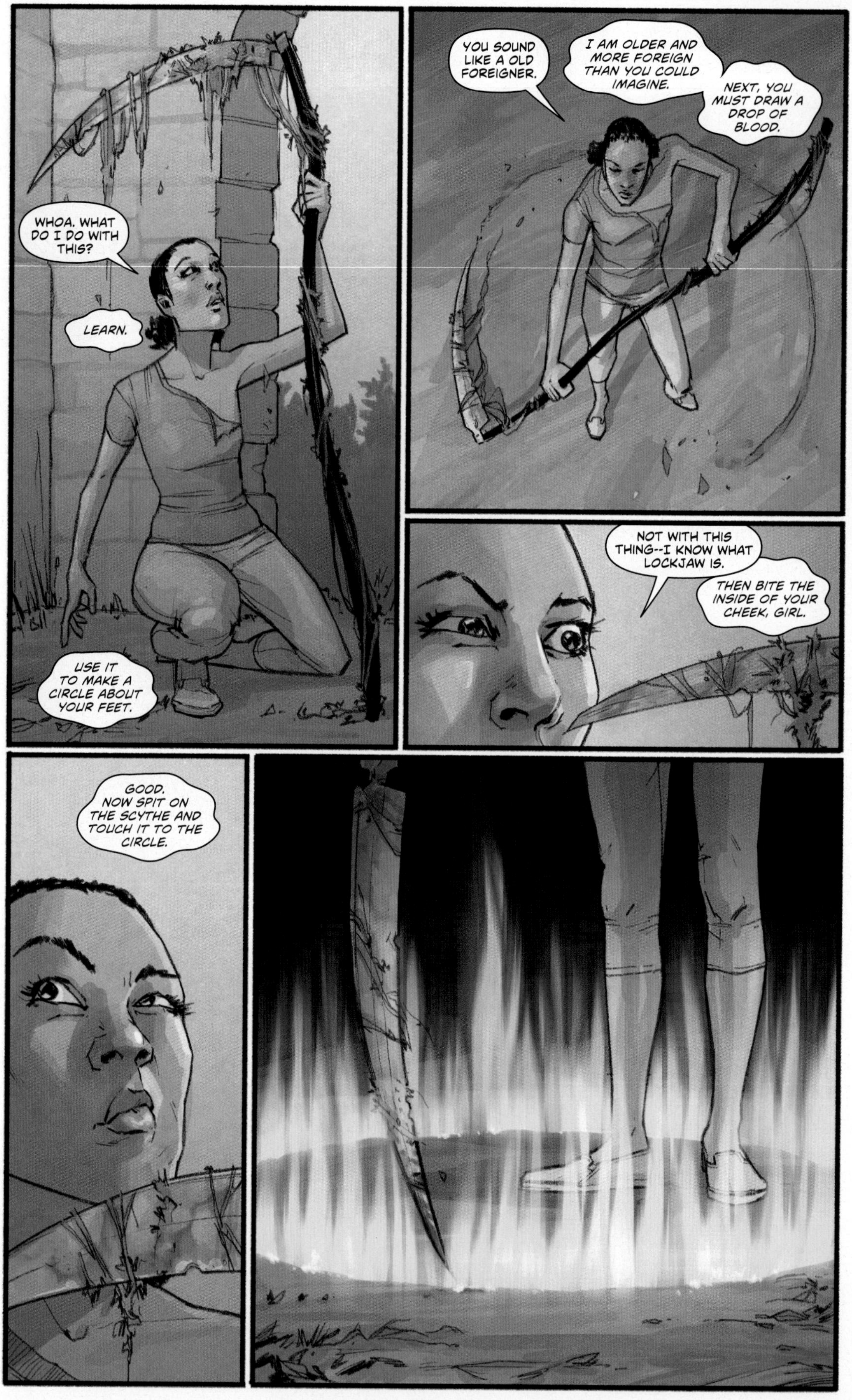

WHOA. WHAT DO I DO WITH THIS?
LEARN.
USE IT TO MAKE A CIRCLE ABOUT YOUR FEET.
YOU SOUND LIKE A OLD FOREIGNER.
I AM OLDER AND MORE FOREIGN THAN YOU COULD IMAGINE.
NEXT, YOU MUST DRAW A DROP OF BLOOD.
NOT WITH THIS THING--I KNOW WHAT LOCKJAW IS.
THEN BITE THE INSIDE OF YOUR CHEEK, GIRL.
GOOD. NOW SPIT ON THE SCYTHE AND TOUCH IT TO THE CIRCLE.

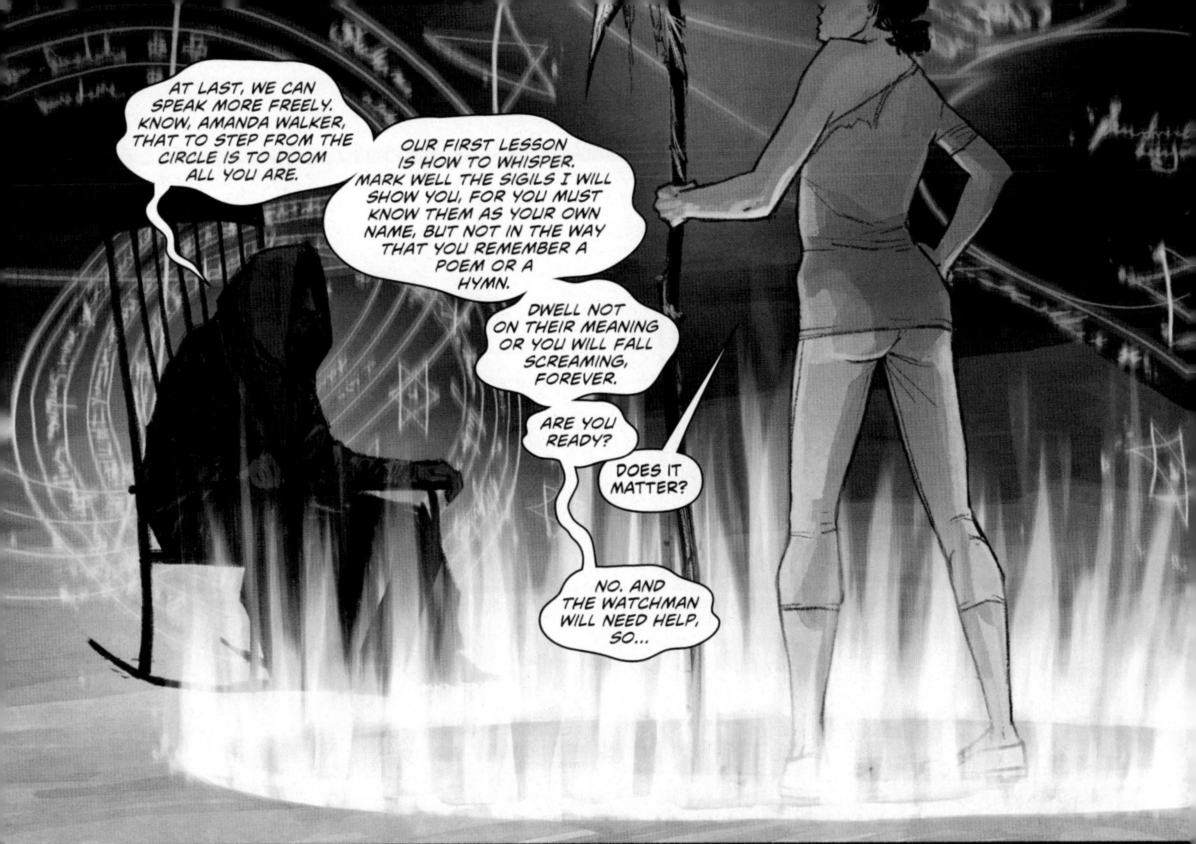
AT LAST, WE CAN SPEAK MORE FREELY. KNOW, AMANDA WALKER, THAT TO STEP FROM THE CIRCLE IS TO DOOM ALL YOU ARE.
OUR FIRST LESSON IS HOW TO WHISPER. MARK WELL THE SIGILS I WILL SHOW YOU, FOR YOU MUST KNOW THEM AS YOUR OWN NAME, BUT NOT IN THE WAY THAT YOU REMEMBER A POEM OR A HYMN.
DWELL NOT ON THEIR MEANING OR YOU WILL FALL SCREAMING, FOREVER.
ARE YOU READY?
DOES IT MATTER?
NO. AND THE WATCHMAN WILL NEED HELP, SO...

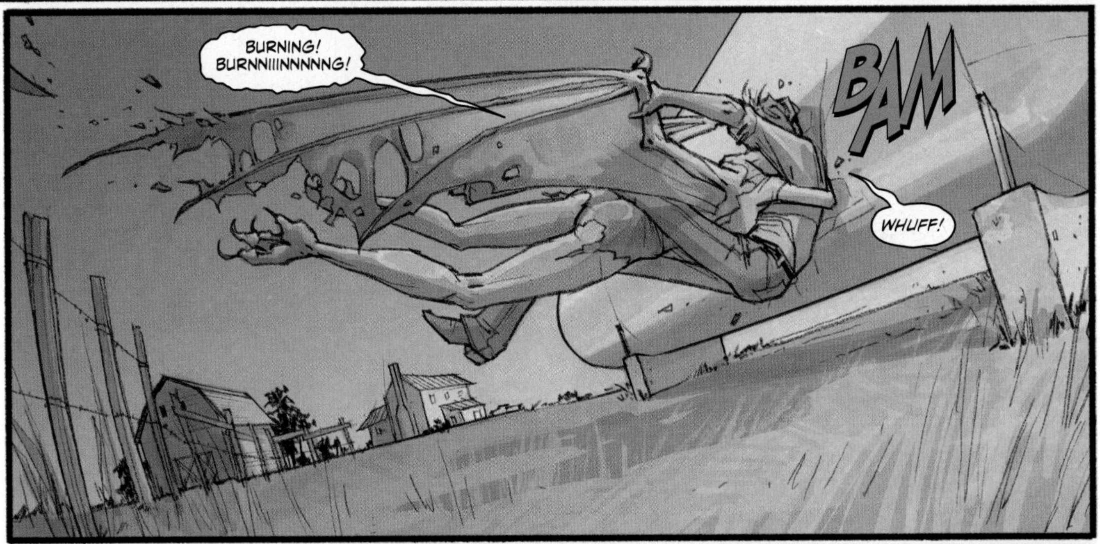
BURNING! BURNNIIINNNNNG!
BAM
WHUFF!

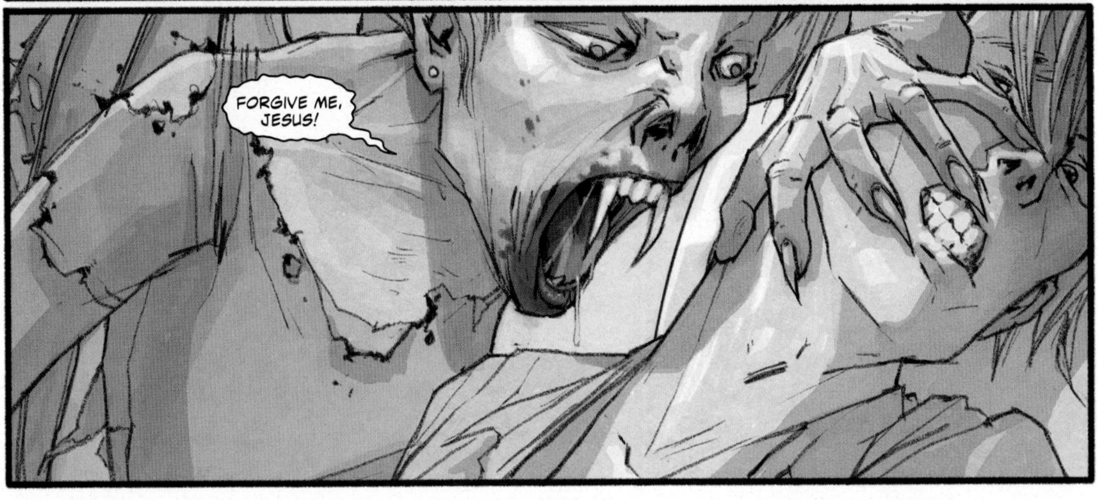
FORGIVE ME, JESUS!

AGGGH'HAAA!

GET OFF!

SORRY 'BOUT THIS, MA'AM.

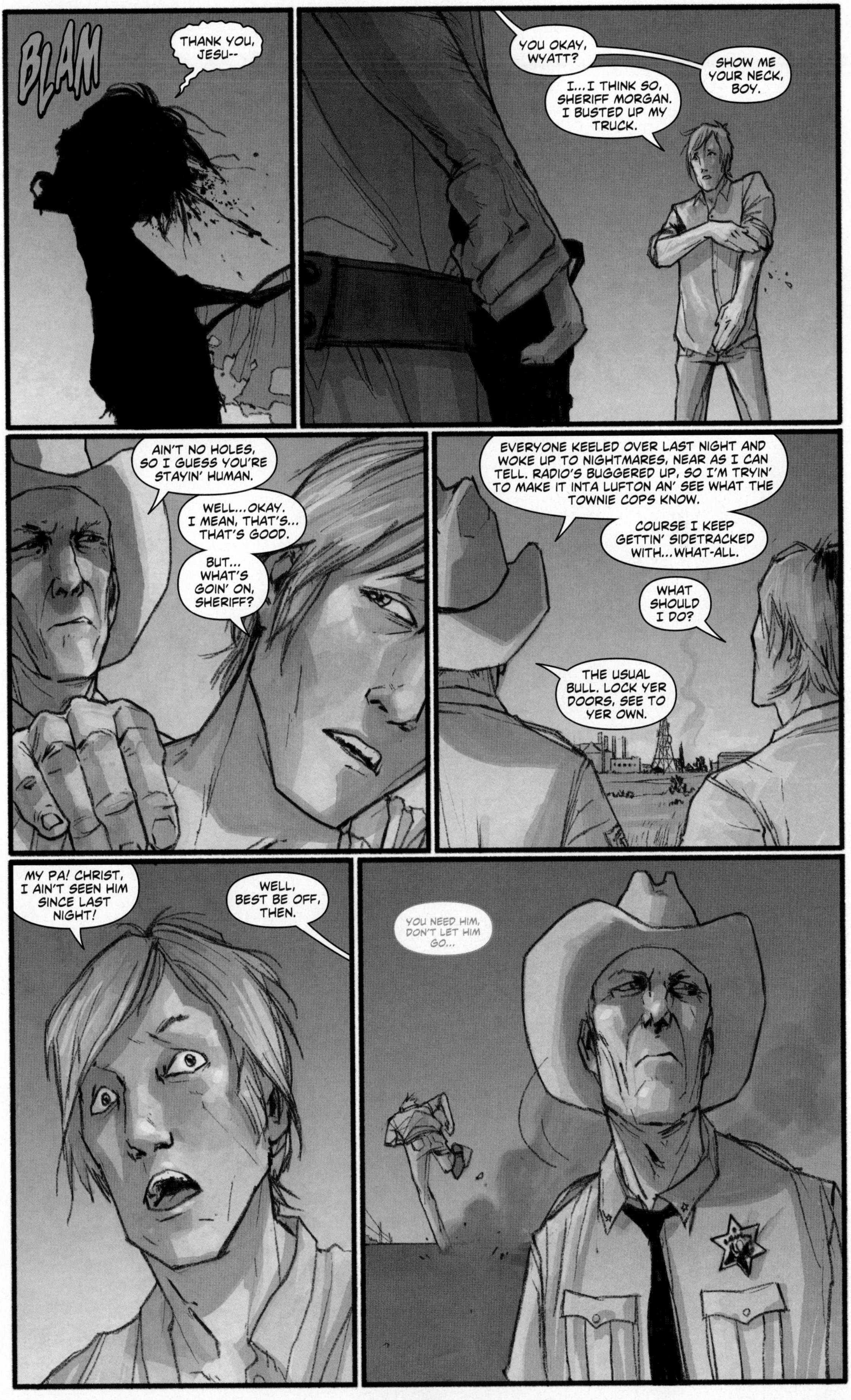
BLAM
THANK YOU, JESU--
YOU OKAY, WYATT?
I...I THINK SO, SHERIFF MORGAN. I BUSTED UP MY TRUCK.
SHOW ME YOUR NECK, BOY.
AIN'T NO HOLES, SO I GUESS YOU'RE STAYIN' HUMAN.
WELL...OKAY. I MEAN, THAT'S... THAT'S GOOD.
BUT... WHAT'S GOIN' ON, SHERIFF?
EVERYONE KEELED OVER LAST NIGHT AND WOKE UP TO NIGHTMARES, NEAR AS I CAN TELL. RADIO'S BUGGERED UP, SO I'M TRYIN' TO MAKE IT INTA LUFTON AN' SEE WHAT THE TOWNIE COPS KNOW.
COURSE I KEEP GETTIN' SIDETRACKED WITH...WHAT-ALL.
WHAT SHOULD I DO?
THE USUAL BULL. LOCK YER DOORS, SEE TO YER OWN.
MY PA! CHRIST, I AIN'T SEEN HIM SINCE LAST NIGHT!
WELL, BEST BE OFF, THEN.
YOU NEED HIM, DON'T LET HIM GO...

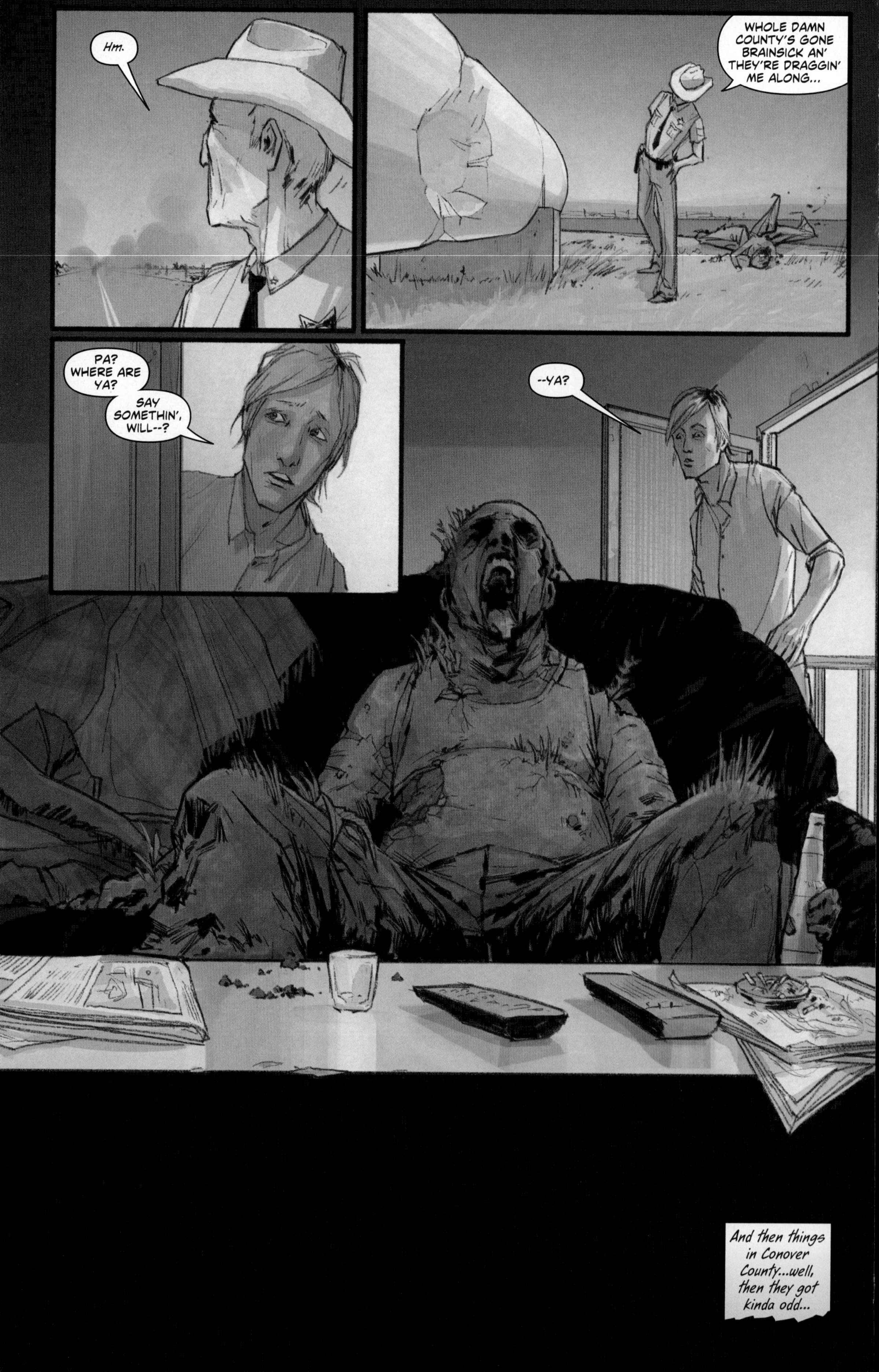
Hm.
WHOLE DAMN COUNTY'S GONE BRAINSICK AN' THEY'RE DRAGGIN' ME ALONG...
PA? WHERE ARE YA?
SAY SOMETHIN', WILL--?
--YA?
And then things in Conover County...well, then they got kinda odd...

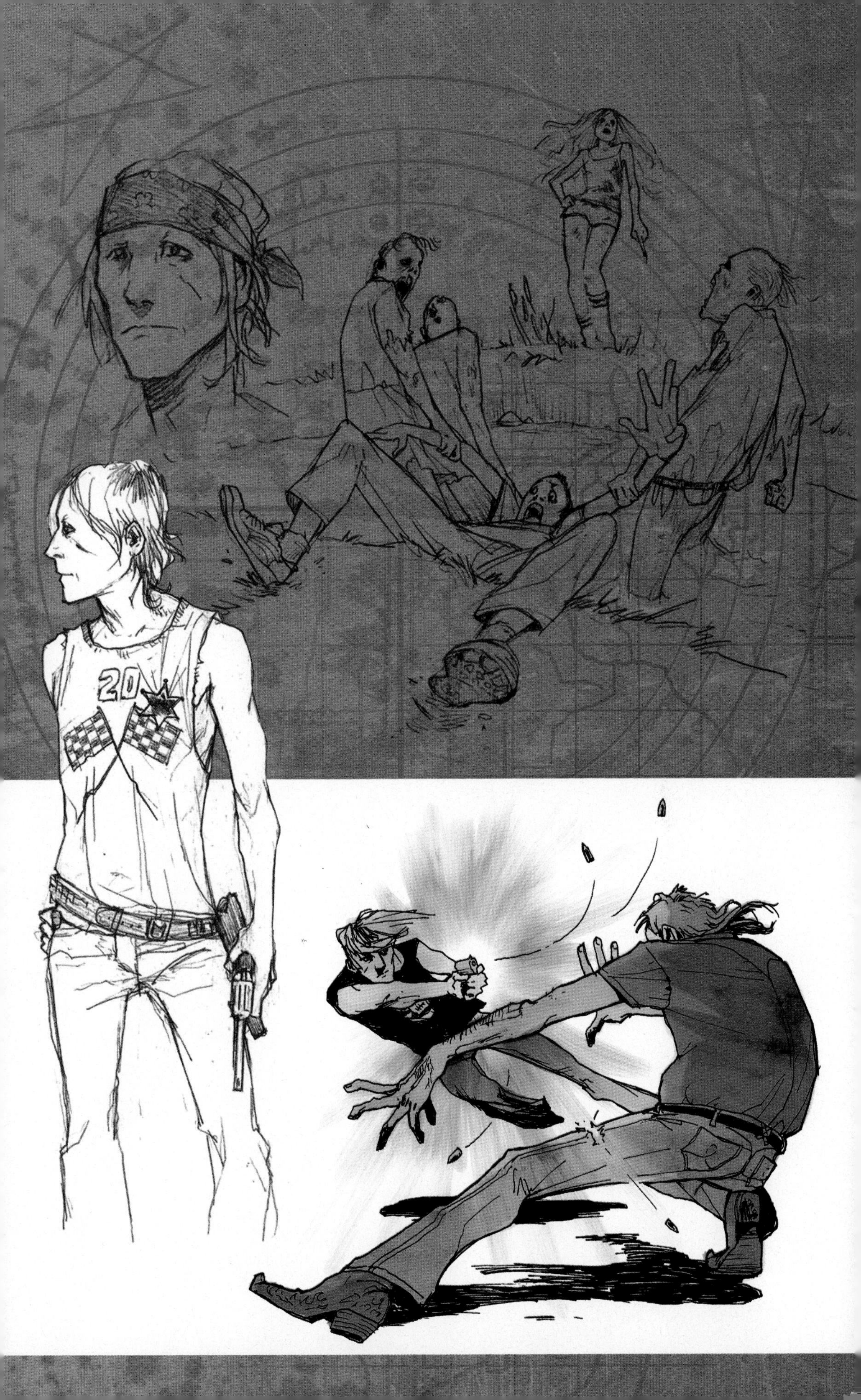
20

CHAPTER TWO

An' The Word Was Law

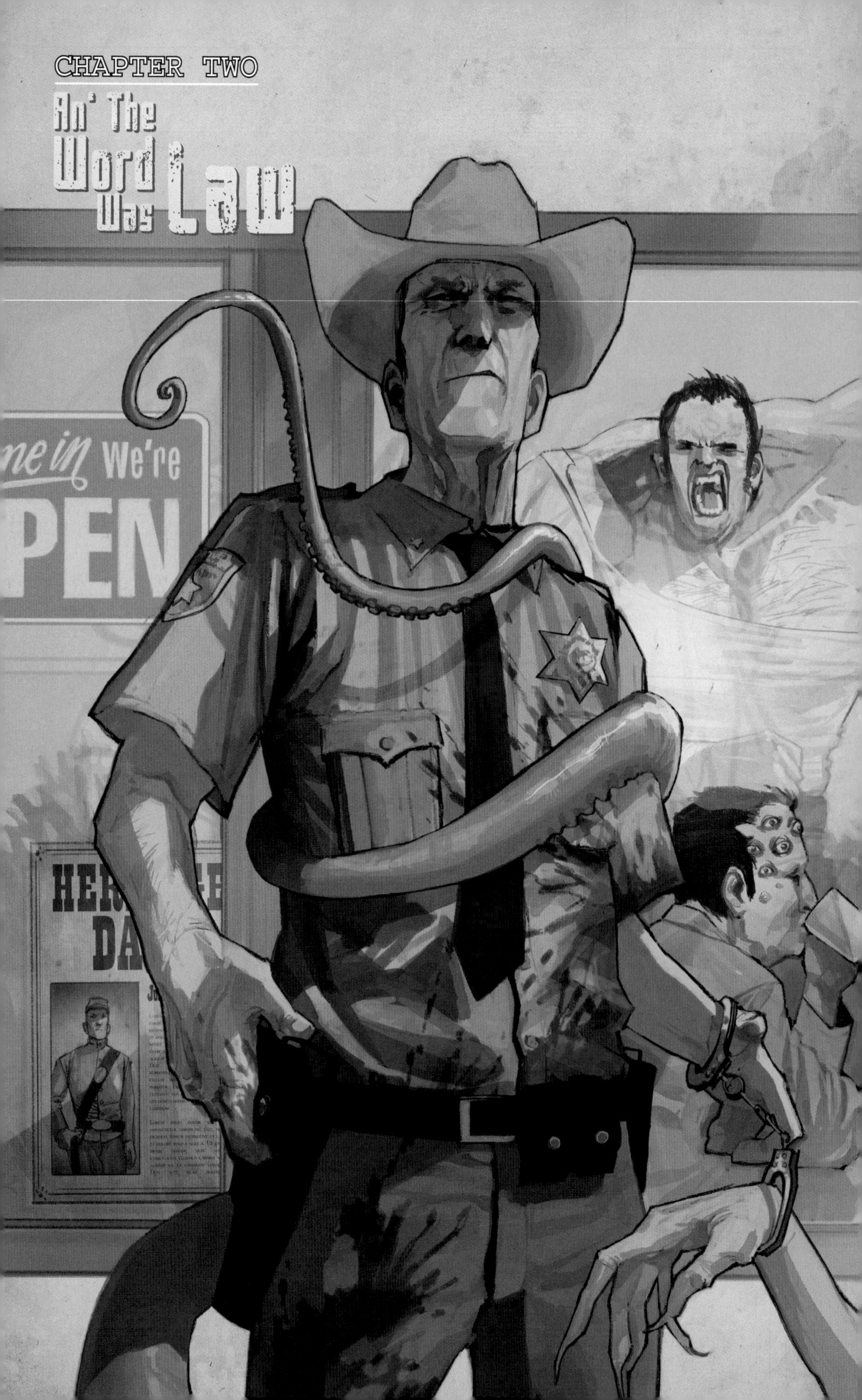

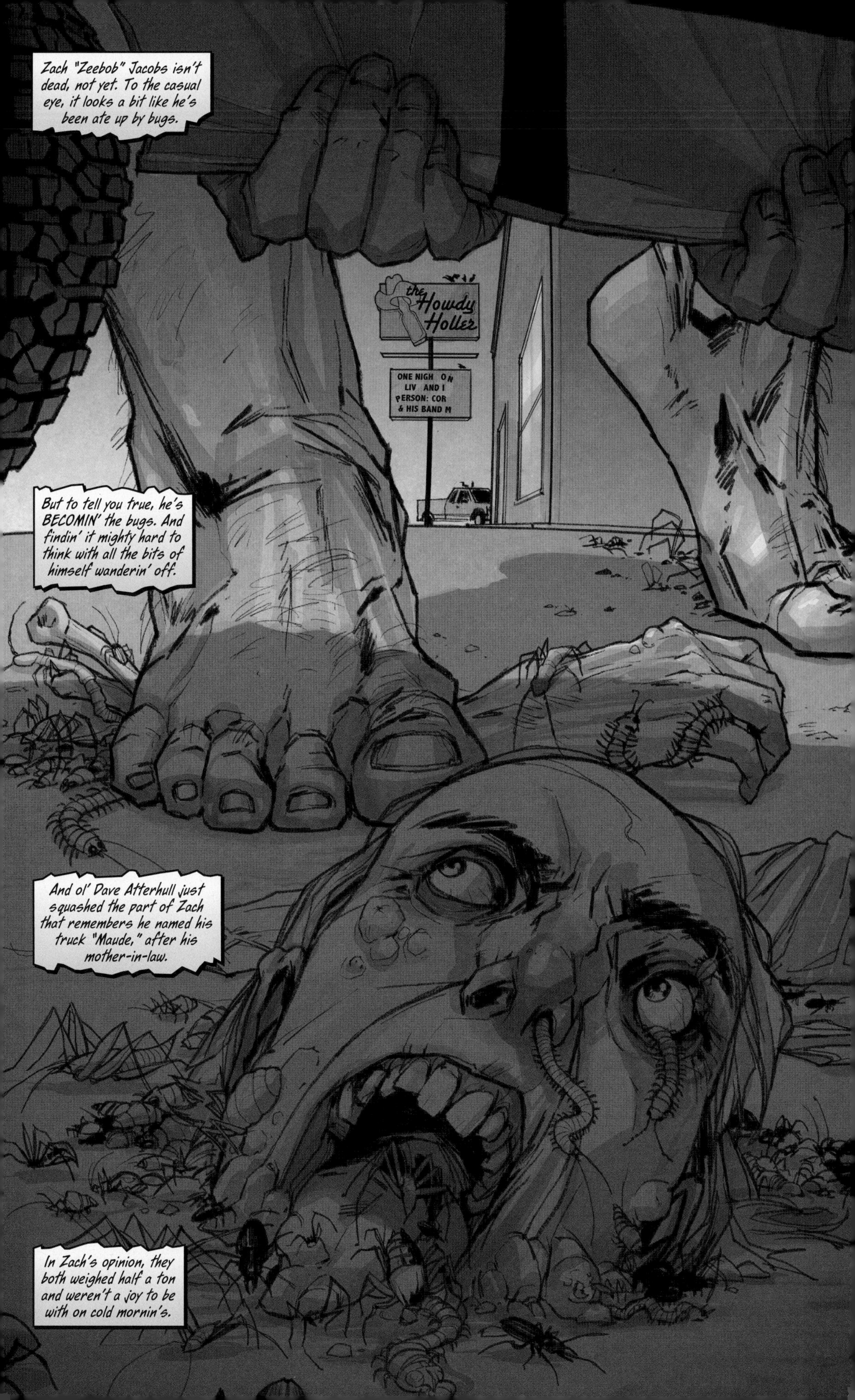
Zach "Zeebob" Jacobs isn't dead, not yet. To the casual eye, it looks a bit like he's been ate up by bugs.
the Howdy Holler
ONE NIGH O
LIV AND I
PERSON: COR
& HIS BAND M
But to tell you true, he's BECOMIN' the bugs. And findin' it mighty hard to think with all the bits of himself wanderin' off.
And ol' Dave Atterhull just squashed the part of Zach that remembers he named his truck "Maude," after his mother-in-law.
In Zach's opinion, they both weighed half a ton and weren't a joy to be with on cold mornin's.

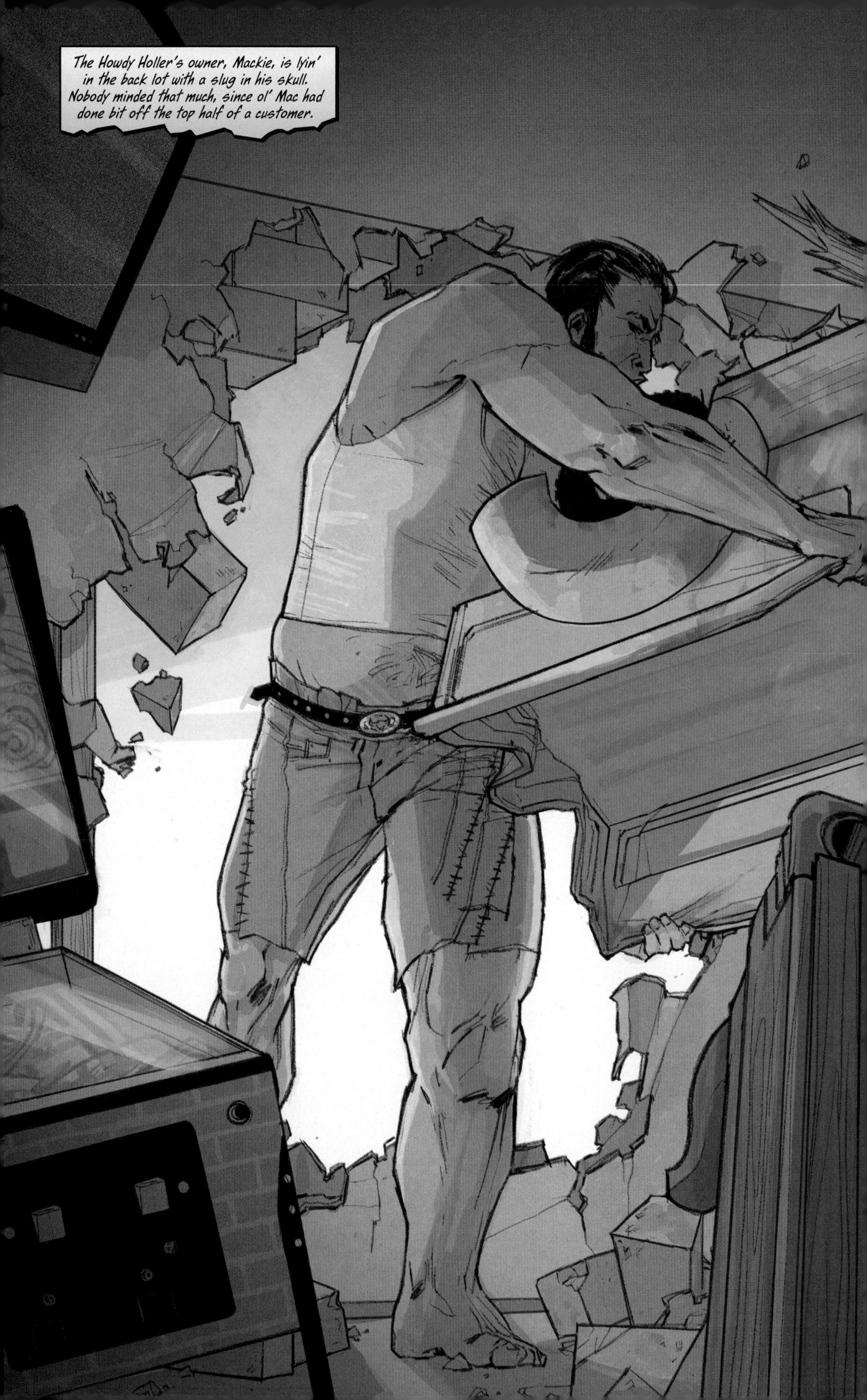
The Howdy Holler's owner, Mackie, is lyin' in the back lot with a slug in his skull. Nobody minded that much, since ol' Mac had done bit off the top half of a customer.

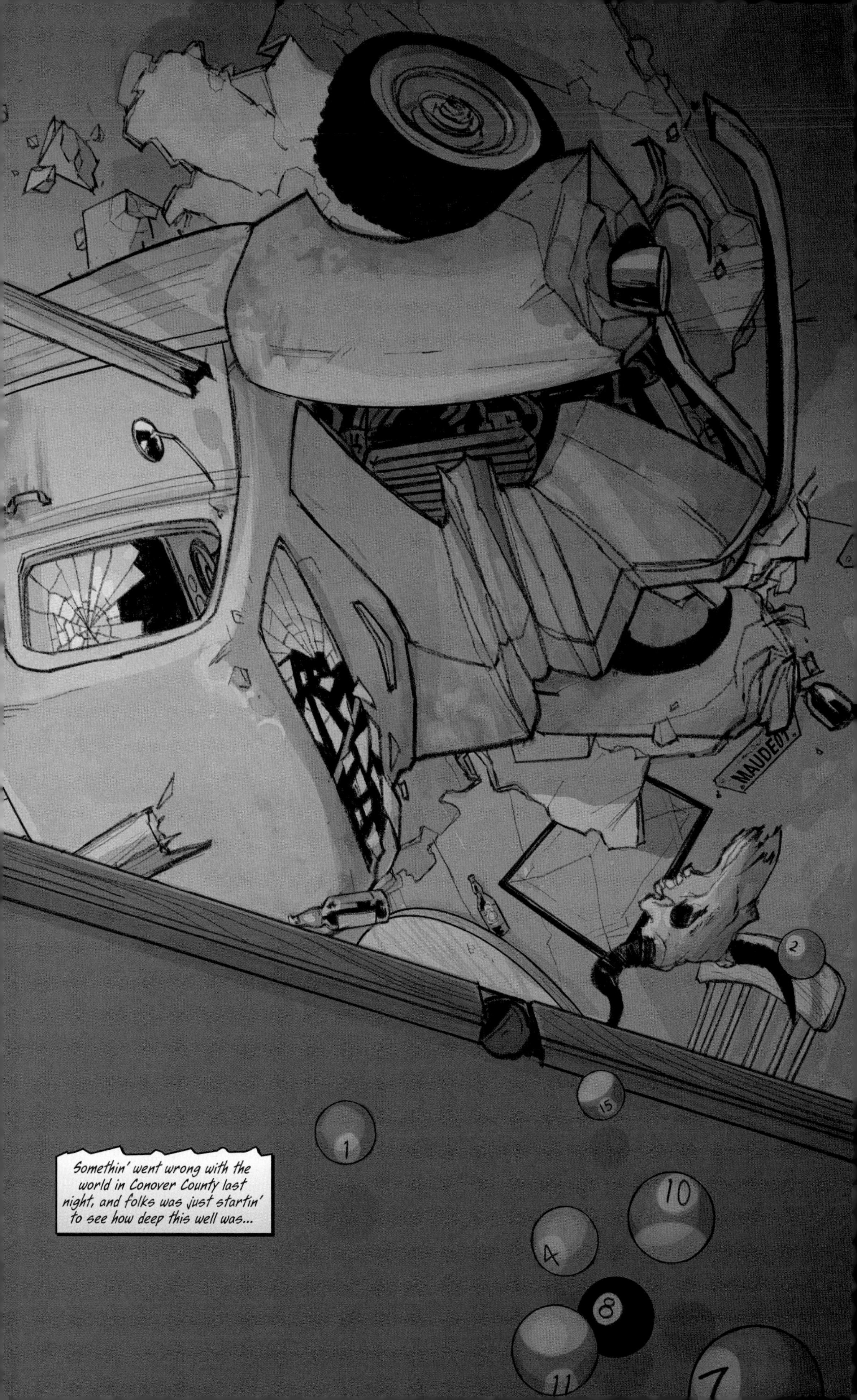
Somethin' went wrong with the world in Conover County last night, and folks was just startin' to see how deep this well was...
MAUDE01

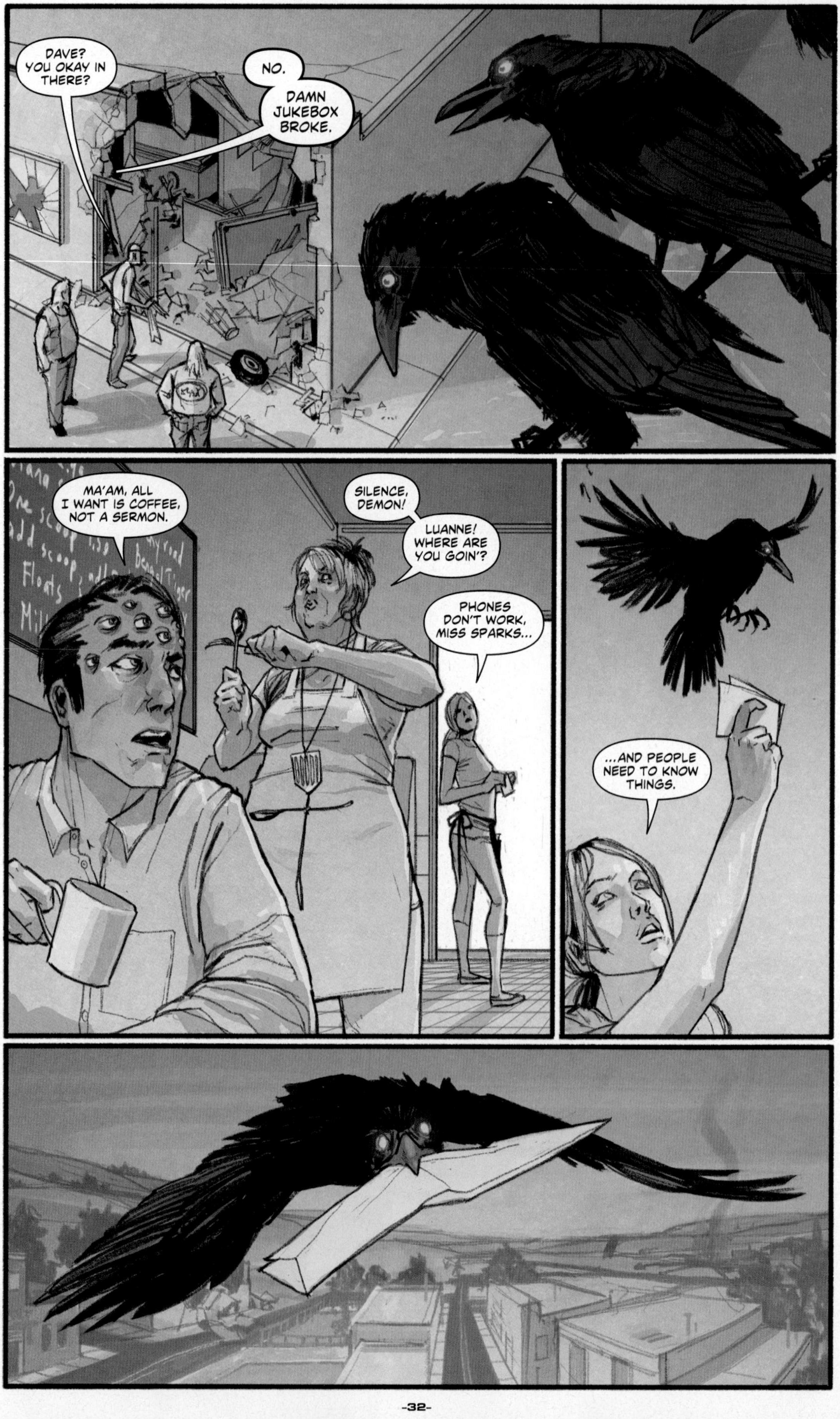
DAVE? YOU OKAY IN THERE?
NO.
DAMN JUKEBOX BROKE.
MA'AM, ALL I WANT IS COFFEE, NOT A SERMON.
SILENCE, DEMON!
LUANNE! WHERE ARE YOU GOIN'?
PHONES DON'T WORK, MISS SPARKS...
...AND PEOPLE NEED TO KNOW THINGS.

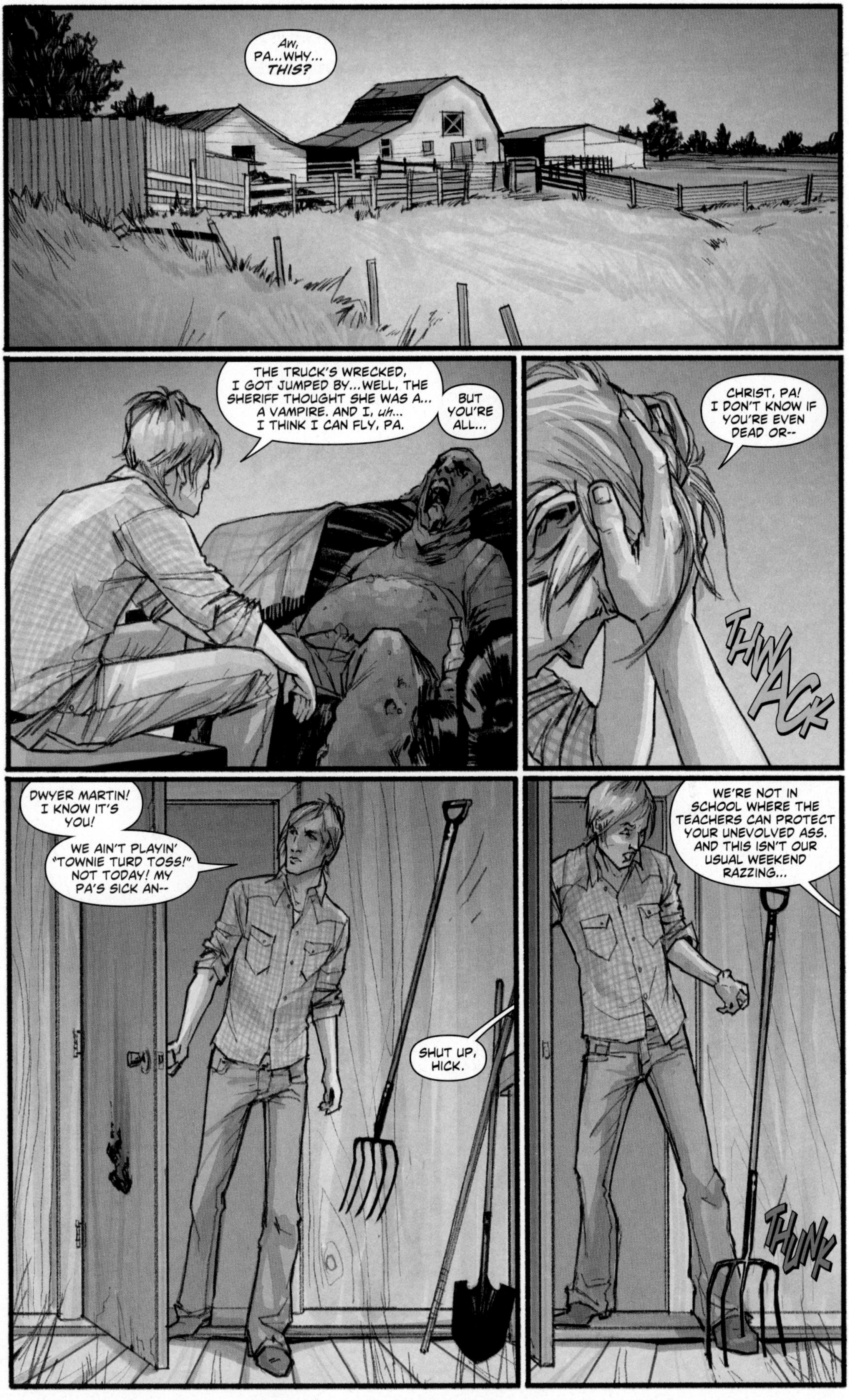
AW, PA...WHY... THIS?
THE TRUCK'S WRECKED, I GOT JUMPED BY...WELL, THE SHERIFF THOUGHT SHE WAS A... A VAMPIRE. AND I, uh... I THINK I CAN FLY, PA.
BUT YOU'RE ALL...
CHRIST, PA! I DON'T KNOW IF YOU'RE EVEN DEAD OR--
THWACK
DWYER MARTIN! I KNOW IT'S YOU!
WE AIN'T PLAYIN' "TOWNIE TURD TOSS!" NOT TODAY! MY PA'S SICK AN--
SHUT UP, HICK.
WE'RE NOT IN SCHOOL WHERE THE TEACHERS CAN PROTECT YOUR UNEVOLVED ASS. AND THIS ISN'T OUR USUAL WEEKEND RAZZING...
THUNK

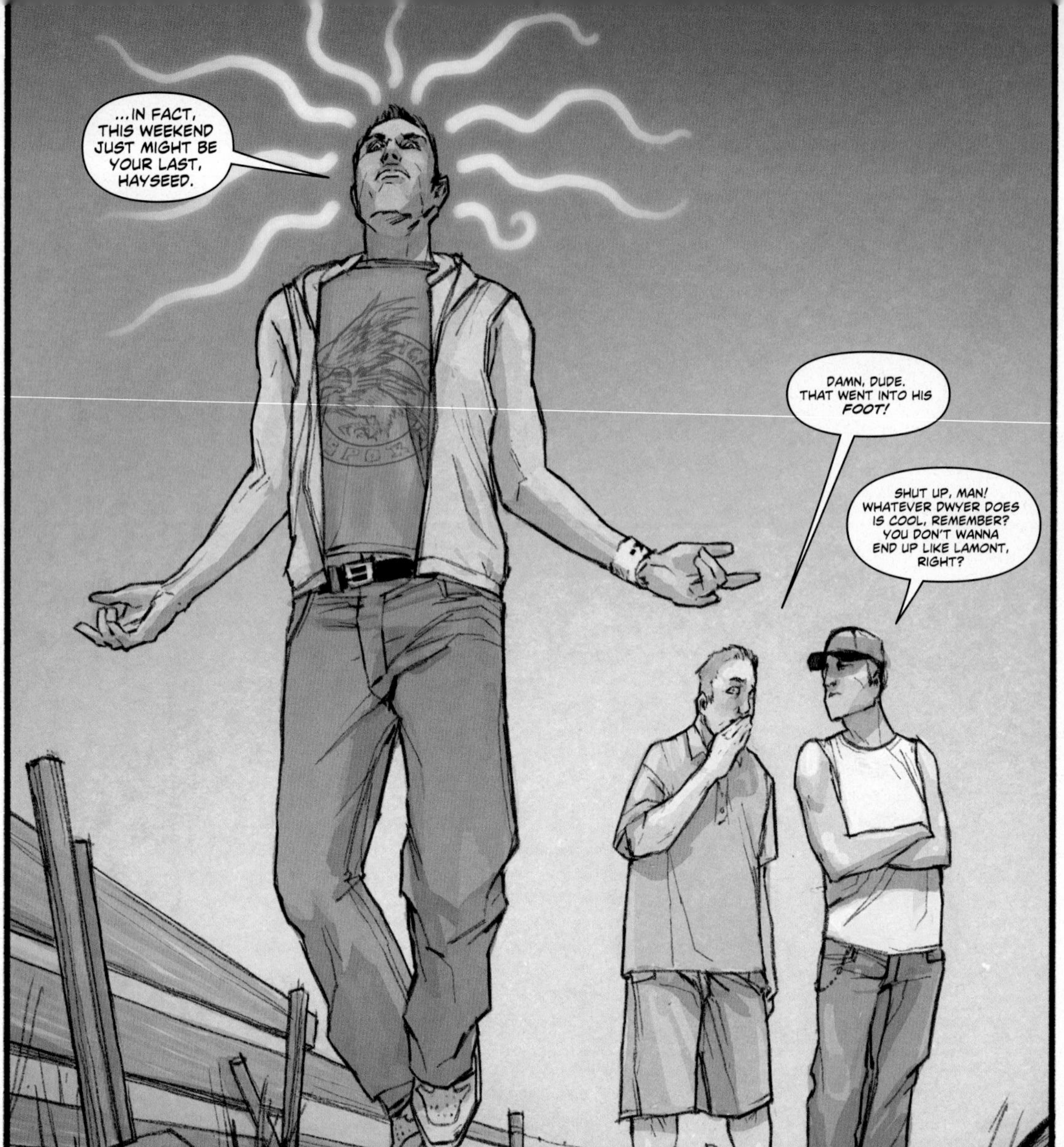
...IN FACT, THIS WEEKEND JUST MIGHT BE YOUR LAST, HAYSEED.
DAMN, DUDE. THAT WENT INTO HIS *FOOT!*
SHUT UP, MAN! WHATEVER DWYER DOES IS COOL, REMEMBER? YOU DON'T WANNA END UP LIKE LAMONT, RIGHT?

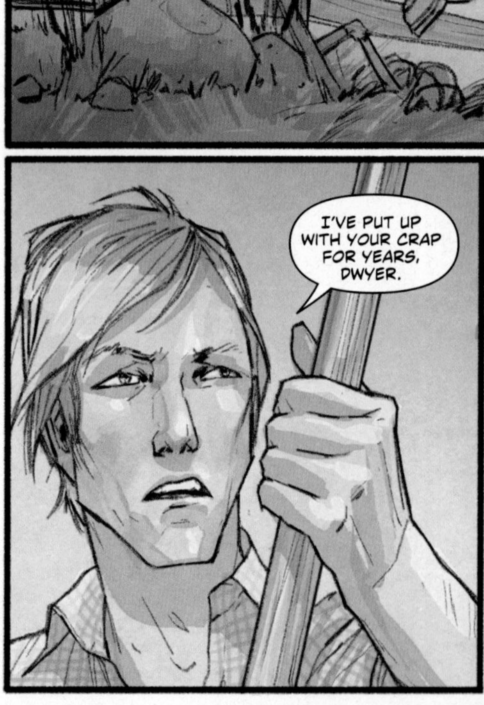
I'VE PUT UP WITH YOUR CRAP FOR YEARS, DWYER.

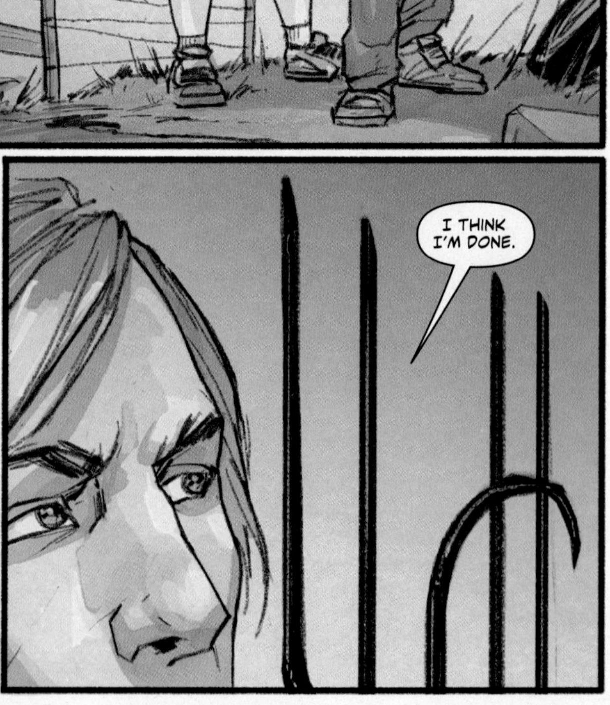
I THINK I'M DONE.

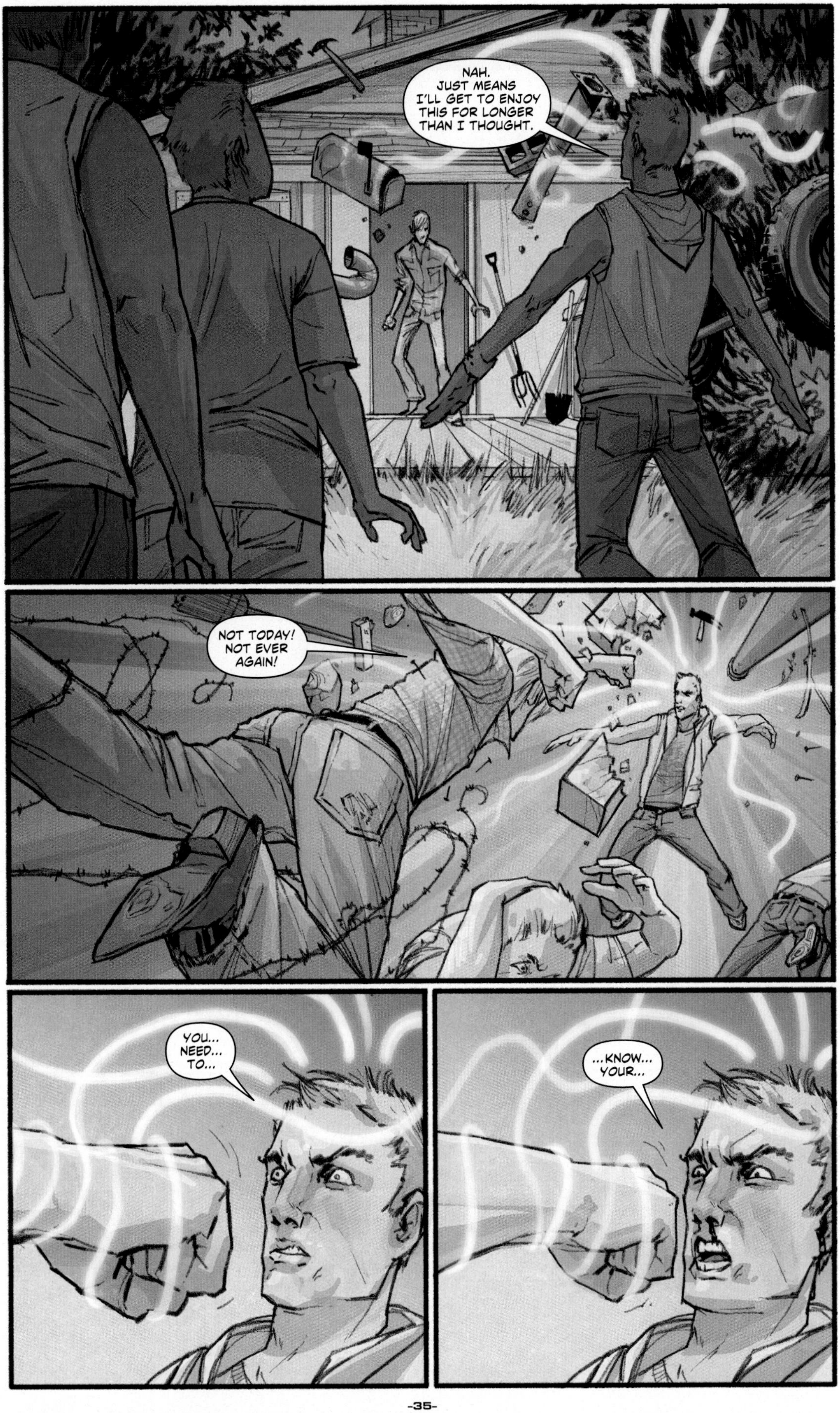
NAH. JUST MEANS I'LL GET TO ENJOY THIS FOR LONGER THAN I THOUGHT.
NOT TODAY! NOT EVER AGAIN!
YOU... NEED... TO...
...KNOW... YOUR...

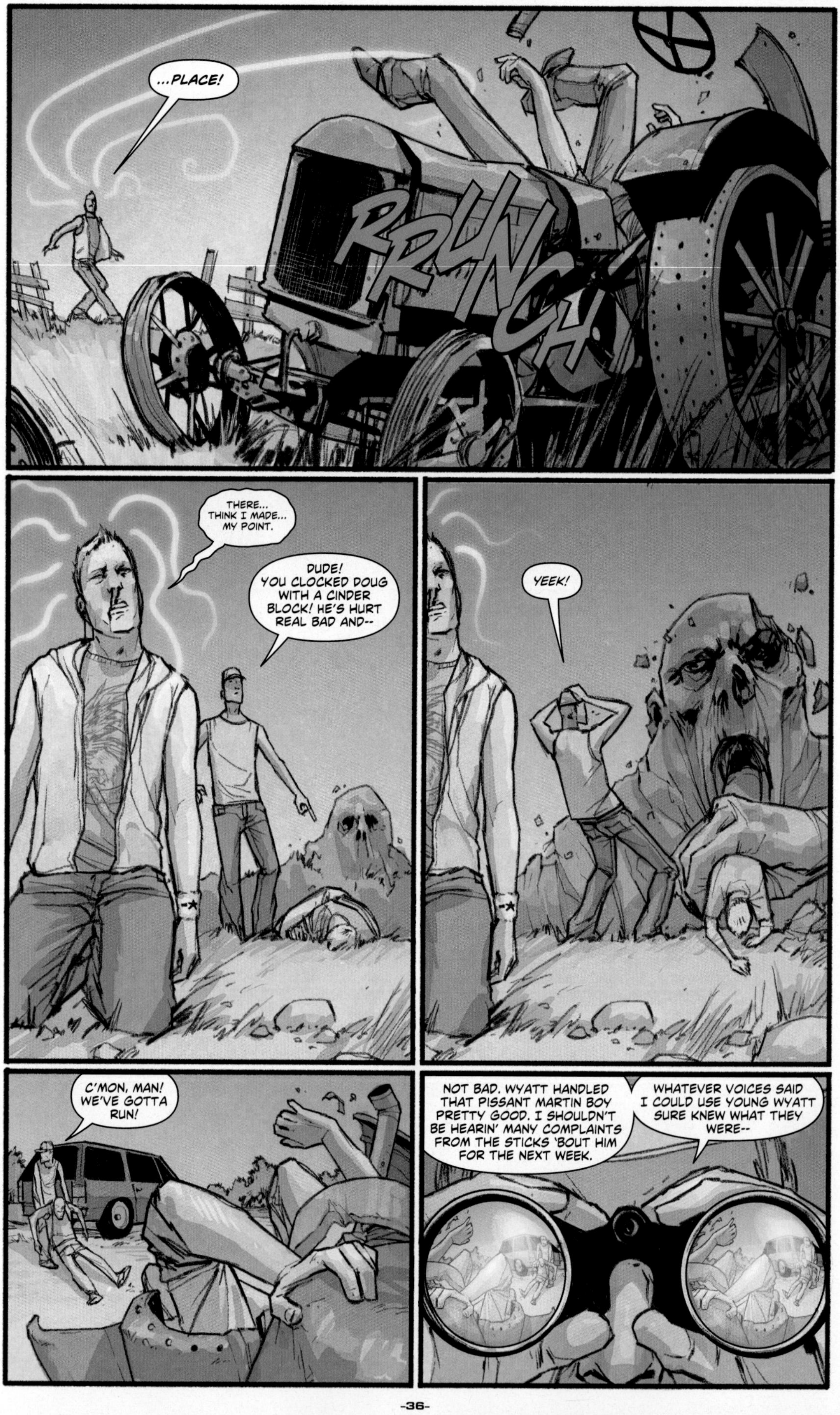
...PLACE!
RRUNCH
THERE... THINK I MADE... MY POINT.
DUDE! YOU CLOCKED DOUG WITH A CINDER BLOCK! HE'S HURT REAL BAD AND--
YEEK!
C'MON, MAN! WE'VE GOTTA RUN!
NOT BAD. WYATT HANDLED THAT PISSANT MARTIN BOY PRETTY GOOD. I SHOULDN'T BE HEARIN' MANY COMPLAINTS FROM THE STICKS 'BOUT HIM FOR THE NEXT WEEK.
WHATEVER VOICES SAID I COULD USE YOUNG WYATT SURE KNEW WHAT THEY WERE--

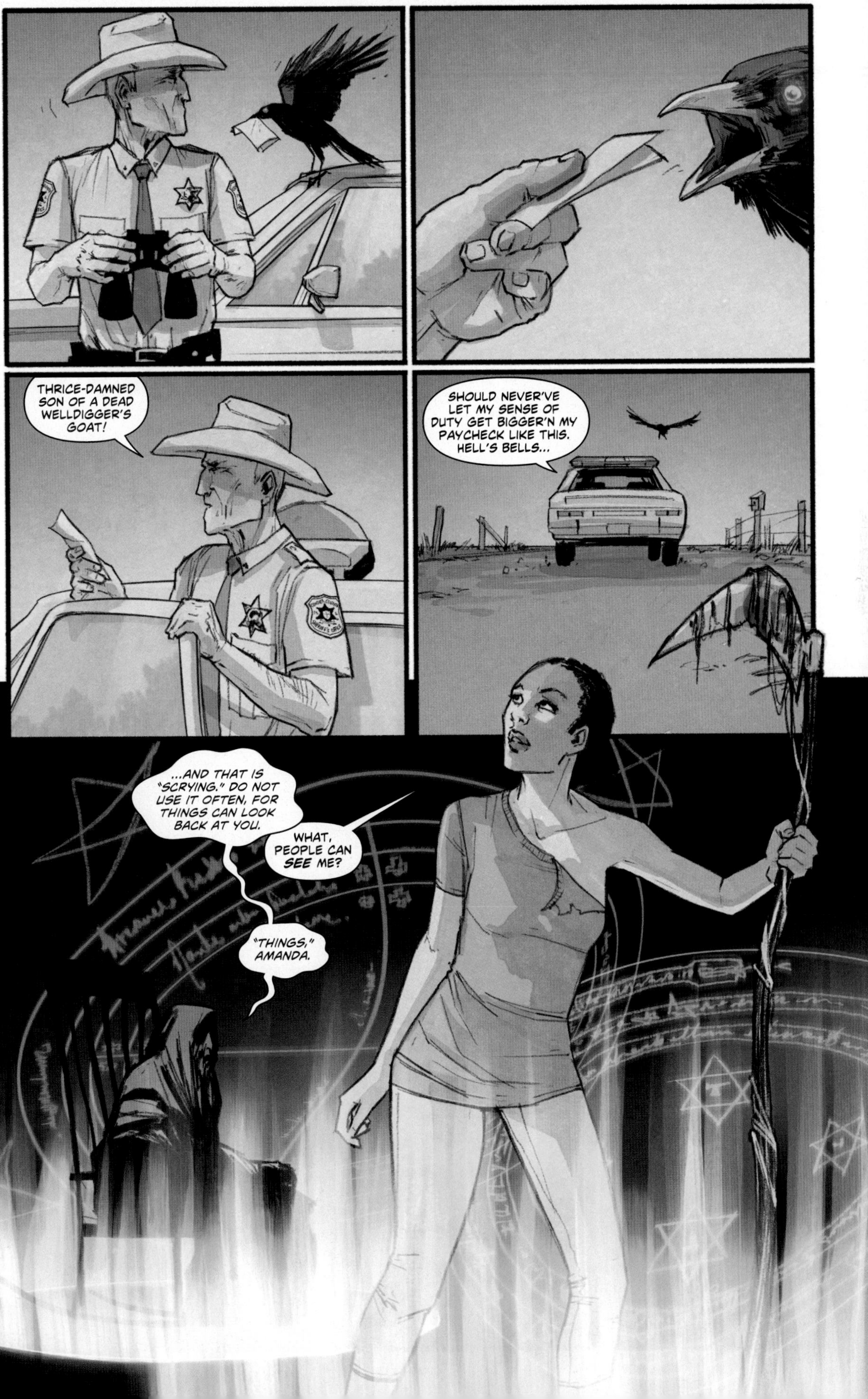
THRICE-DAMNED SON OF A DEAD WELLDIGGER'S GOAT!
SHOULD NEVER'VE LET MY SENSE OF DUTY GET BIGGER'N MY PAYCHECK LIKE THIS. HELL'S BELLS...
...AND THAT IS "SCRYING." DO NOT USE IT OFTEN, FOR THINGS CAN LOOK BACK AT YOU.
WHAT, PEOPLE CAN SEE ME?
"THINGS," AMANDA.

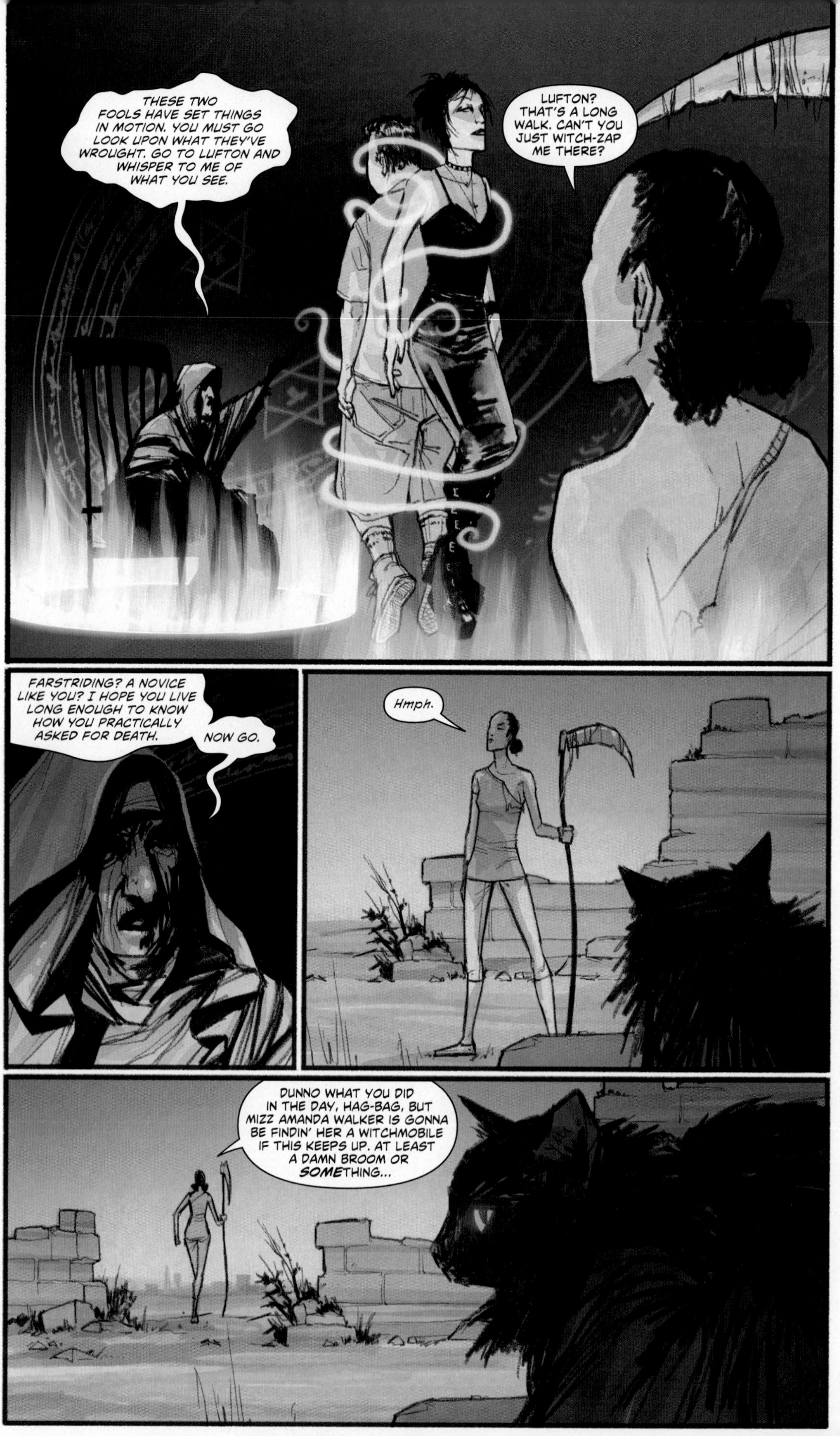
THESE TWO FOOLS HAVE SET THINGS IN MOTION. YOU MUST GO LOOK UPON WHAT THEY'VE WROUGHT. GO TO LUFTON AND WHISPER TO ME OF WHAT YOU SEE.
LUFTON? THAT'S A LONG WALK. CAN'T YOU JUST WITCH-ZAP ME THERE?
FARSTRIDING? A NOVICE LIKE YOU? I HOPE YOU LIVE LONG ENOUGH TO KNOW HOW YOU PRACTICALLY ASKED FOR DEATH.
NOW GO.
Hmph.
DUNNO WHAT YOU DID IN THE DAY, HAG-BAG, BUT MIZZ AMANDA WALKER IS GONNA BE FINDIN' HER A WITCHMOBILE IF THIS KEEPS UP. AT LEAST A DAMN BROOM OR SOMETHING...

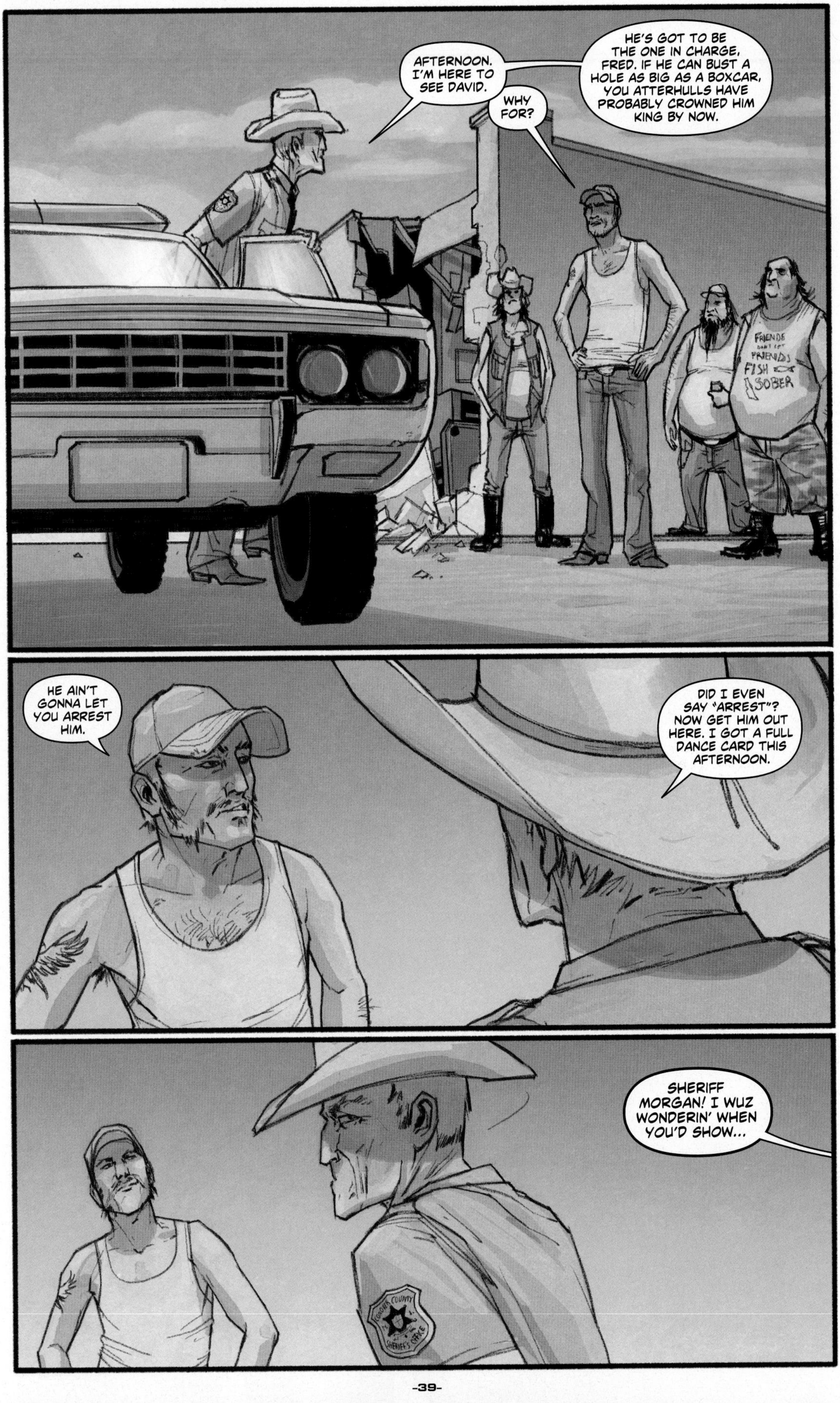
AFTERNOON. I'M HERE TO SEE DAVID.
WHY FOR?
HE'S GOT TO BE THE ONE IN CHARGE, FRED. IF HE CAN BUST A HOLE AS BIG AS A BOXCAR, YOU ATTERHULLS HAVE PROBABLY CROWNED HIM KING BY NOW.
FRIENDS DON'T LET FRIENDS FISH SOBER
HE AIN'T GONNA LET YOU ARREST HIM.
DID I EVEN SAY "ARREST"? NOW GET HIM OUT HERE. I GOT A FULL DANCE CARD THIS AFTERNOON.
SHERIFF MORGAN! I WUZ WONDERIN' WHEN YOU'D SHOW...

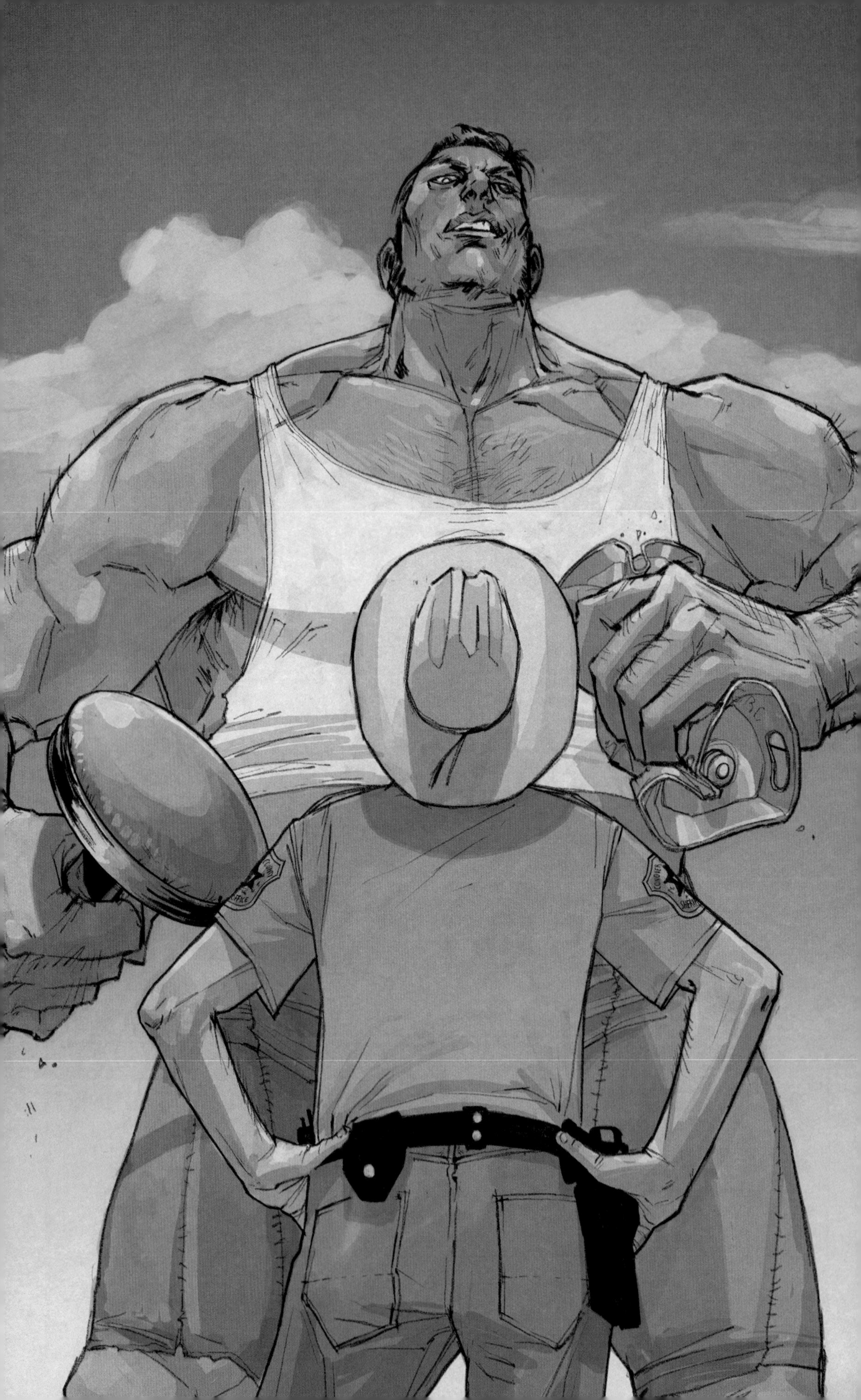

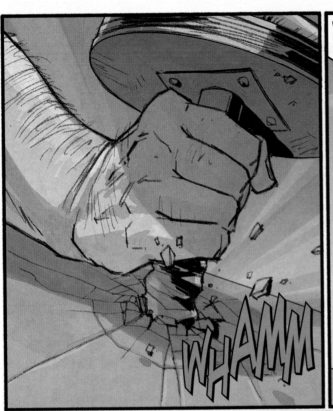

WELL, SHERIFF? DON'CHA KNOW HOW T' USE A STOOL?

WHAMM

THESE ARE WHAT THEY CALL "INTERESTIN' TIMES," MR. ATTERHULL. IN LIGHT OF THAT, I'M WILLIN' TO LET A FEW THINGS SLIDE.

WHATCHOO GONNA DO? SHOOT ME?

MAYBE IF I HAD A GATLING ON MY HIP, IT'D TAKE MORE'N MY PEA-SHOOTER TO DROP YOU, I RECKON.

BUT FRED HERE IS ANOTHER STORY. SO HOW ABOUT YOU SHUT UP AND LISTEN FOR A SPELL?

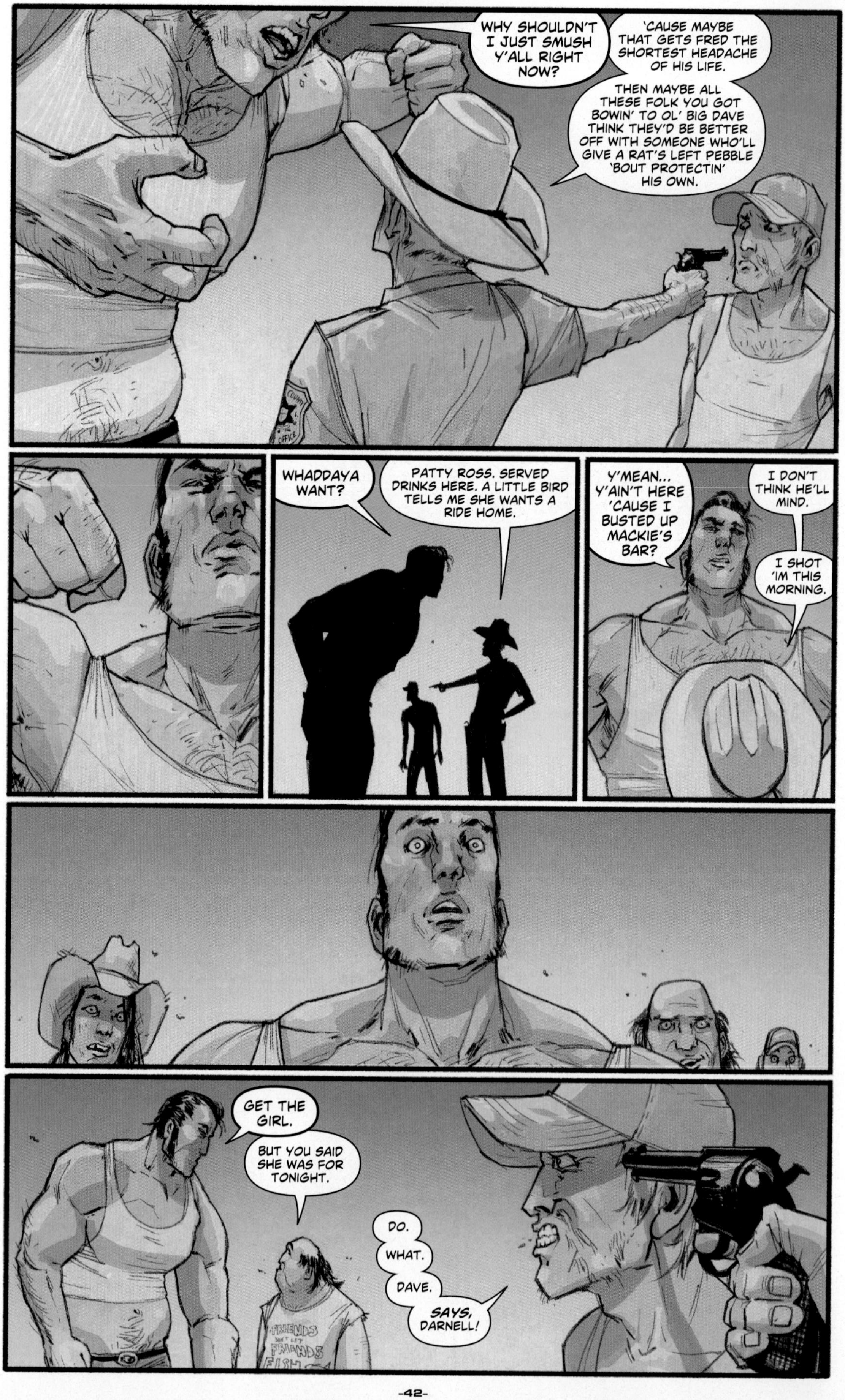
WHY SHOULDN'T I JUST SMUSH Y'ALL RIGHT NOW?
'CAUSE MAYBE THAT GETS FRED THE SHORTEST HEADACHE OF HIS LIFE.
THEN MAYBE ALL THESE FOLK YOU GOT BOWIN' TO OL' BIG DAVE THINK THEY'D BE BETTER OFF WITH SOMEONE WHO'LL GIVE A RAT'S LEFT PEBBLE 'BOUT PROTECTIN' HIS OWN.
WHADDAYA WANT?
PATTY ROSS. SERVED DRINKS HERE. A LITTLE BIRD TELLS ME SHE WANTS A RIDE HOME.
Y'MEAN... Y'AIN'T HERE 'CAUSE I BUSTED UP MACKIE'S BAR?
I DON'T THINK HE'LL MIND.
I SHOT 'IM THIS MORNING.
GET THE GIRL.
BUT YOU SAID SHE WAS FOR TONIGHT.
DO.
WHAT.
DAVE.
SAYS, DARNELL!

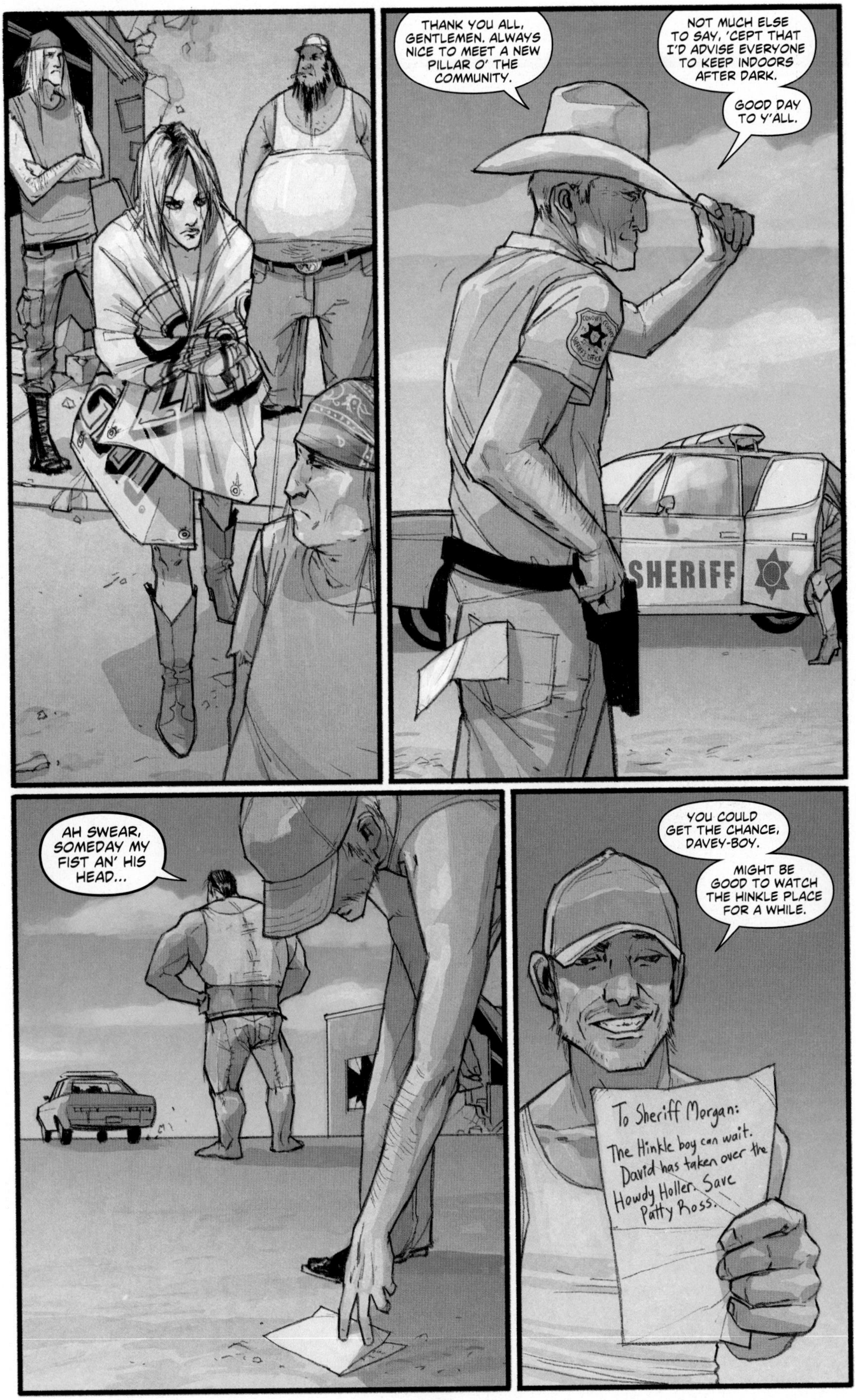
THANK YOU ALL, GENTLEMEN. ALWAYS NICE TO MEET A NEW PILLAR O' THE COMMUNITY.
NOT MUCH ELSE TO SAY, 'CEPT THAT I'D ADVISE EVERYONE TO KEEP INDOORS AFTER DARK.
GOOD DAY TO Y'ALL.
SHERIFF
AH SWEAR, SOMEDAY MY FIST AN' HIS HEAD...
YOU COULD GET THE CHANCE, DAVEY-BOY.
MIGHT BE GOOD TO WATCH THE HINKLE PLACE FOR A WHILE.
To Sheriff Morgan:
The Hinkle boy can wait. David has taken over the Howdy Holler. Save Patty Ross.

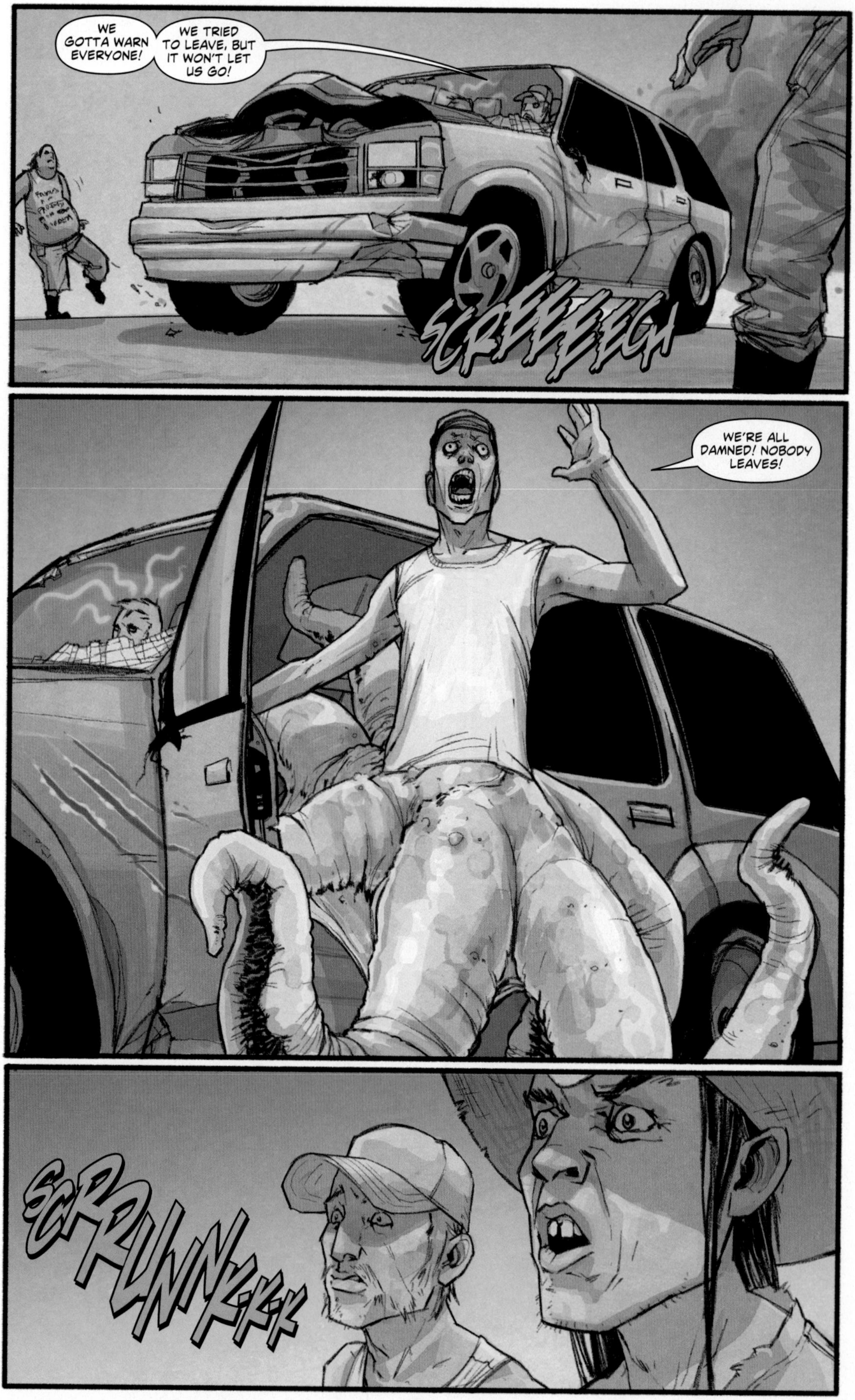
WE GOTTA WARN EVERYONE!
WE TRIED TO LEAVE, BUT IT WON'T LET US GO!
SCREEEECH
WE'RE ALL DAMNED! NOBODY LEAVES!
SCRUNNK-K-K

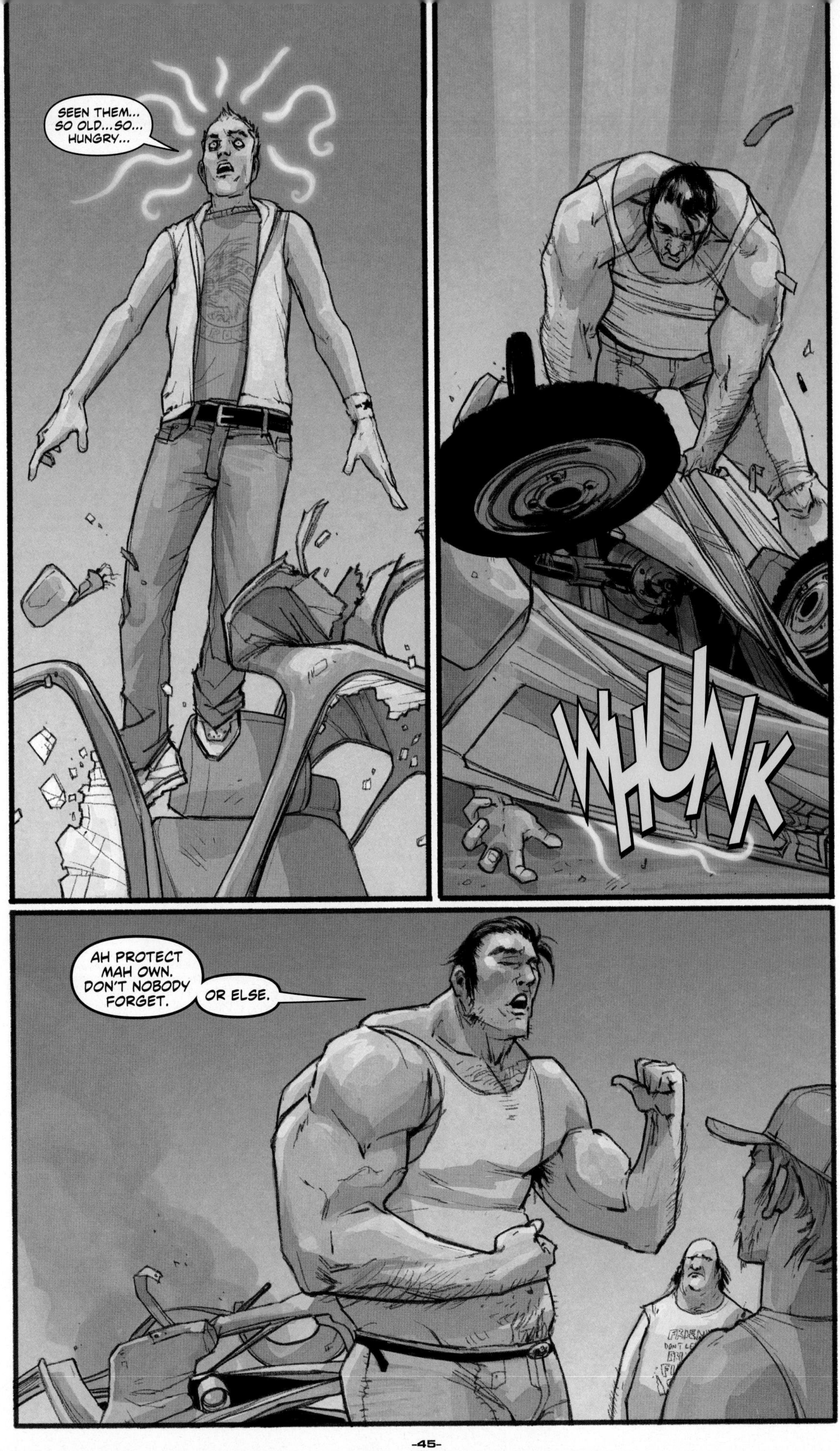
SEEN THEM... SO OLD...SO... HUNGRY...
WHUNK
AH PROTECT MAH OWN. DON'T NOBODY FORGET.
OR ELSE.

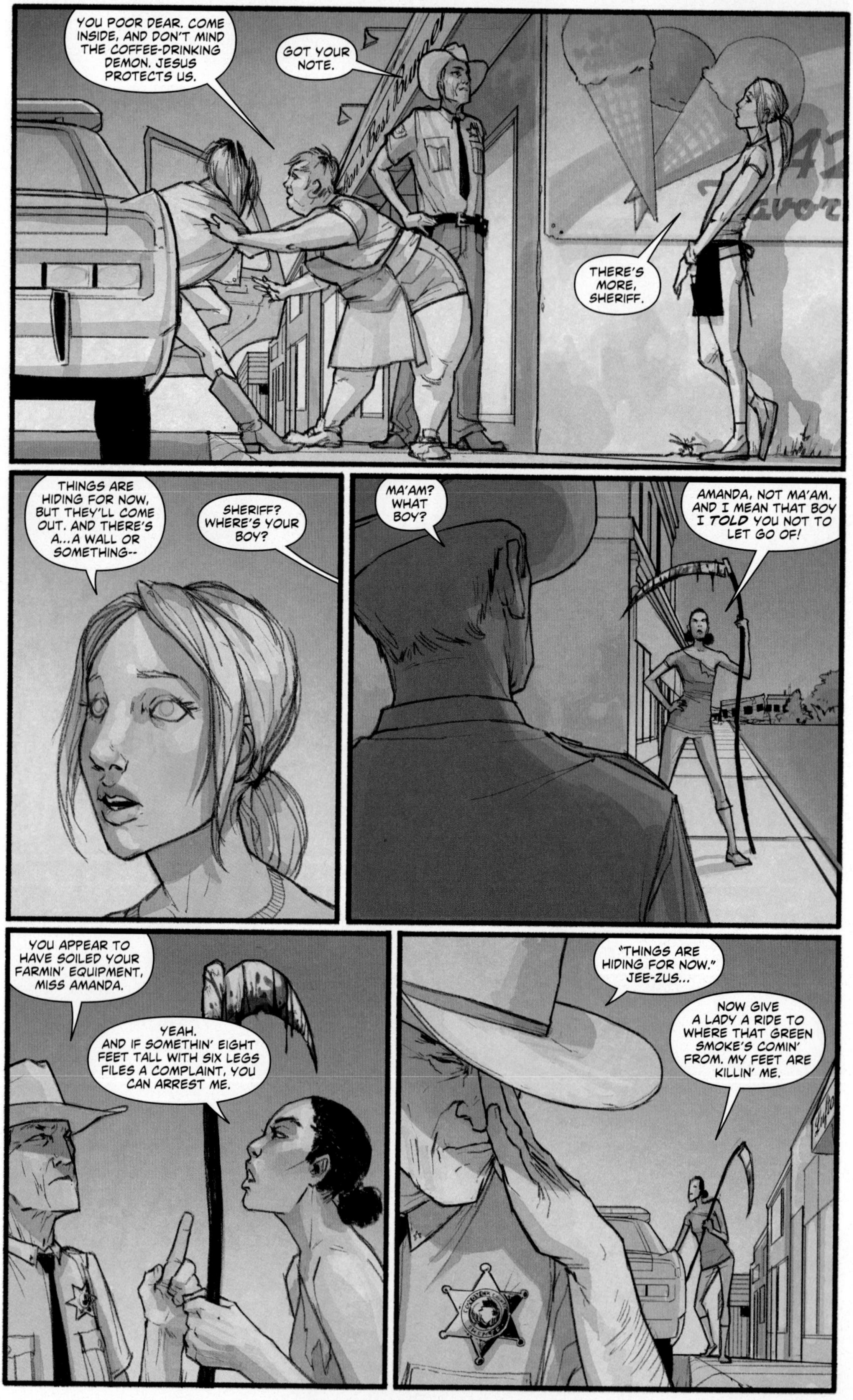
YOU POOR DEAR. COME INSIDE, AND DON'T MIND THE COFFEE-DRINKING DEMON. JESUS PROTECTS US.
GOT YOUR NOTE.
THERE'S MORE, SHERIFF.
THINGS ARE HIDING FOR NOW, BUT THEY'LL COME OUT. AND THERE'S A...A WALL OR SOMETHING--
SHERIFF? WHERE'S YOUR BOY?
MA'AM? WHAT BOY?
AMANDA, NOT MA'AM. AND I MEAN THAT BOY I *TOLD* YOU NOT TO LET GO OF!
YOU APPEAR TO HAVE SOILED YOUR FARMIN' EQUIPMENT, MISS AMANDA.
YEAH. AND IF SOMETHIN' EIGHT FEET TALL WITH SIX LEGS FILES A COMPLAINT, YOU CAN ARREST ME.
"THINGS ARE HIDING FOR NOW." JEE-ZUS...
NOW GIVE A LADY A RIDE TO WHERE THAT GREEN SMOKE'S COMIN' FROM. MY FEET ARE KILLIN' ME.

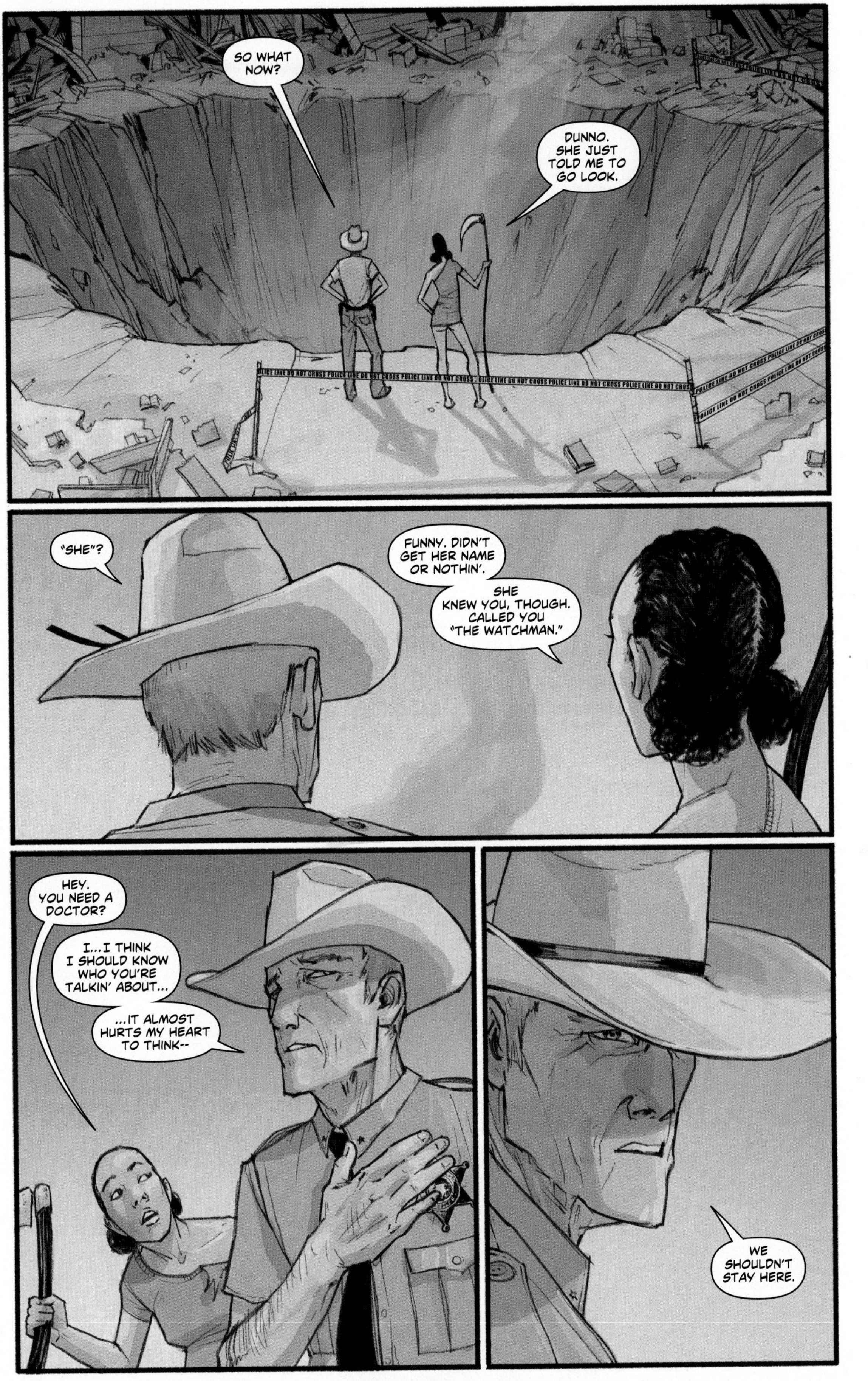
SO WHAT NOW?
DUNNO. SHE JUST TOLD ME TO GO LOOK.
POLICE LINE DO NOT CROSS POLICE LINE DO NOT CROSS
"SHE"?
FUNNY. DIDN'T GET HER NAME OR NOTHIN'.
SHE KNEW YOU, THOUGH. CALLED YOU "THE WATCHMAN."
HEY. YOU NEED A DOCTOR?
I...I THINK I SHOULD KNOW WHO YOU'RE TALKIN' ABOUT...
...IT ALMOST HURTS MY HEART TO THINK--
WE SHOULDN'T STAY HERE.

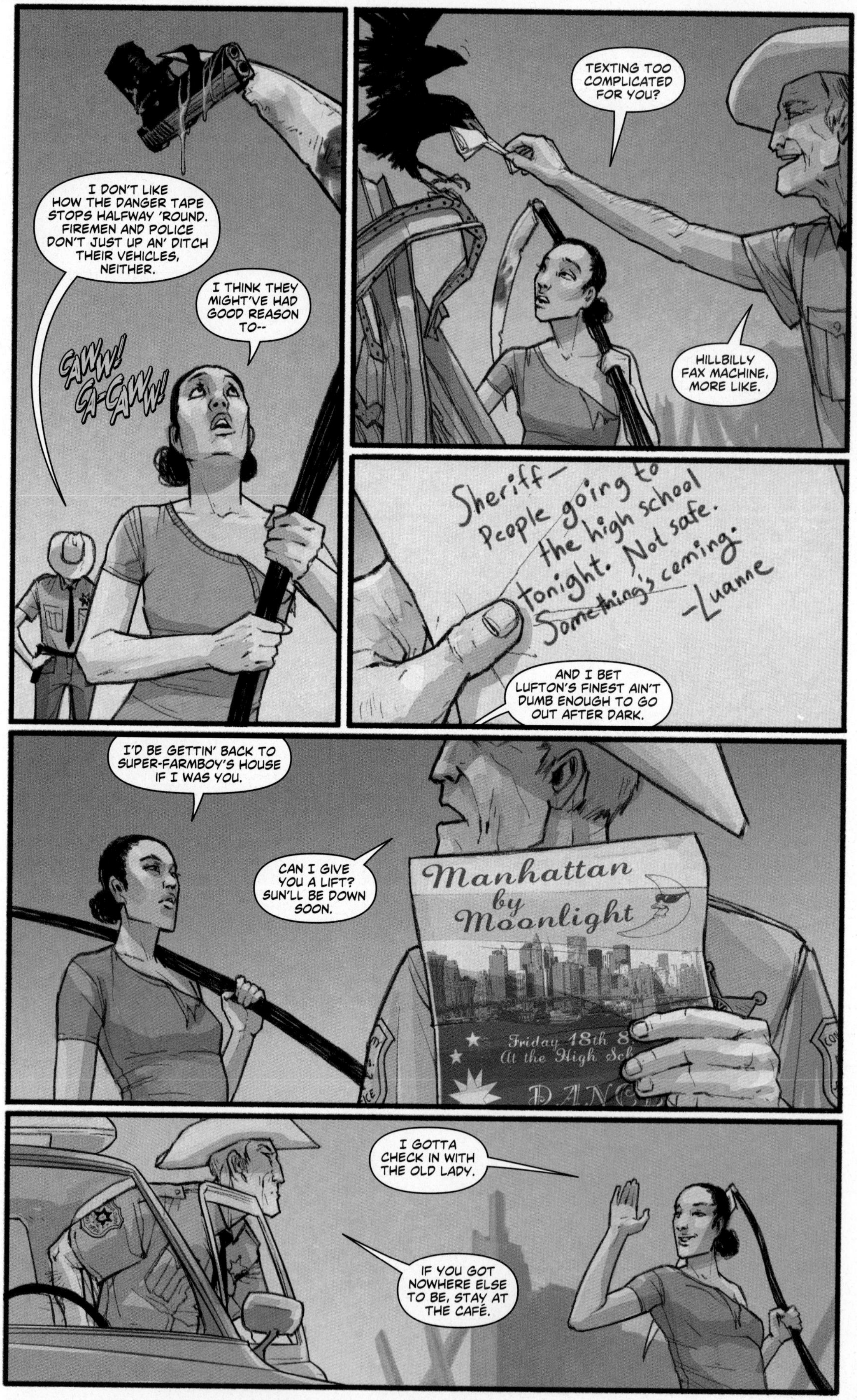

I DON'T LIKE HOW THE DANGER TAPE STOPS HALFWAY 'ROUND. FIREMEN AND POLICE DON'T JUST UP AN' DITCH THEIR VEHICLES, NEITHER.
I THINK THEY MIGHT'VE HAD GOOD REASON TO--
CAWW! CA-CAWW!
TEXTING TOO COMPLICATED FOR YOU?
HILLBILLY FAX MACHINE, MORE LIKE.
Sheriff— People going to the high school tonight. Not safe. Something's coming. -Luanne
AND I BET LUFTON'S FINEST AIN'T DUMB ENOUGH TO GO OUT AFTER DARK.
I'D BE GETTIN' BACK TO SUPER-FARMBOY'S HOUSE IF I WAS YOU.
CAN I GIVE YOU A LIFT? SUN'LL BE DOWN SOON.
Manhattan by Moonlight
Friday 18th 8
At the High Sch
I GOTTA CHECK IN WITH THE OLD LADY.
IF YOU GOT NOWHERE ELSE TO BE, STAY AT THE CAFÉ.

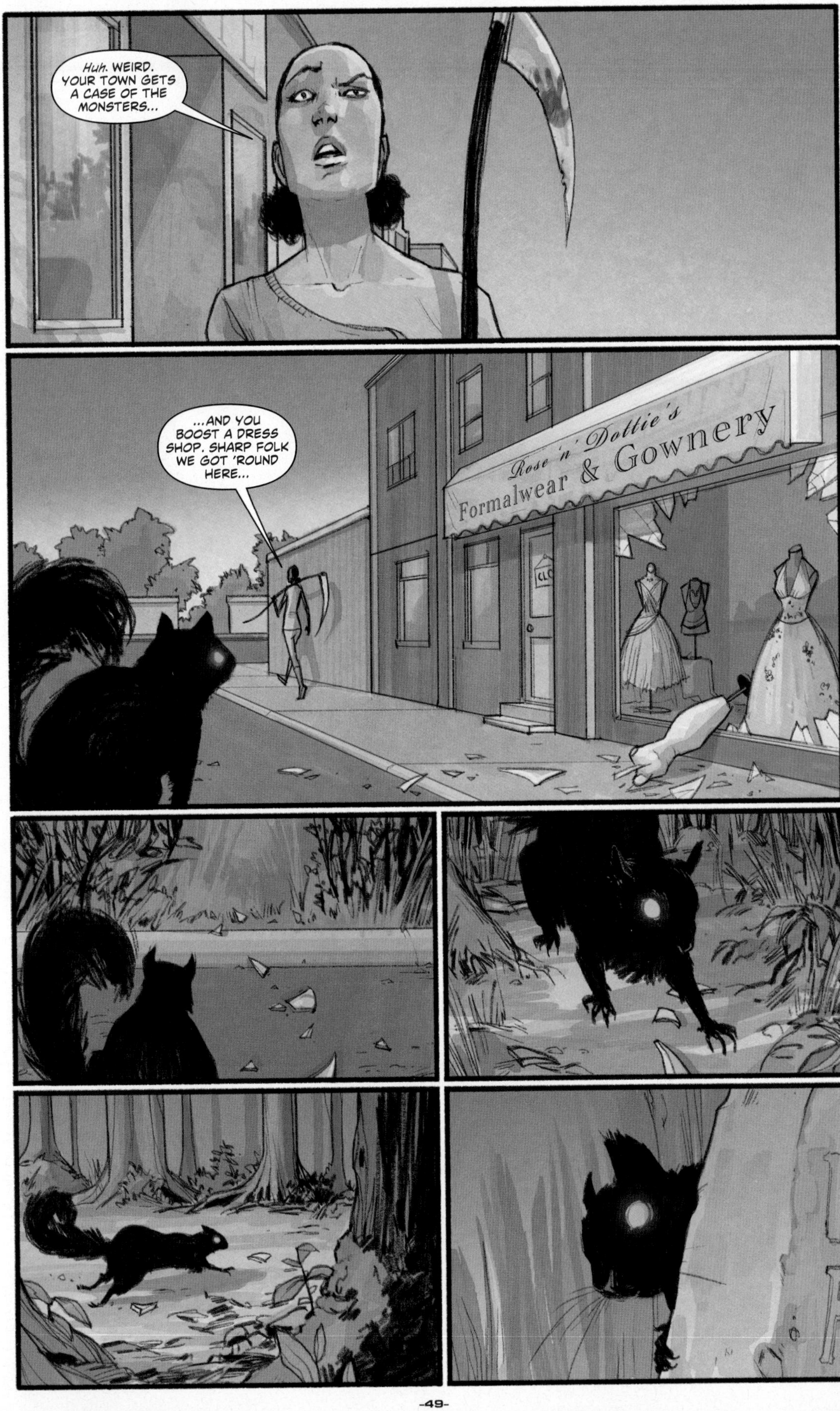

Huh. WEIRD. YOUR TOWN GETS A CASE OF THE MONSTERS...
...AND YOU BOOST A DRESS SHOP. SHARP FOLK WE GOT 'ROUND HERE...
Rose 'n' Dottie's
Formalwear & Gownery

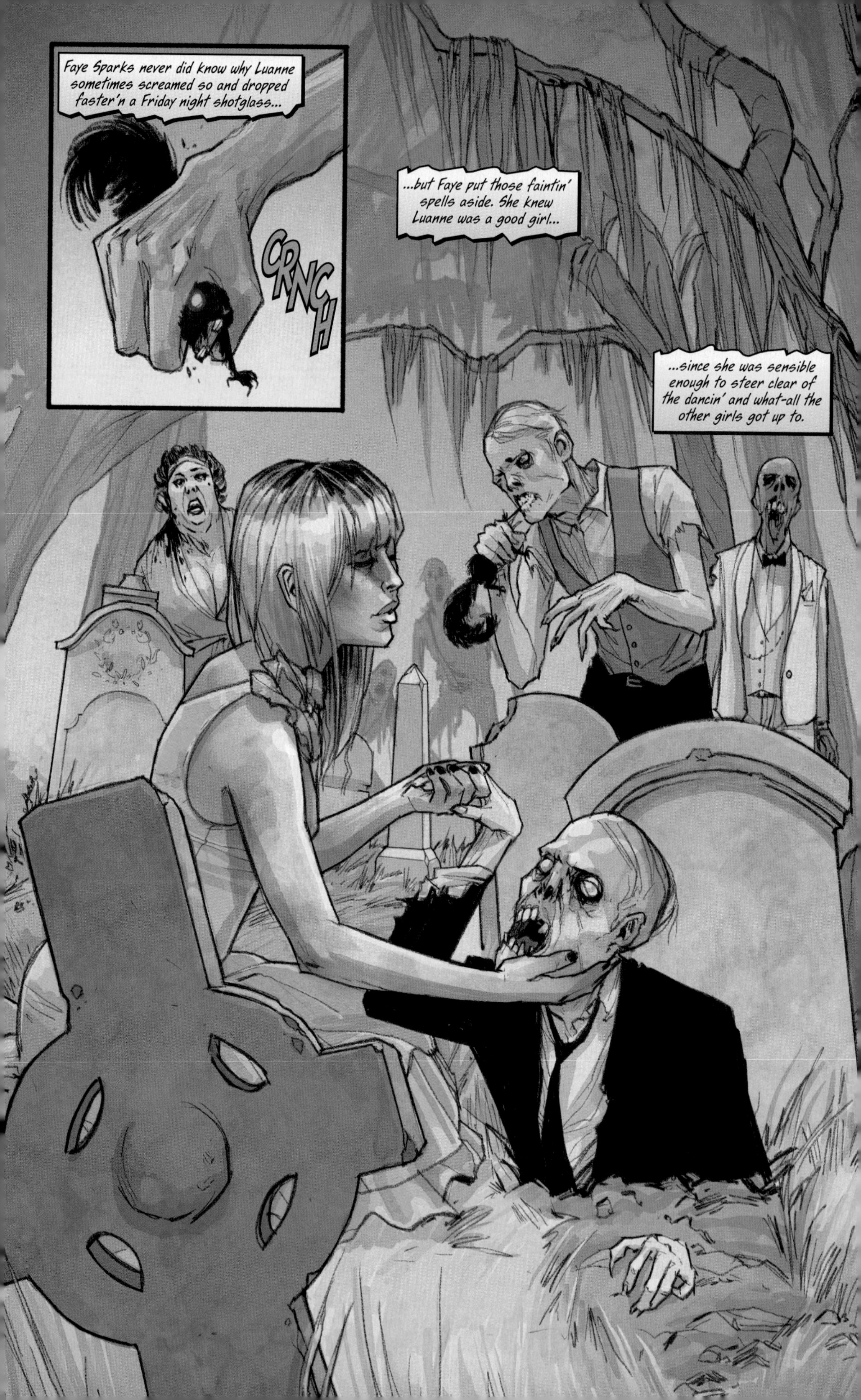
Faye Sparks never did know why Luanne sometimes screamed so and dropped faster'n a Friday night shotglass...
CRNCH
...but Faye put those faintin' spells aside. She knew Luanne was a good girl...
...since she was sensible enough to steer clear of the dancin' and what-all the other girls got up to.

CHAPTER THREE

A Time to MOURN, an' a Time to DANCE

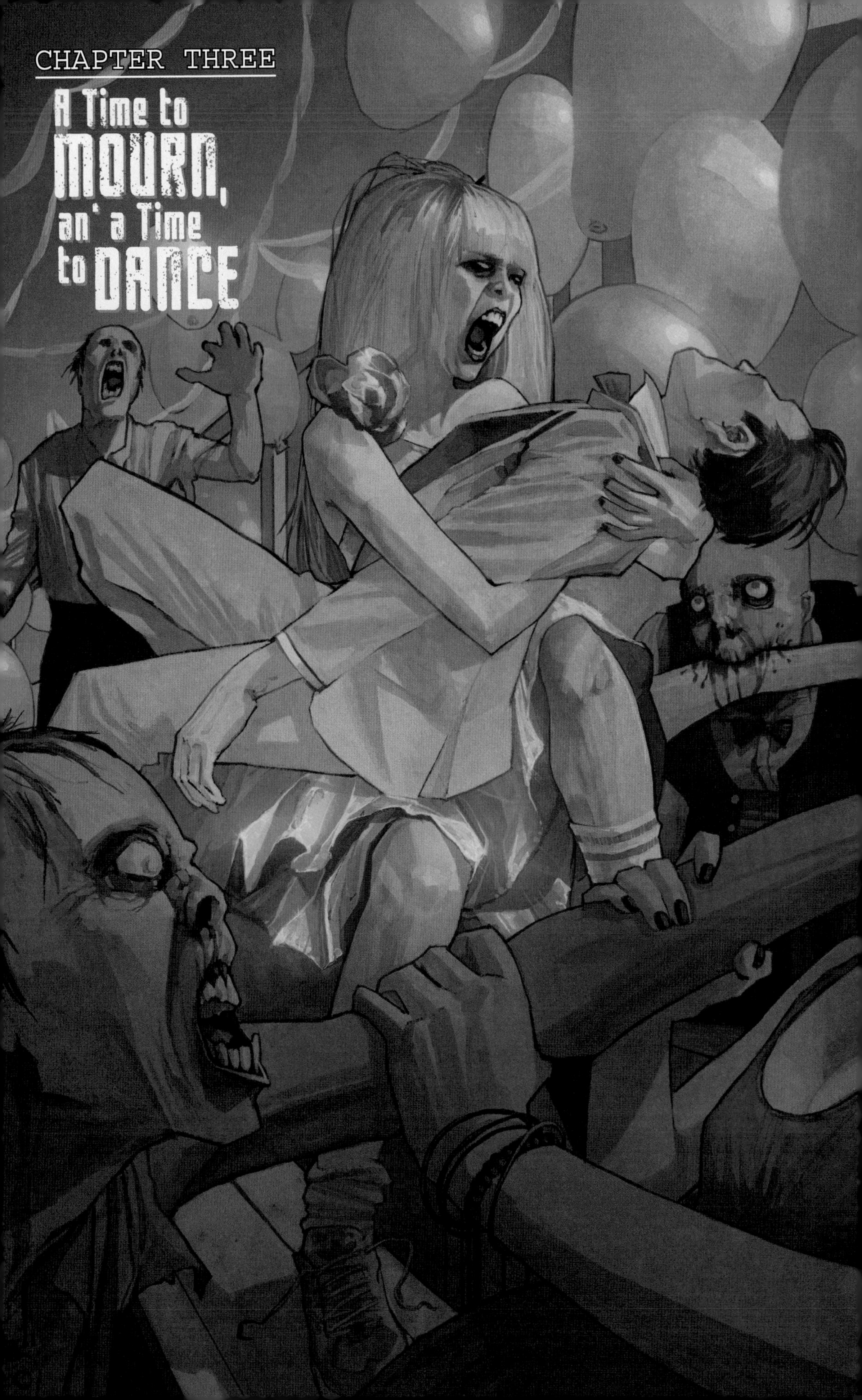

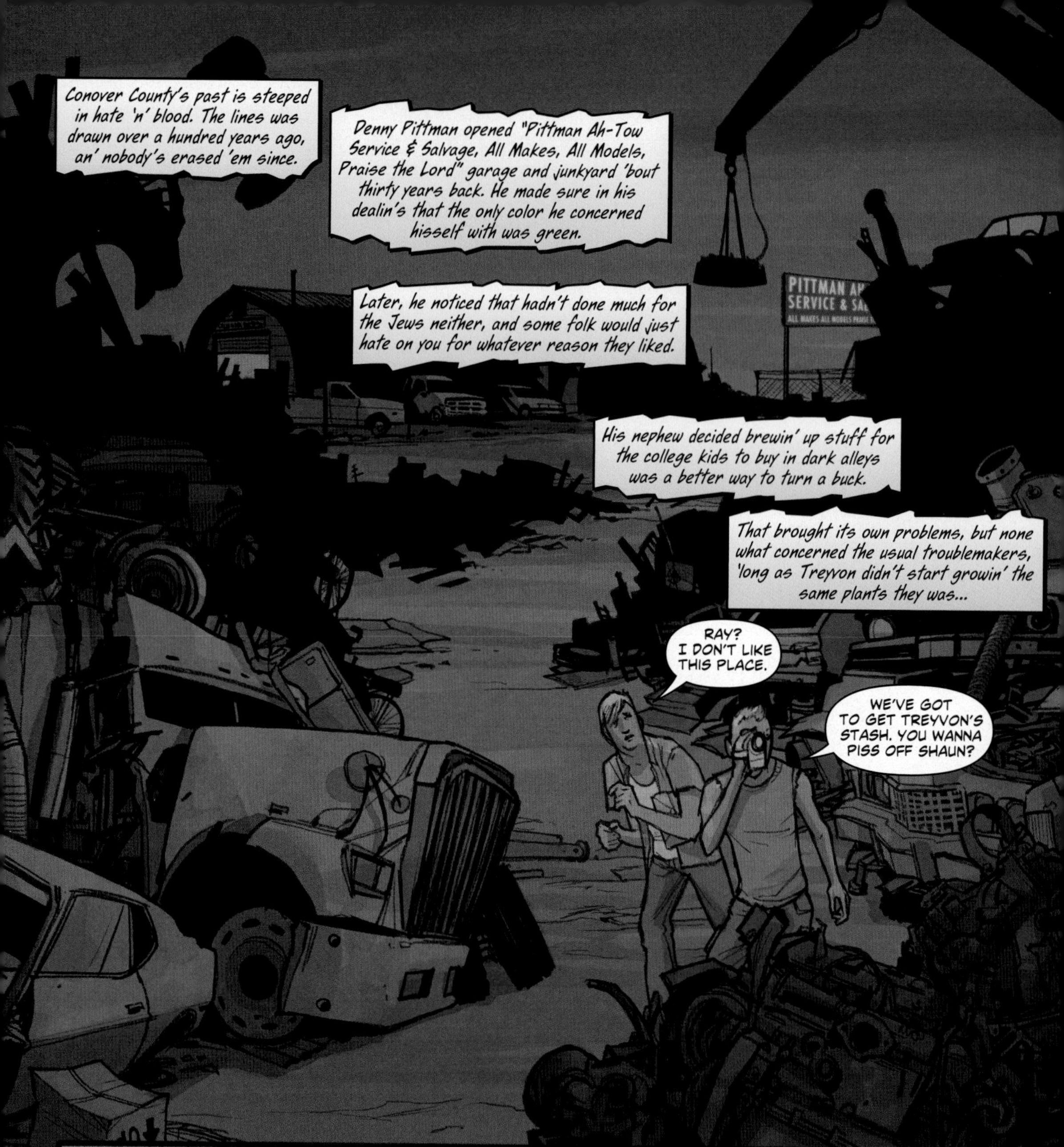
Conover County's past is steeped in hate 'n' blood. The lines was drawn over a hundred years ago, an' nobody's erased 'em since.
Denny Pittman opened "Pittman Ah-Tow Service & Salvage, All Makes, All Models, Praise the Lord" garage and junkyard 'bout thirty years back. He made sure in his dealin's that the only color he concerned hisself with was green.
Later, he noticed that hadn't done much for the Jews neither, and some folk would just hate on you for whatever reason they liked.
His nephew decided brewin' up stuff for the college kids to buy in dark alleys was a better way to turn a buck.
That brought its own problems, but none what concerned the usual troublemakers, 'long as Treyvon didn't start growin' the same plants they was...
RAY? I DON'T LIKE THIS PLACE.
WE'VE GOT TO GET TREYVON'S STASH. YOU WANNA PISS OFF SHAUN?

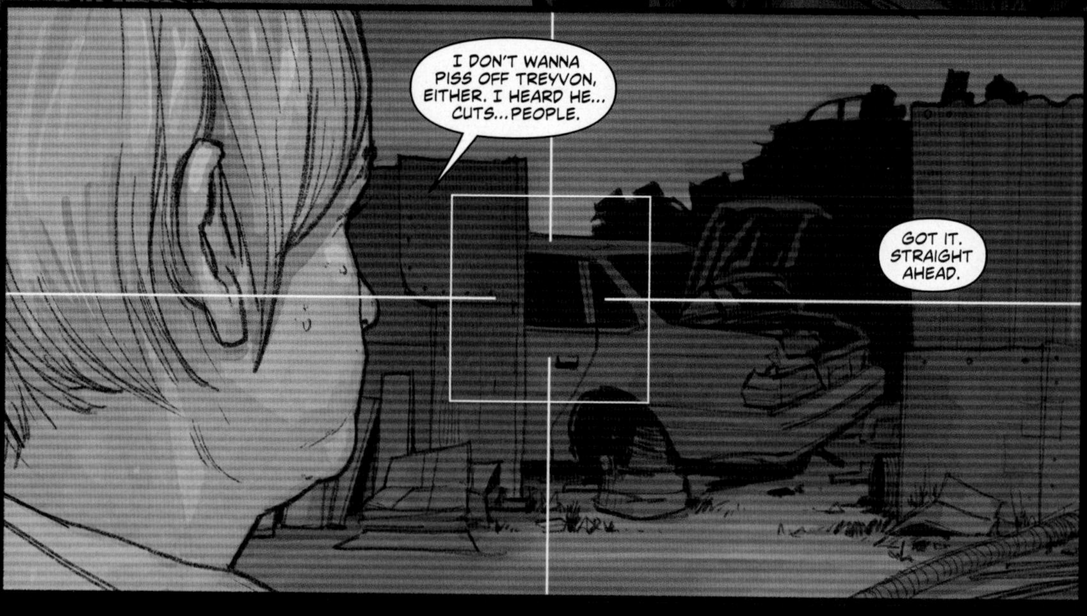
I DON'T WANNA PISS OFF TREYVON, EITHER. I HEARD HE... CUTS...PEOPLE.
GOT IT. STRAIGHT AHEAD.

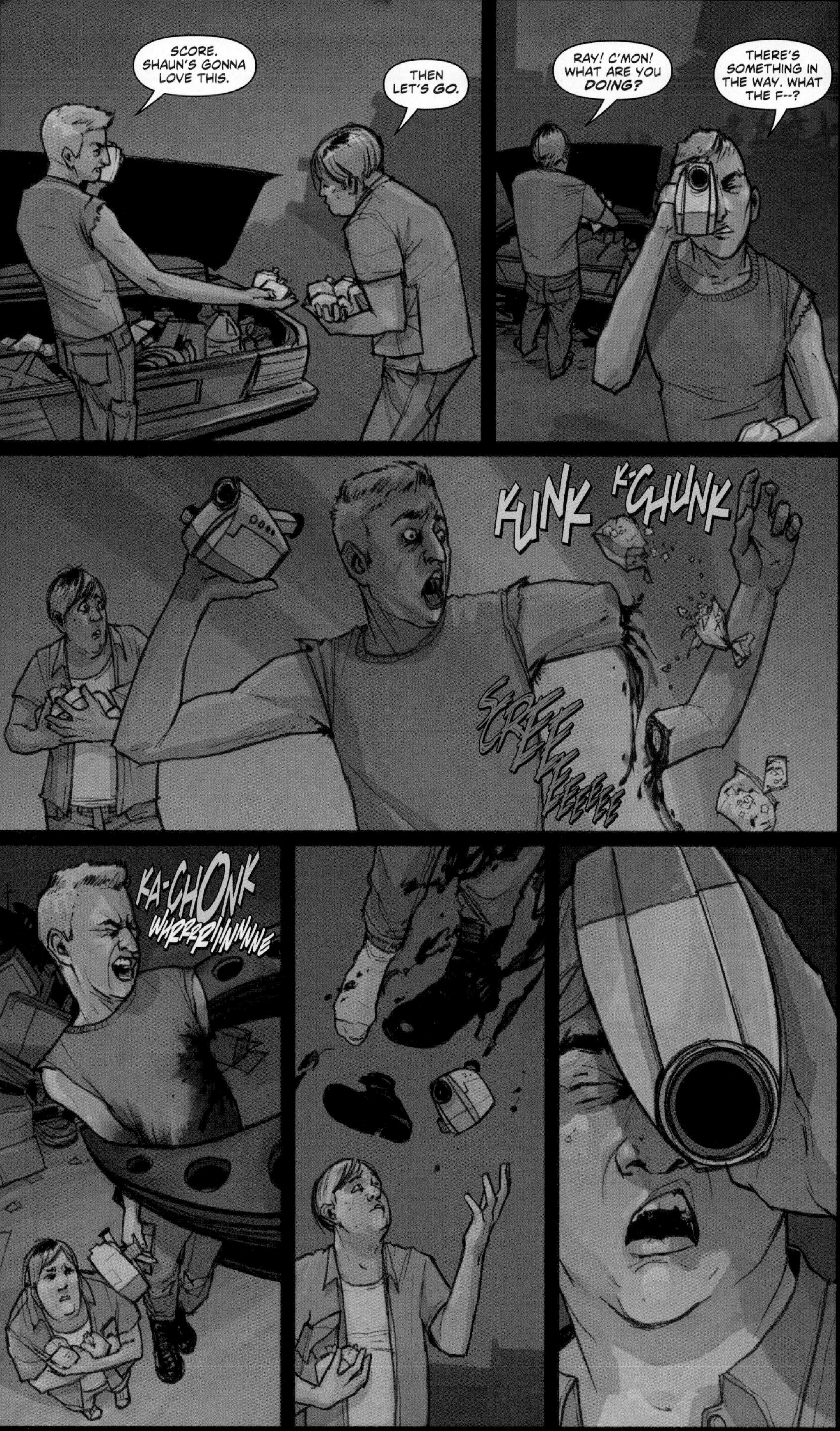
SCORE. SHAUN'S GONNA LOVE THIS.
THEN LET'S GO.
RAY! C'MON! WHAT ARE YOU DOING?
THERE'S SOMETHING IN THE WAY. WHAT THE F--?
KUNK
K-CHUNK
SCREEEEEEEEE
KA-CHONK
WHRRRRIINNNNE

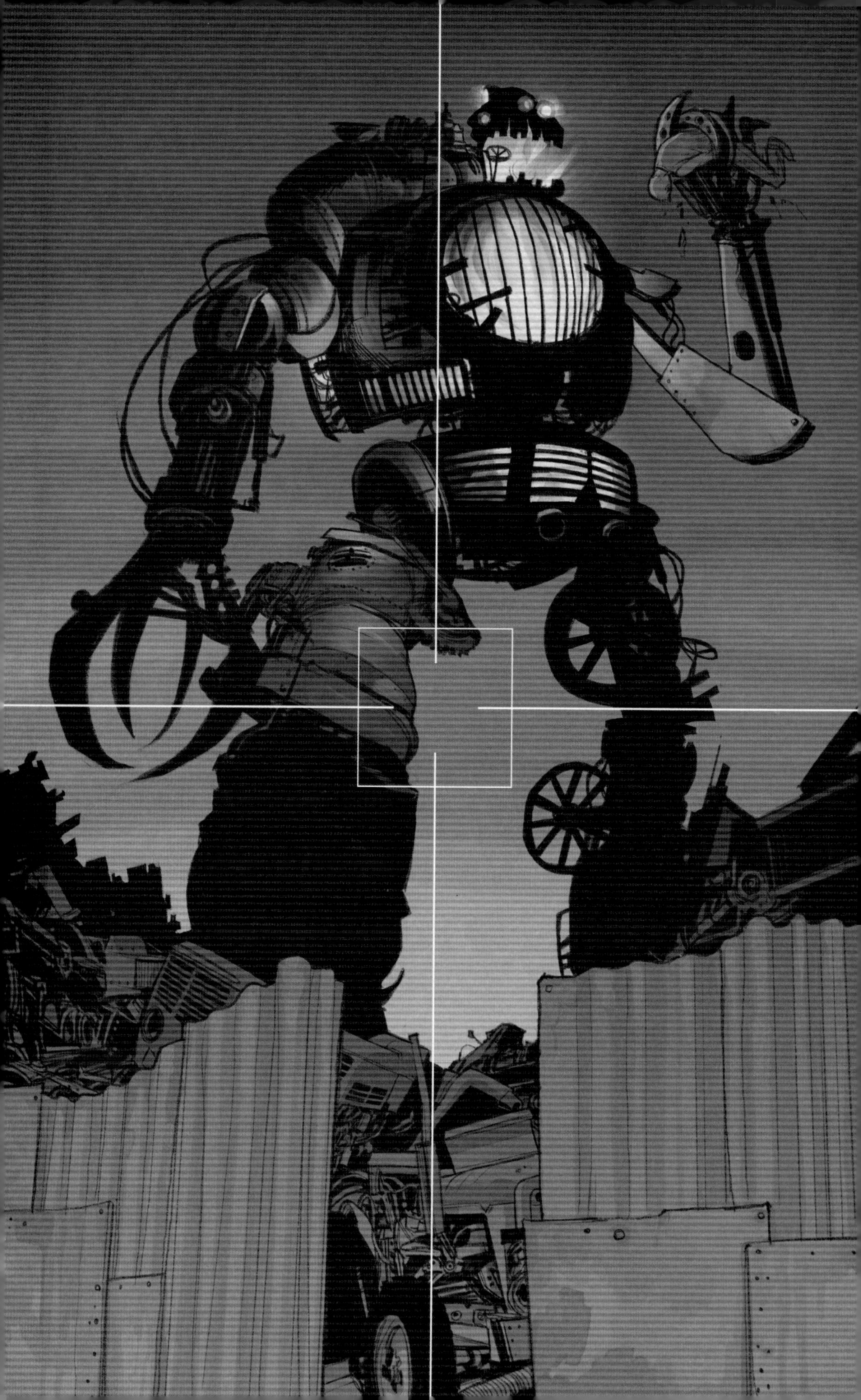

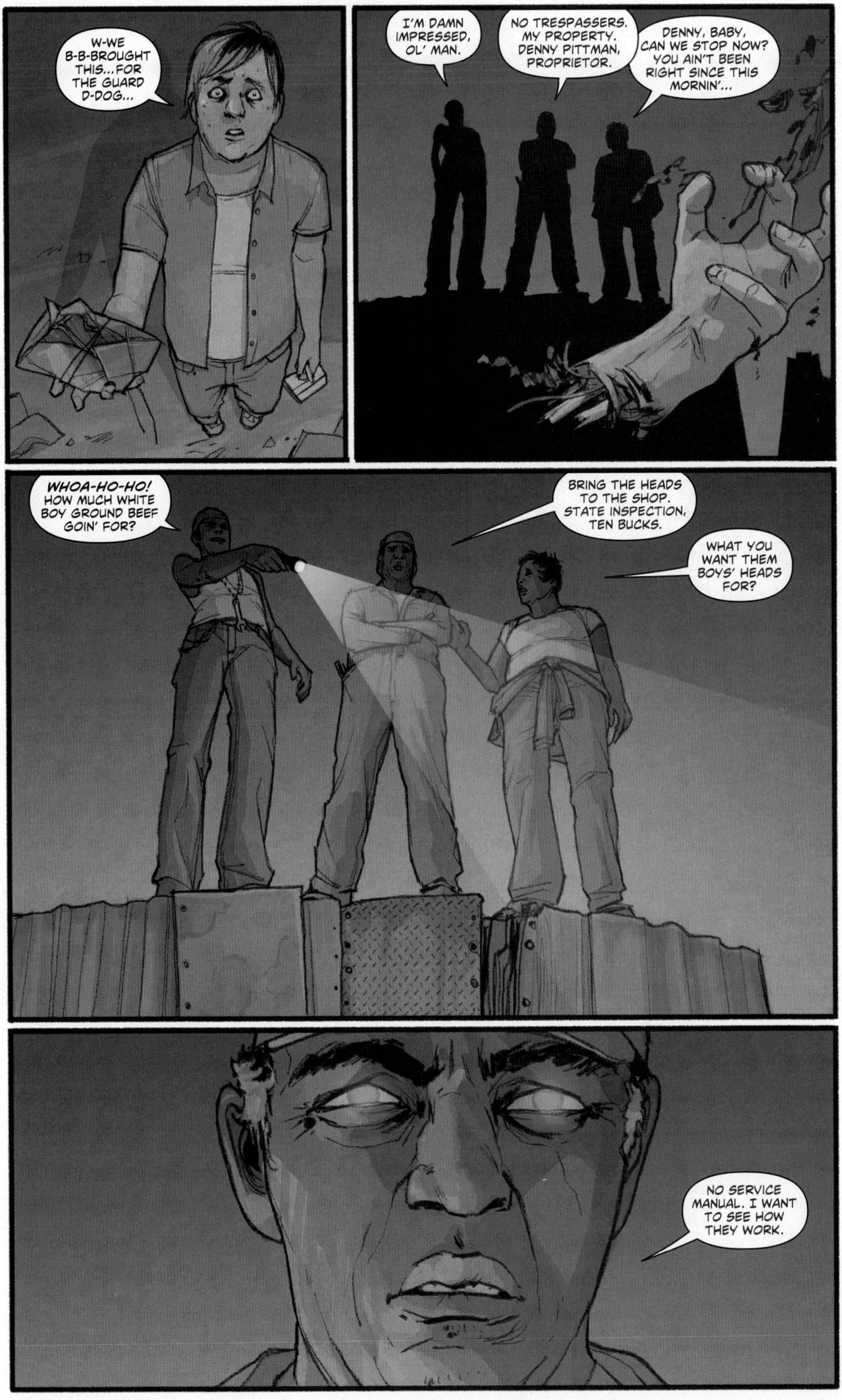
W-WE B-B-BROUGHT THIS...FOR THE GUARD D-DOG...
I'M DAMN IMPRESSED, OL' MAN.
NO TRESPASSERS. MY PROPERTY. DENNY PITTMAN, PROPRIETOR.
DENNY, BABY, CAN WE STOP NOW? YOU AIN'T BEEN RIGHT SINCE THIS MORNIN'...
WHOA-HO-HO! HOW MUCH WHITE BOY GROUND BEEF GOIN' FOR?
BRING THE HEADS TO THE SHOP. STATE INSPECTION, TEN BUCKS.
WHAT YOU WANT THEM BOYS' HEADS FOR?
NO SERVICE MANUAL. I WANT TO SEE HOW THEY WORK.

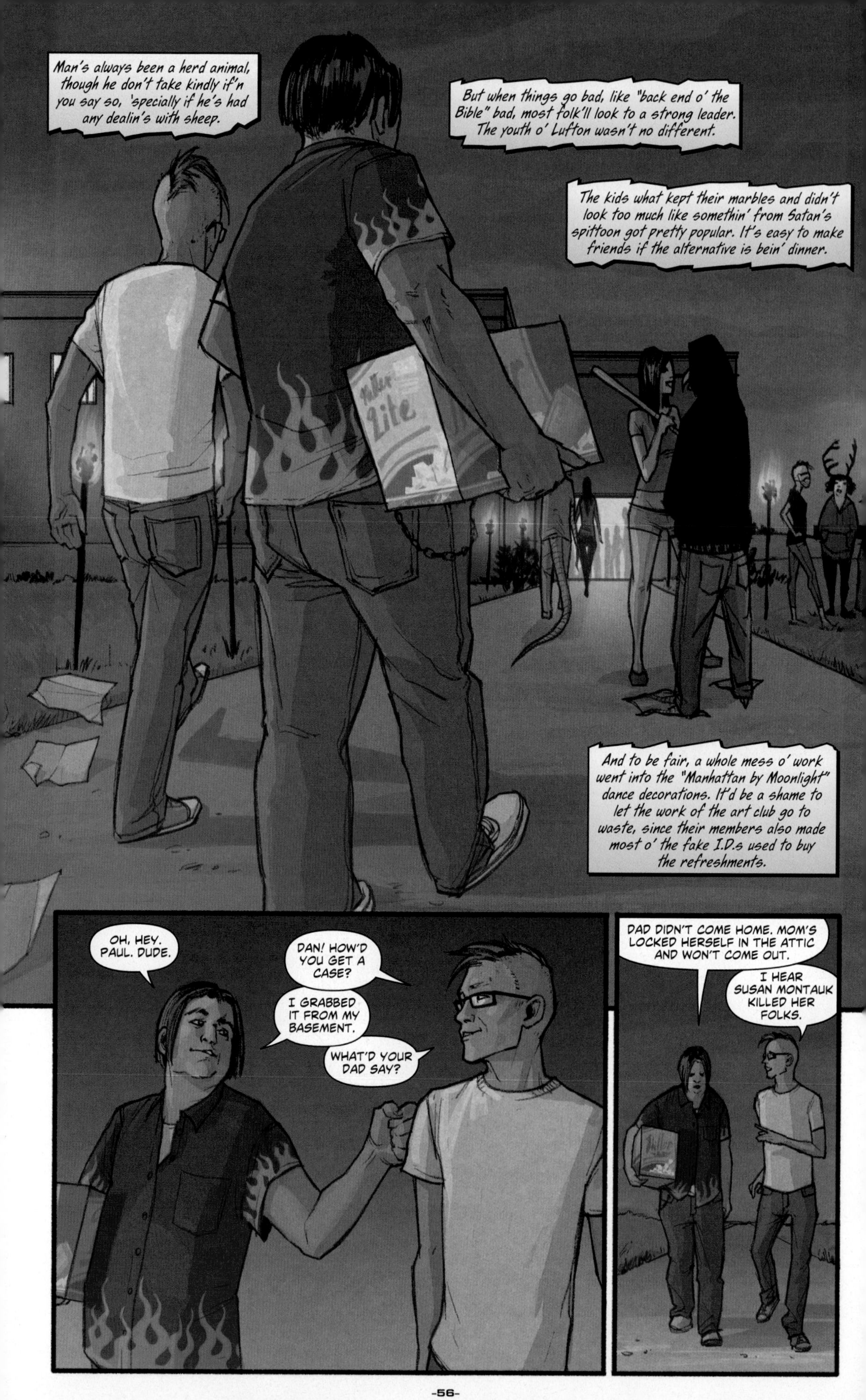
Man's always been a herd animal, though he don't take kindly if'n you say so, 'specially if he's had any dealin's with sheep.
But when things go bad, like "back end o' the Bible" bad, most folk'll look to a strong leader. The youth o' Lufton wasn't no different.
The kids what kept their marbles and didn't look too much like somethin' from Satan's spittoon got pretty popular. It's easy to make friends if the alternative is bein' dinner.
And to be fair, a whole mess o' work went into the "Manhattan by Moonlight" dance decorations. It'd be a shame to let the work of the art club go to waste, since their members also made most o' the fake I.D.s used to buy the refreshments.
OH, HEY. PAUL. DUDE.
DAN! HOW'D YOU GET A CASE?
I GRABBED IT FROM MY BASEMENT.
WHAT'D YOUR DAD SAY?
DAD DIDN'T COME HOME. MOM'S LOCKED HERSELF IN THE ATTIC AND WON'T COME OUT.
I HEAR SUSAN MONTAUK KILLED HER FOLKS.

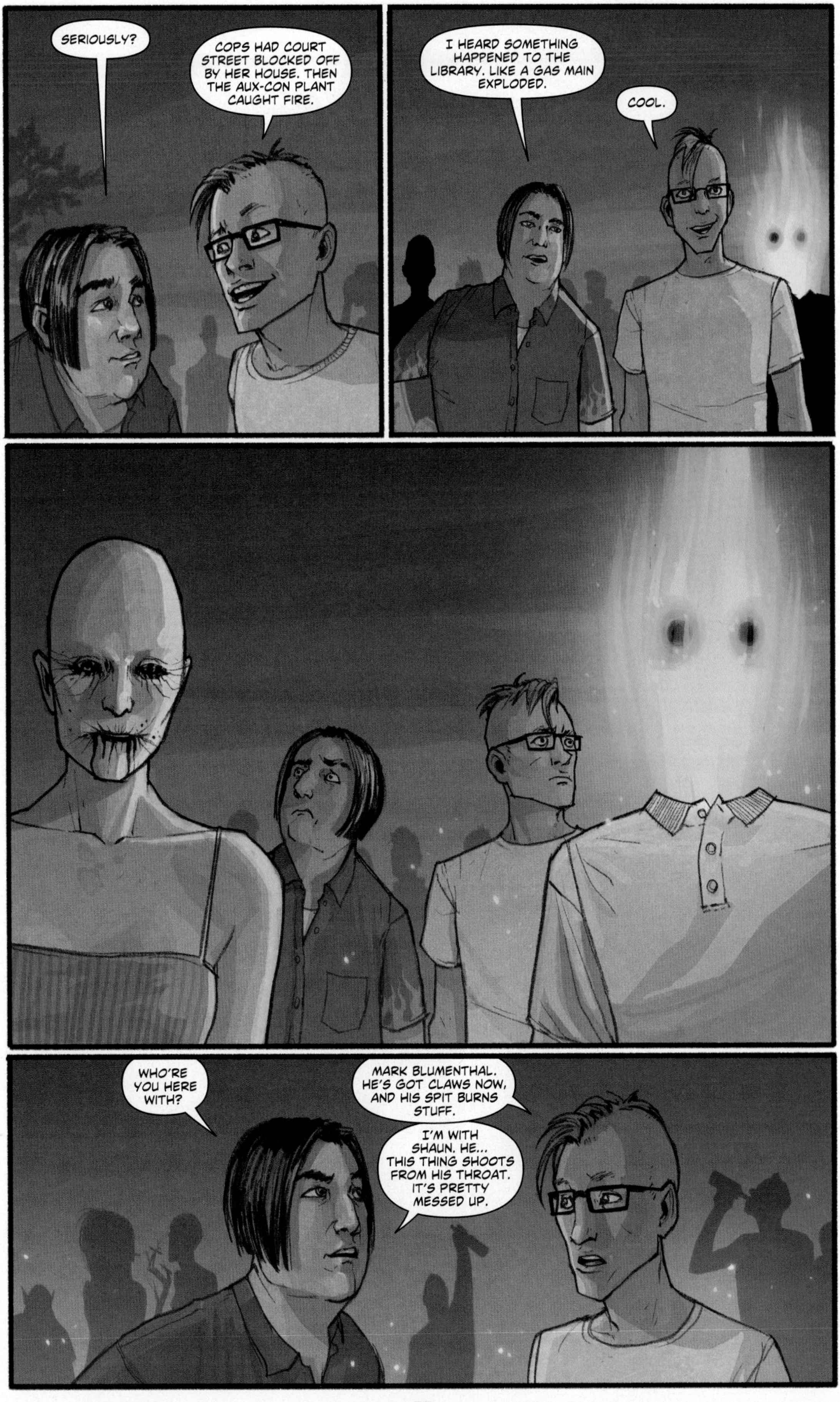
SERIOUSLY?
COPS HAD COURT STREET BLOCKED OFF BY HER HOUSE. THEN THE AUX-CON PLANT CAUGHT FIRE.
I HEARD SOMETHING HAPPENED TO THE LIBRARY. LIKE A GAS MAIN EXPLODED.
COOL.
WHO'RE YOU HERE WITH?
MARK BLUMENTHAL. HE'S GOT CLAWS NOW, AND HIS SPIT BURNS STUFF.
I'M WITH SHAUN. HE... THIS THING SHOOTS FROM HIS THROAT. IT'S PRETTY MESSED UP.

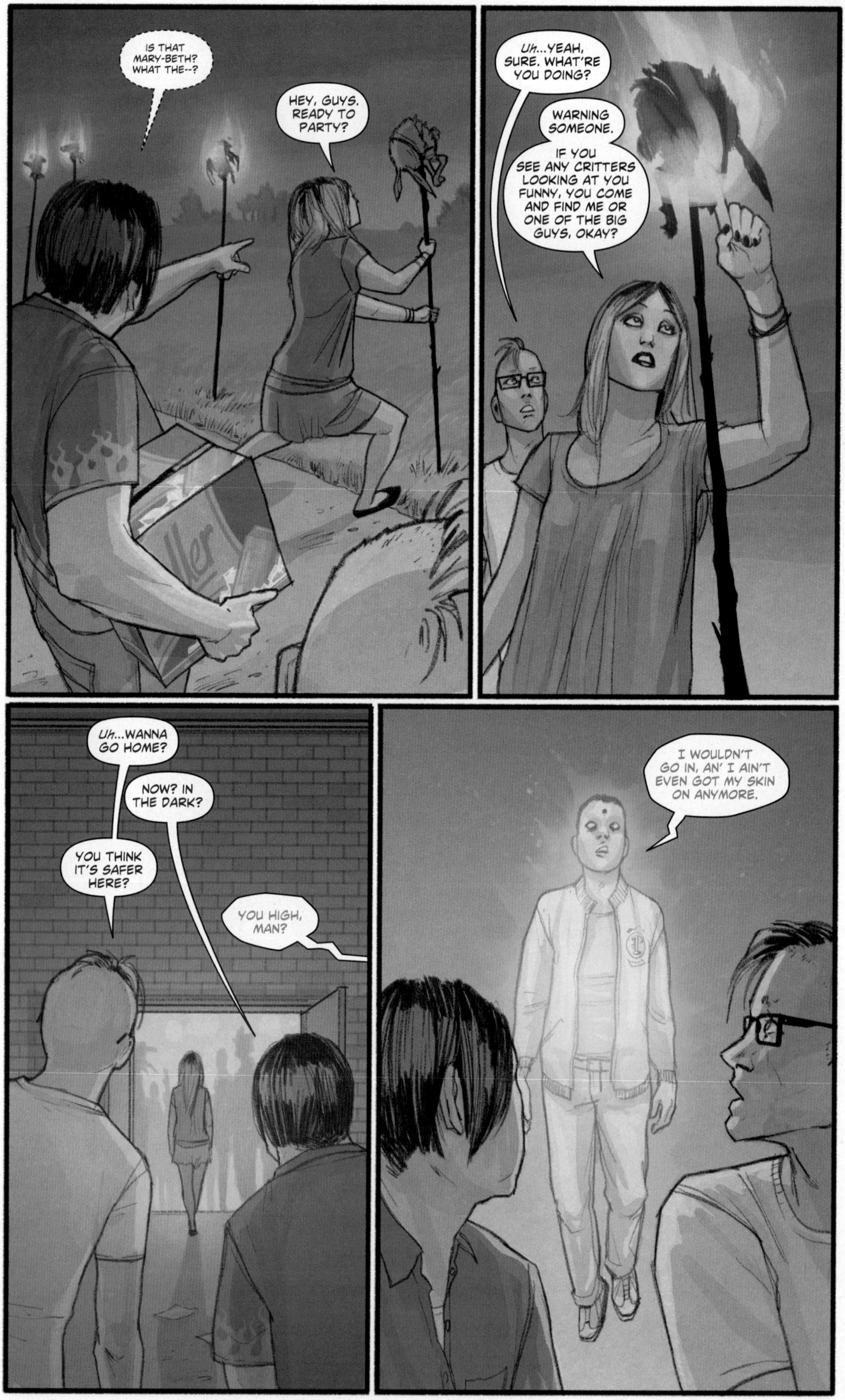
IS THAT MARY-BETH? WHAT THE--?
HEY, GUYS. READY TO PARTY?
Uh...YEAH, SURE. WHAT'RE YOU DOING?
WARNING SOMEONE.
IF YOU SEE ANY CRITTERS LOOKING AT YOU FUNNY, YOU COME AND FIND ME OR ONE OF THE BIG GUYS, OKAY?
Uh...WANNA GO HOME?
NOW? IN THE DARK?
YOU THINK IT'S SAFER HERE?
YOU HIGH, MAN?
I WOULDN'T GO IN, AN' I AIN'T EVEN GOT MY SKIN ON ANYMORE.

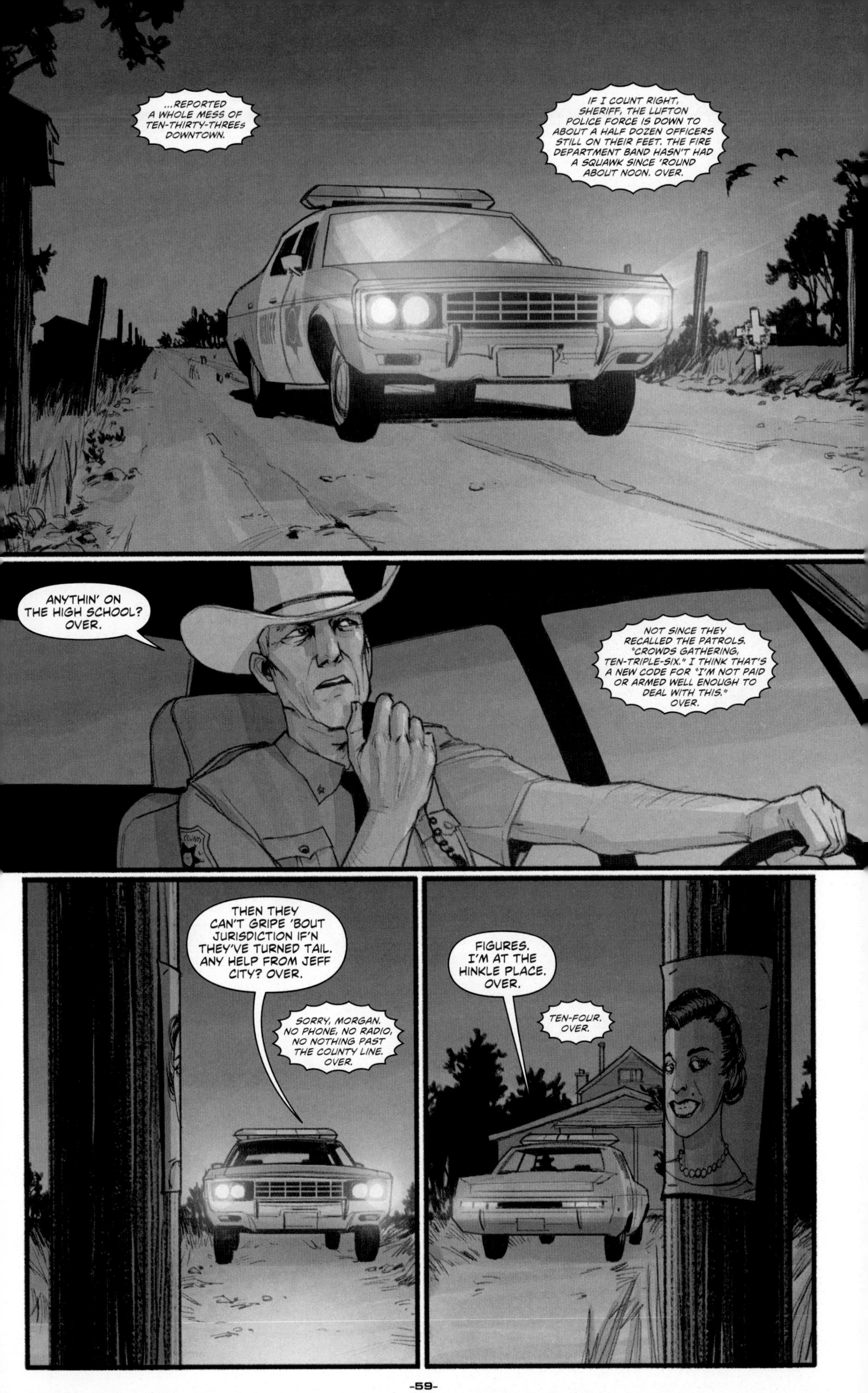
...REPORTED A WHOLE MESS OF TEN-THIRTY-THREES DOWNTOWN.
IF I COUNT RIGHT, SHERIFF, THE LUFTON POLICE FORCE IS DOWN TO ABOUT A HALF DOZEN OFFICERS STILL ON THEIR FEET. THE FIRE DEPARTMENT BAND HASN'T HAD A SQUAWK SINCE 'ROUND ABOUT NOON. OVER.
ANYTHIN' ON THE HIGH SCHOOL? OVER.
NOT SINCE THEY RECALLED THE PATROLS. "CROWDS GATHERING, TEN-TRIPLE-SIX." I THINK THAT'S A NEW CODE FOR "I'M NOT PAID OR ARMED WELL ENOUGH TO DEAL WITH THIS." OVER.
THEN THEY CAN'T GRIPE 'BOUT JURISDICTION IF'N THEY'VE TURNED TAIL. ANY HELP FROM JEFF CITY? OVER.
SORRY, MORGAN. NO PHONE, NO RADIO, NO NOTHING PAST THE COUNTY LINE. OVER.
FIGURES. I'M AT THE HINKLE PLACE. OVER.
TEN-FOUR. OVER.

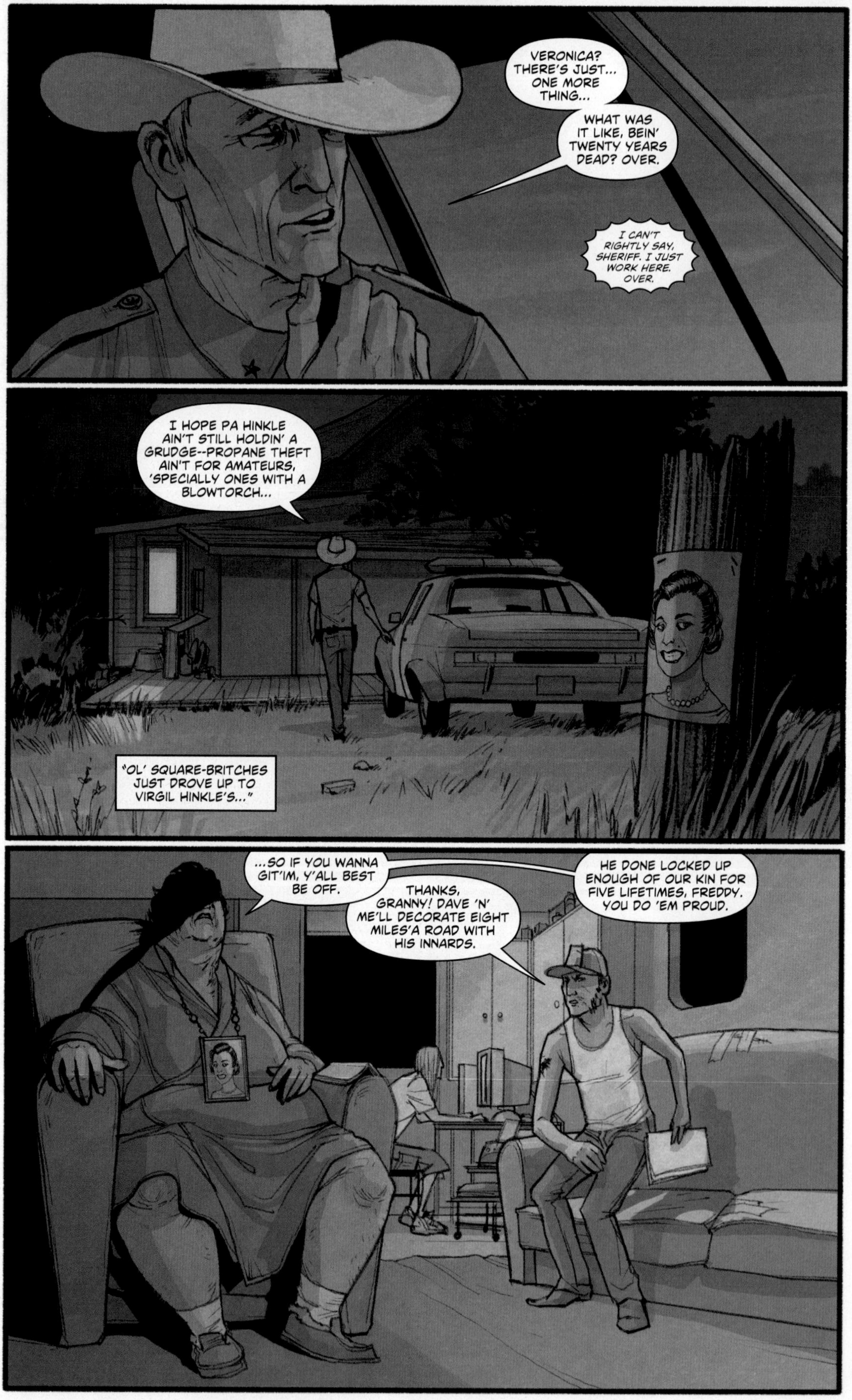
VERONICA? THERE'S JUST... ONE MORE THING...
WHAT WAS IT LIKE, BEIN' TWENTY YEARS DEAD? OVER.
I CAN'T RIGHTLY SAY, SHERIFF. I JUST WORK HERE. OVER.
I HOPE PA HINKLE AIN'T STILL HOLDIN' A GRUDGE--PROPANE THEFT AIN'T FOR AMATEURS, 'SPECIALLY ONES WITH A BLOWTORCH...
"OL' SQUARE-BRITCHES JUST DROVE UP TO VIRGIL HINKLE'S..."
...SO IF YOU WANNA GIT'IM, Y'ALL BEST BE OFF.
HE DONE LOCKED UP ENOUGH OF OUR KIN FOR FIVE LIFETIMES, FREDDY. YOU DO 'EM PROUD.
THANKS, GRANNY! DAVE 'N' ME'LL DECORATE EIGHT MILES'A ROAD WITH HIS INNARDS.

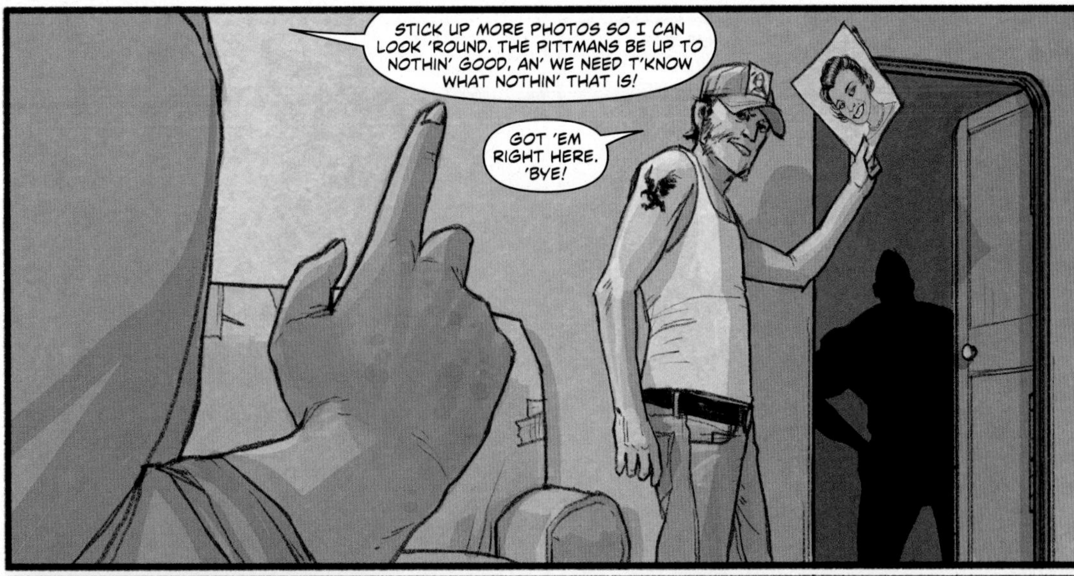
STICK UP MORE PHOTOS SO I CAN LOOK 'ROUND. THE PITTMANS BE UP TO NOTHIN' GOOD, AN' WE NEED T'KNOW WHAT NOTHIN' THAT IS!
GOT 'EM RIGHT HERE. 'BYE!

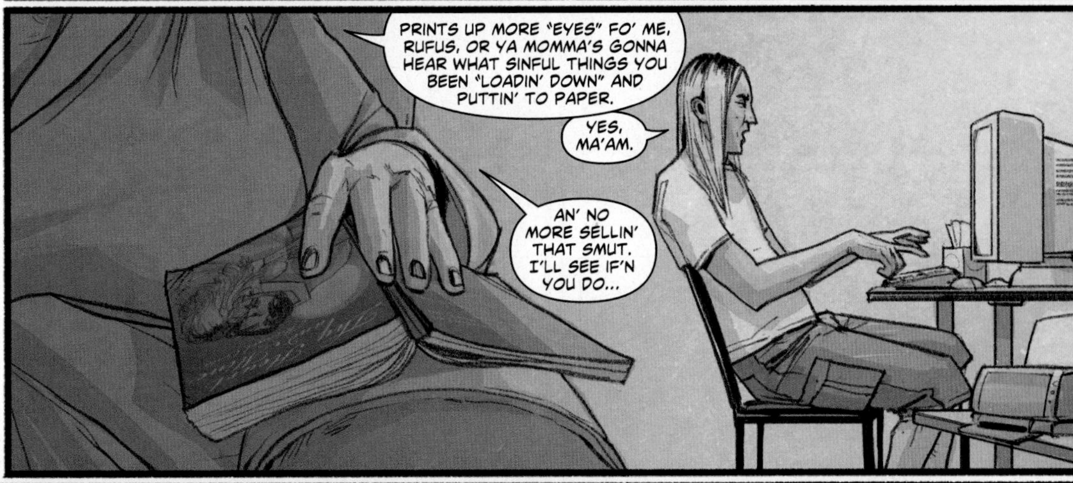
PRINTS UP MORE "EYES" FO' ME, RUFUS, OR YA MOMMA'S GONNA HEAR WHAT SINFUL THINGS YOU BEEN "LOADIN' DOWN" AND PUTTIN' TO PAPER.
YES, MA'AM.
AN' NO MORE SELLIN' THAT SMUT. I'LL SEE IF'N YOU DO...

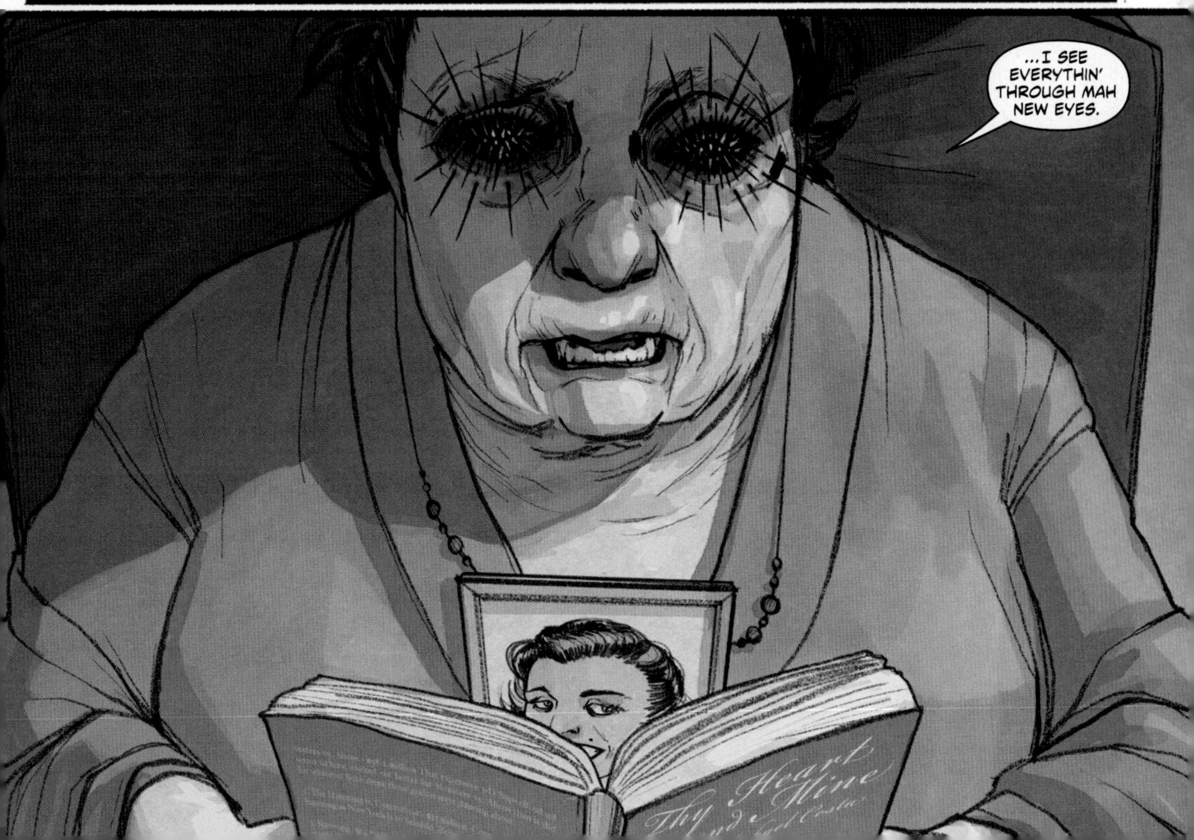
...I SEE EVERYTHIN' THROUGH MAH NEW EYES.
Thy Heart Mine

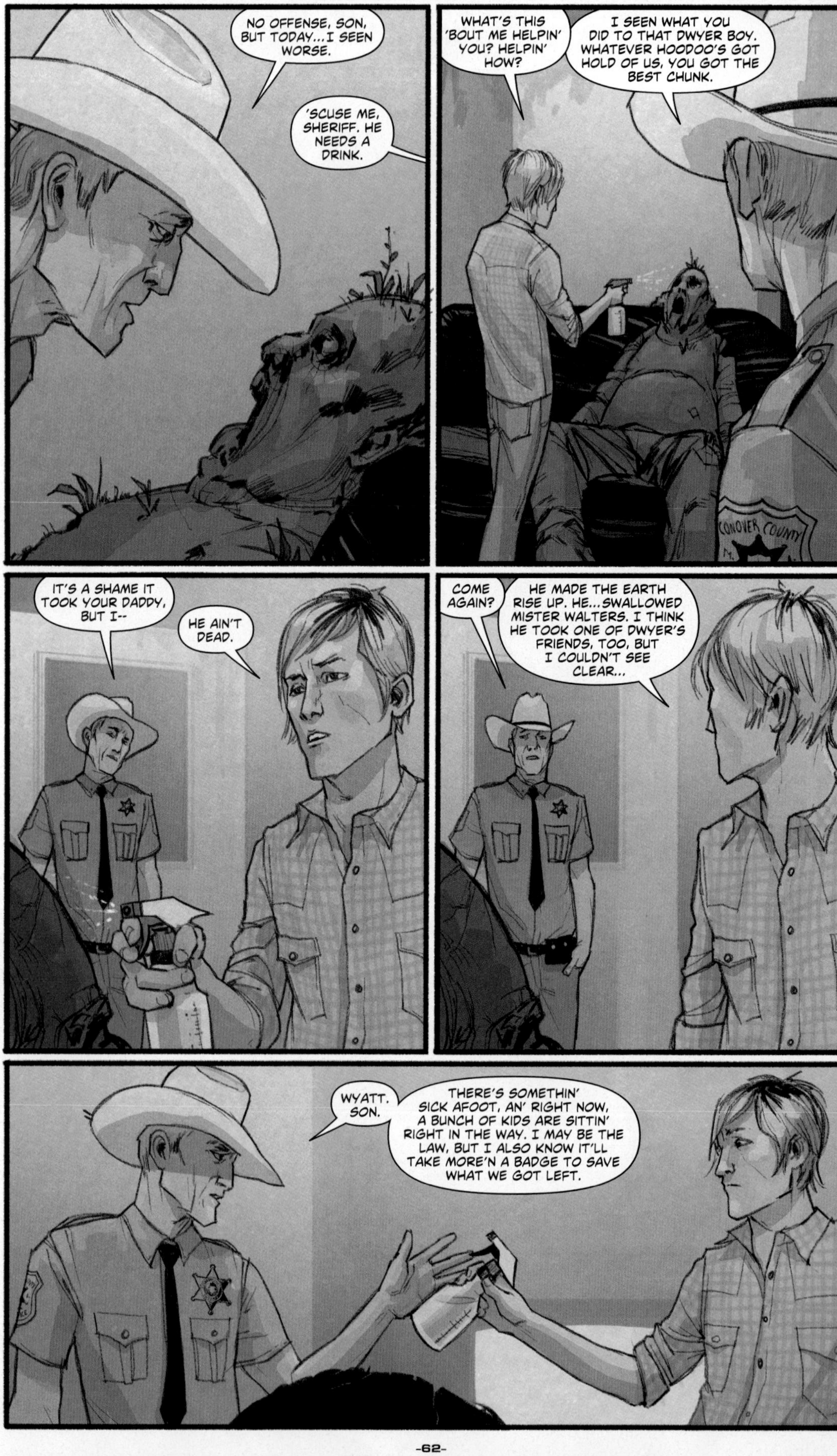
NO OFFENSE, SON, BUT TODAY...I SEEN WORSE.
'SCUSE ME, SHERIFF. HE NEEDS A DRINK.
WHAT'S THIS 'BOUT ME HELPIN' YOU? HELPIN' HOW?
I SEEN WHAT YOU DID TO THAT DWYER BOY. WHATEVER HOODOO'S GOT HOLD OF US, YOU GOT THE BEST CHUNK.
CONOVER COUNTY
IT'S A SHAME IT TOOK YOUR DADDY, BUT I--
HE AIN'T DEAD.
COME AGAIN?
HE MADE THE EARTH RISE UP. HE...SWALLOWED MISTER WALTERS. I THINK HE TOOK ONE OF DWYER'S FRIENDS, TOO, BUT I COULDN'T SEE CLEAR...
WYATT. SON.
THERE'S SOMETHIN' SICK AFOOT, AN' RIGHT NOW, A BUNCH OF KIDS ARE SITTIN' RIGHT IN THE WAY. I MAY BE THE LAW, BUT I ALSO KNOW IT'LL TAKE MORE'N A BADGE TO SAVE WHAT WE GOT LEFT.

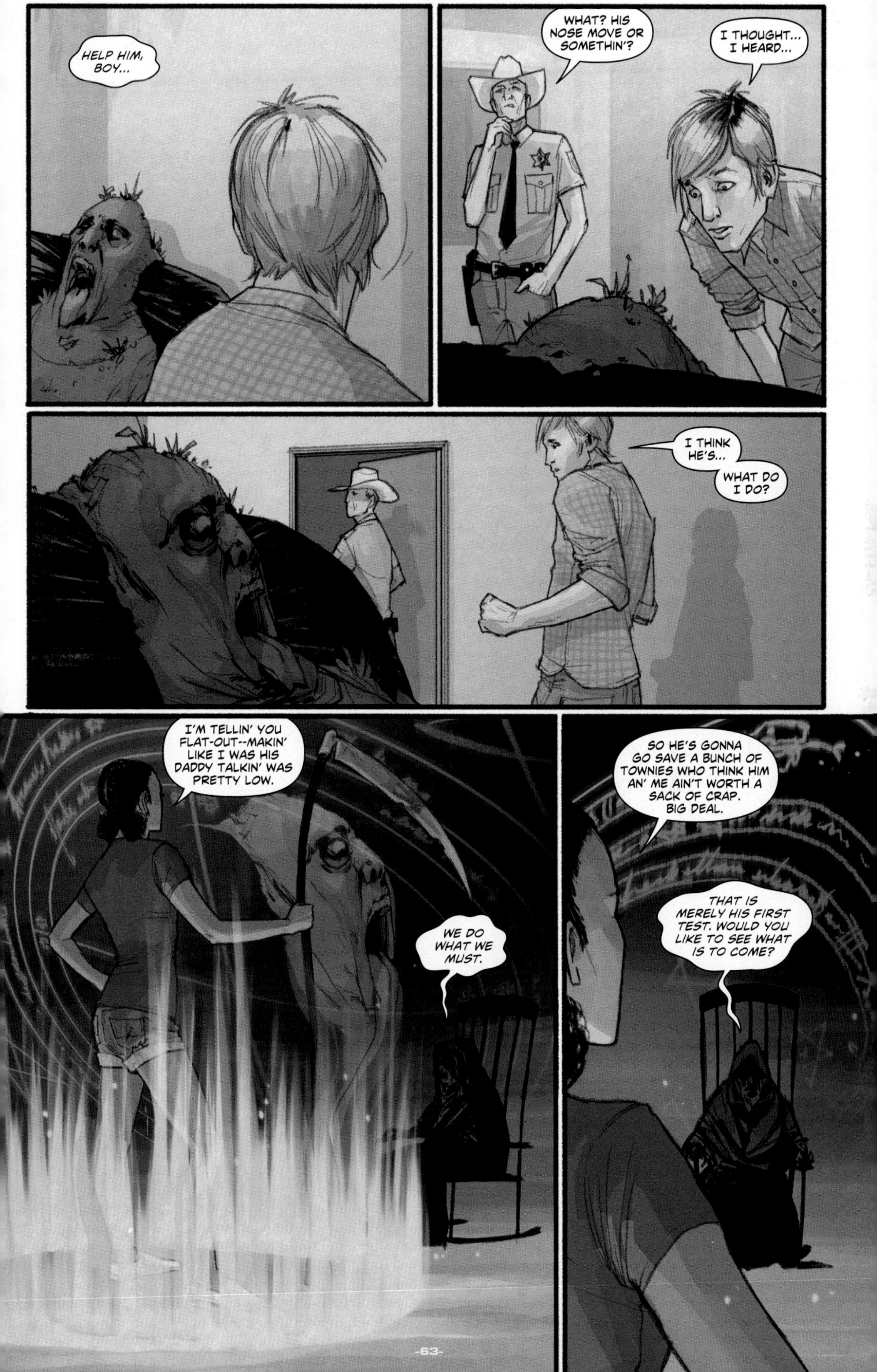
HELP HIM, BOY...
WHAT? HIS NOSE MOVE OR SOMETHIN'?
I THOUGHT... I HEARD...
I THINK HE'S...
WHAT DO I DO?
I'M TELLIN' YOU FLAT-OUT--MAKIN' LIKE I WAS HIS DADDY TALKIN' WAS PRETTY LOW.
WE DO WHAT WE MUST.
SO HE'S GONNA GO SAVE A BUNCH OF TOWNIES WHO THINK HIM AN' ME AIN'T WORTH A SACK OF CRAP. BIG DEAL.
THAT IS MERELY HIS FIRST TEST. WOULD YOU LIKE TO SEE WHAT IS TO COME?

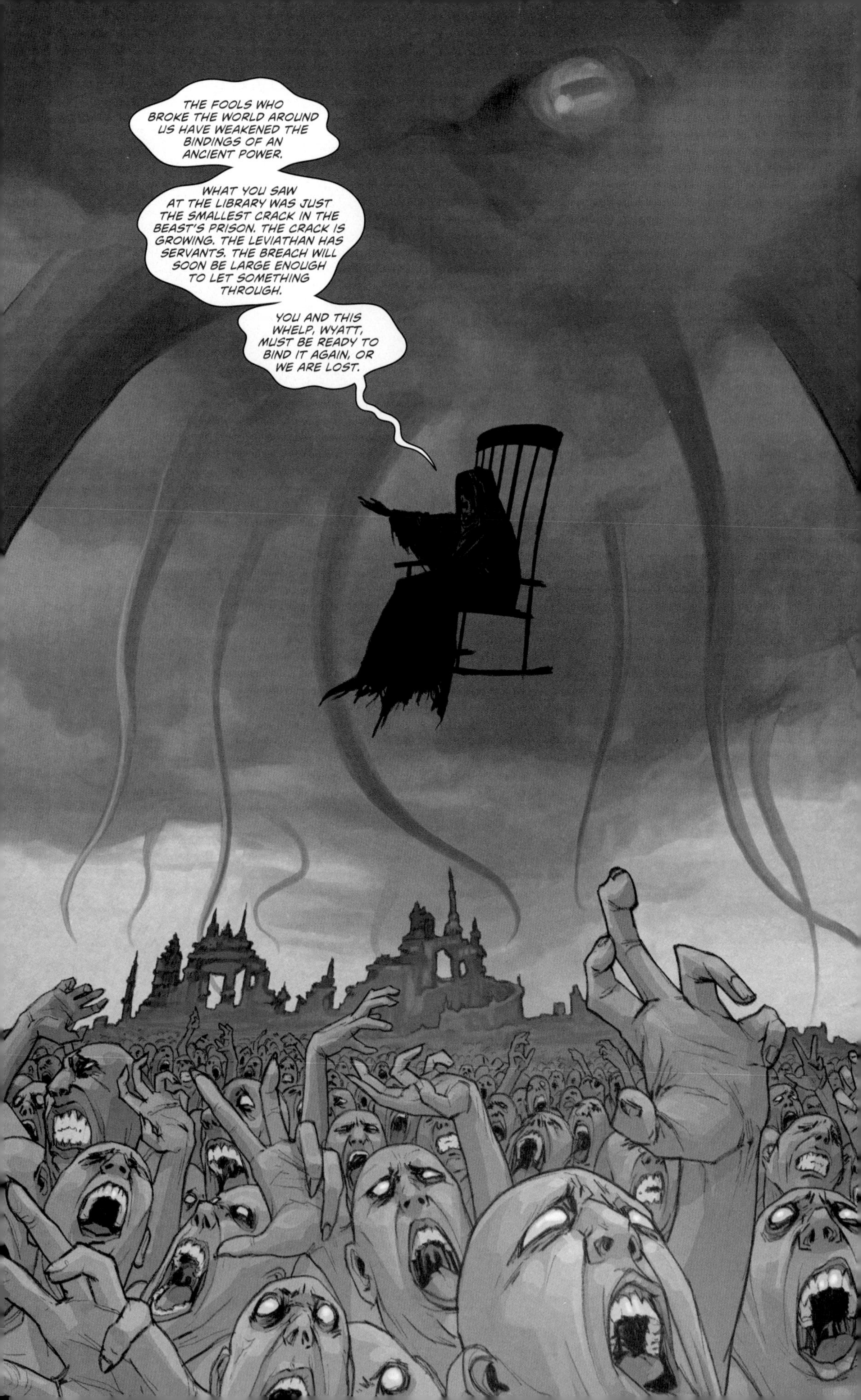
THE FOOLS WHO BROKE THE WORLD AROUND US HAVE WEAKENED THE BINDINGS OF AN ANCIENT POWER.
WHAT YOU SAW AT THE LIBRARY WAS JUST THE SMALLEST CRACK IN THE BEAST'S PRISON. THE CRACK IS GROWING. THE LEVIATHAN HAS SERVANTS. THE BREACH WILL SOON BE LARGE ENOUGH TO LET SOMETHING THROUGH.
YOU AND THIS WHELP, WYATT, MUST BE READY TO BIND IT AGAIN, OR WE ARE LOST.

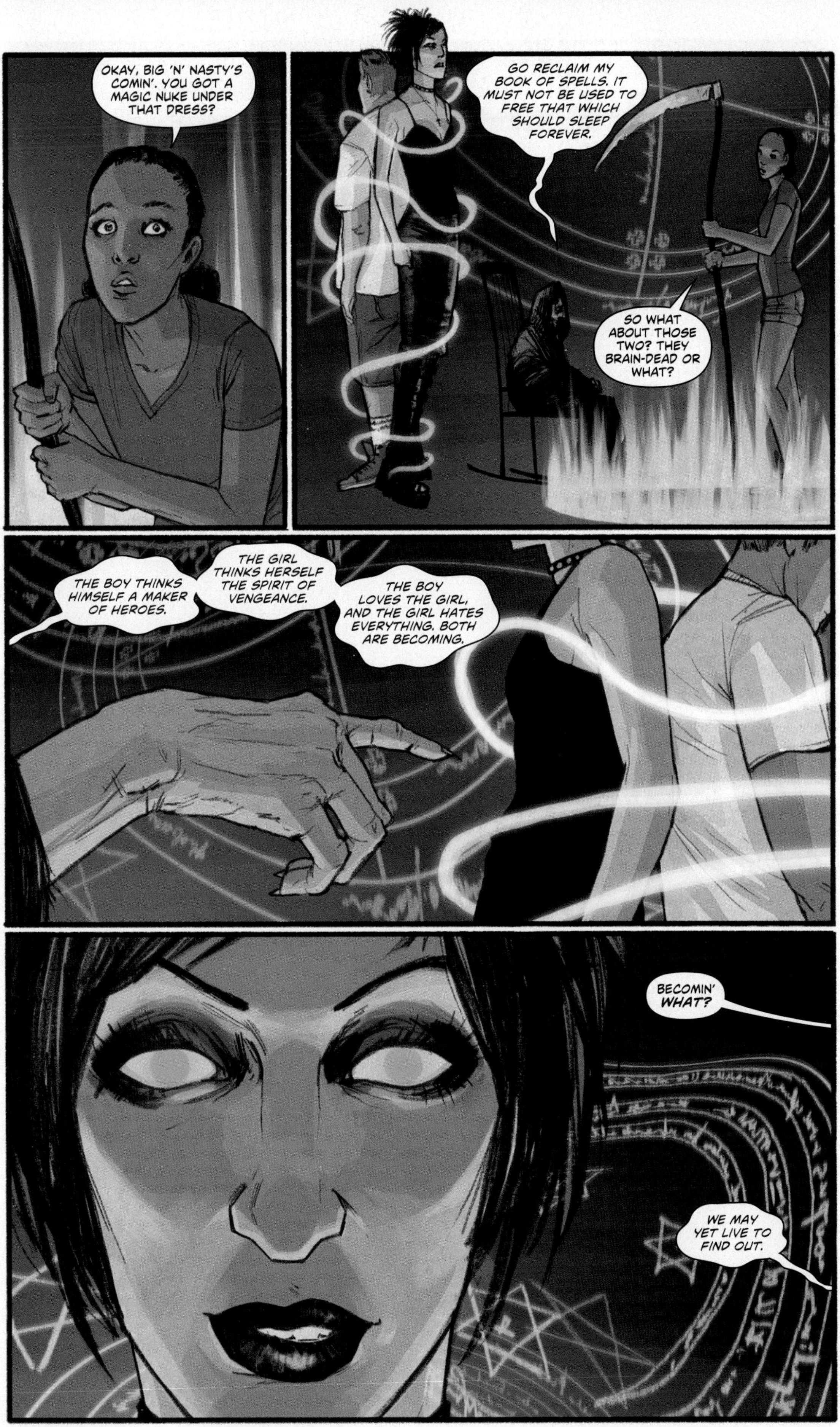
OKAY, BIG 'N' NASTY'S COMIN'. YOU GOT A MAGIC NUKE UNDER THAT DRESS?
GO RECLAIM MY BOOK OF SPELLS. IT MUST NOT BE USED TO FREE THAT WHICH SHOULD SLEEP FOREVER.
SO WHAT ABOUT THOSE TWO? THEY BRAIN-DEAD OR WHAT?
THE BOY THINKS HIMSELF A MAKER OF HEROES.
THE GIRL THINKS HERSELF THE SPIRIT OF VENGEANCE.
THE BOY LOVES THE GIRL, AND THE GIRL HATES EVERYTHING. BOTH ARE BECOMING.
BECOMIN' WHAT?
WE MAY YET LIVE TO FIND OUT.

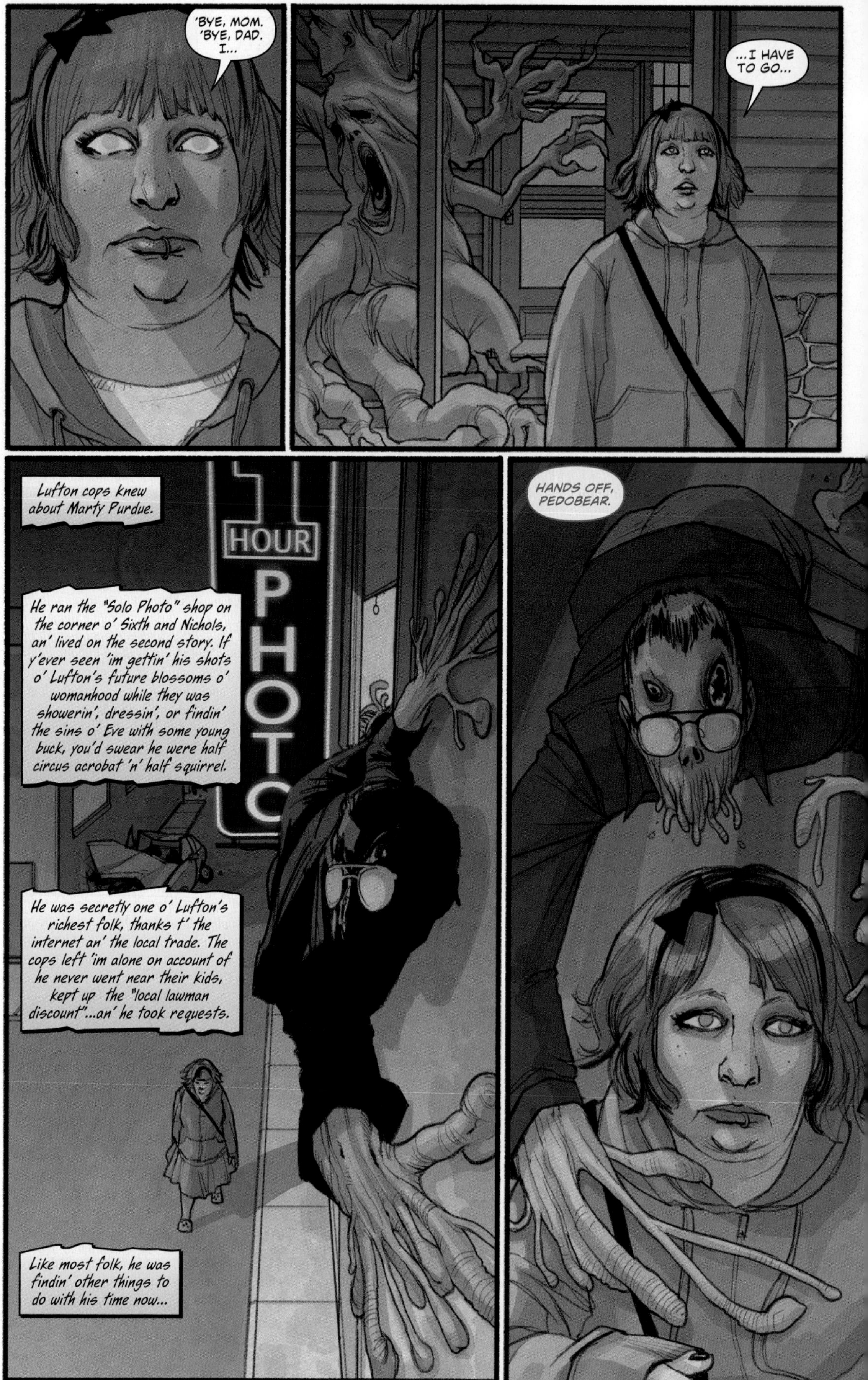

'BYE, MOM. 'BYE, DAD. I...
...I HAVE TO GO...
Lufton cops knew about Marty Purdue.
1 HOUR PHOTO
He ran the "Solo Photo" shop on the corner o' Sixth and Nichols, an' lived on the second story. If y'ever seen 'im gettin' his shots o' Lufton's future blossoms o' womanhood while they was showerin', dressin', or findin' the sins o' Eve with some young buck, you'd swear he were half circus acrobat 'n' half squirrel.
He was secretly one o' Lufton's richest folk, thanks t' the internet an' the local trade. The cops left 'im alone on account of he never went near their kids, kept up the "local lawman discount"...an' he took requests.
Like most folk, he was findin' other things to do with his time now...
HANDS OFF, PEDOBEAR.

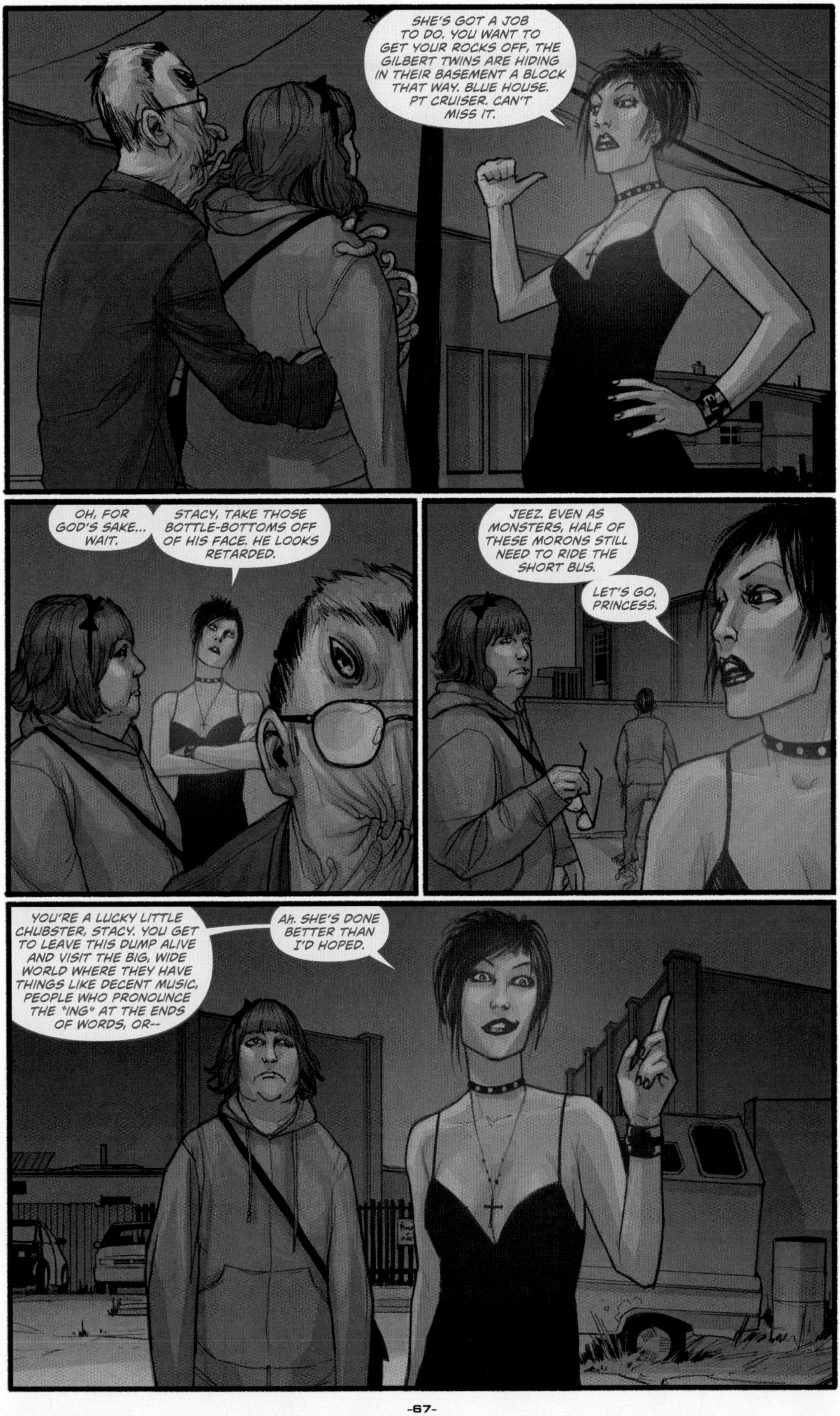
SHE'S GOT A JOB TO DO. YOU WANT TO GET YOUR ROCKS OFF, THE GILBERT TWINS ARE HIDING IN THEIR BASEMENT A BLOCK THAT WAY. BLUE HOUSE. PT CRUISER. CAN'T MISS IT.
OH, FOR GOD'S SAKE... WAIT.
STACY, TAKE THOSE BOTTLE-BOTTOMS OFF OF HIS FACE. HE LOOKS RETARDED.
JEEZ. EVEN AS MONSTERS, HALF OF THESE MORONS STILL NEED TO RIDE THE SHORT BUS.
LET'S GO, PRINCESS.
YOU'RE A LUCKY LITTLE CHUBSTER, STACY. YOU GET TO LEAVE THIS DUMP ALIVE AND VISIT THE BIG, WIDE WORLD WHERE THEY HAVE THINGS LIKE DECENT MUSIC, PEOPLE WHO PRONOUNCE THE "ING" AT THE ENDS OF WORDS, OR--
Ah. SHE'S DONE BETTER THAN I'D HOPED.

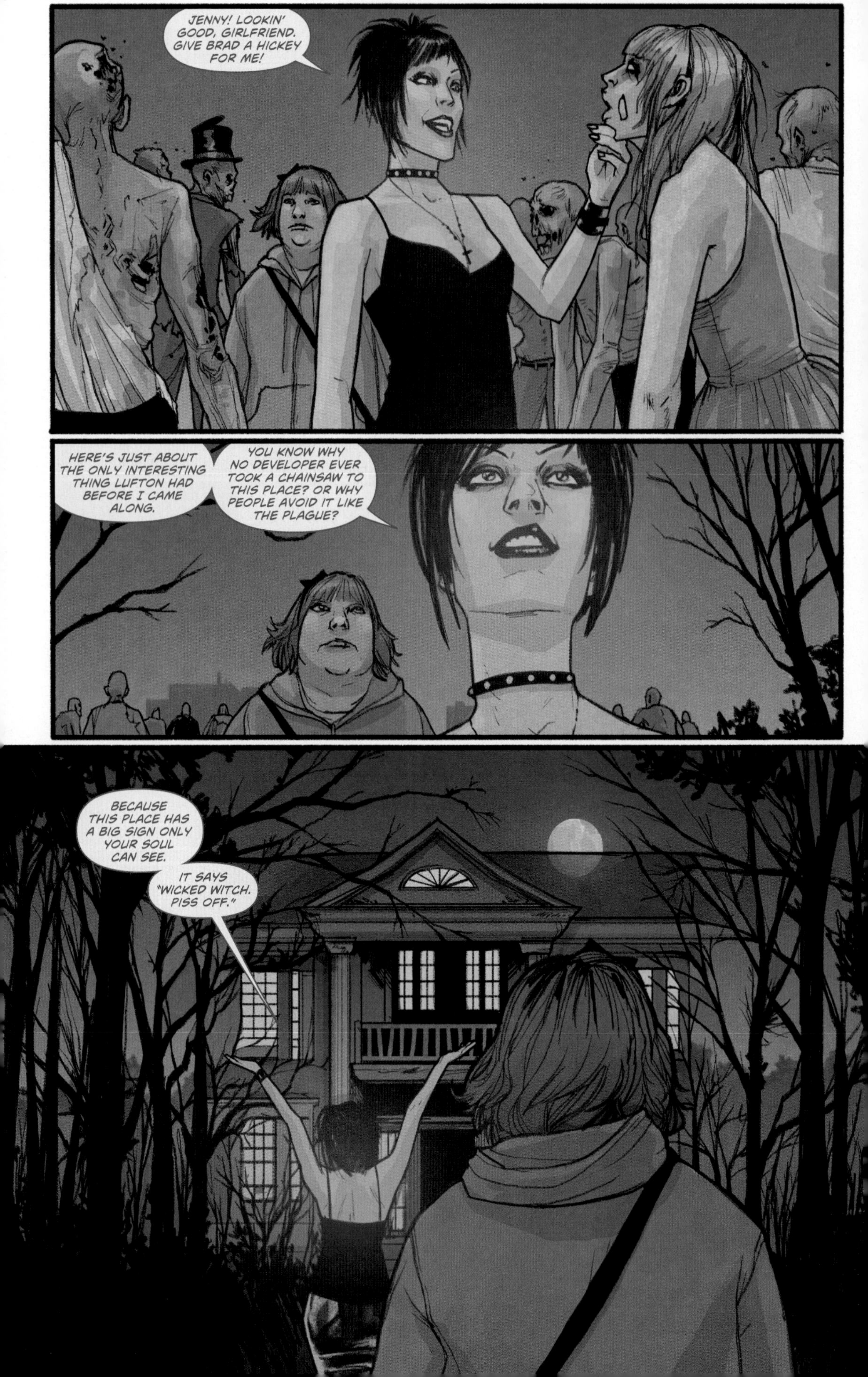
JENNY! LOOKIN' GOOD, GIRLFRIEND. GIVE BRAD A HICKEY FOR ME!
HERE'S JUST ABOUT THE ONLY INTERESTING THING LUFTON HAD BEFORE I CAME ALONG.
YOU KNOW WHY NO DEVELOPER EVER TOOK A CHAINSAW TO THIS PLACE? OR WHY PEOPLE AVOID IT LIKE THE PLAGUE?
BECAUSE THIS PLACE HAS A BIG SIGN ONLY YOUR SOUL CAN SEE.
IT SAYS "WICKED WITCH. PISS OFF."

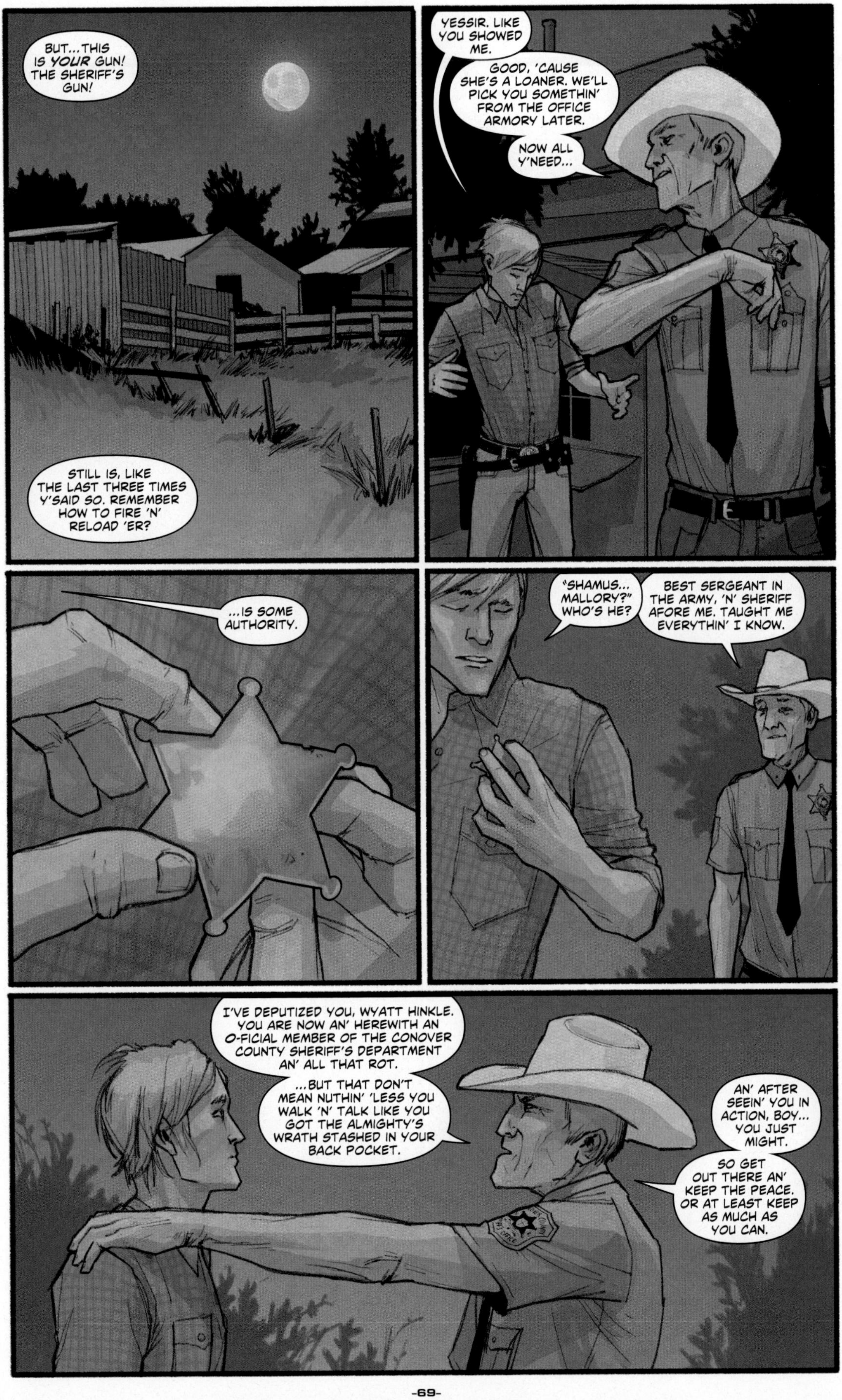
BUT... THIS IS *YOUR* GUN! THE SHERIFF'S GUN!
STILL IS, LIKE THE LAST THREE TIMES Y'SAID SO. REMEMBER HOW TO FIRE 'N' RELOAD 'ER?
YESSIR. LIKE YOU SHOWED ME.
GOOD, 'CAUSE SHE'S A LOANER. WE'LL PICK YOU SOMETHIN' FROM THE OFFICE ARMORY LATER.
NOW ALL Y'NEED...
...IS SOME AUTHORITY.
"SHAMUS... MALLORY?" WHO'S HE?
BEST SERGEANT IN THE ARMY, 'N' SHERIFF AFORE ME. TAUGHT ME EVERYTHIN' I KNOW.
I'VE DEPUTIZED YOU, WYATT HINKLE. YOU ARE NOW AN' HEREWITH AN O-FICIAL MEMBER OF THE CONOVER COUNTY SHERIFF'S DEPARTMENT AN' ALL THAT ROT.
...BUT THAT DON'T MEAN NUTHIN' 'LESS YOU WALK 'N' TALK LIKE YOU GOT THE ALMIGHTY'S WRATH STASHED IN YOUR BACK POCKET.
AN' AFTER SEEIN' YOU IN ACTION, BOY... YOU JUST MIGHT.
SO GET OUT THERE AN' KEEP THE PEACE. OR AT LEAST KEEP AS MUCH AS YOU CAN.

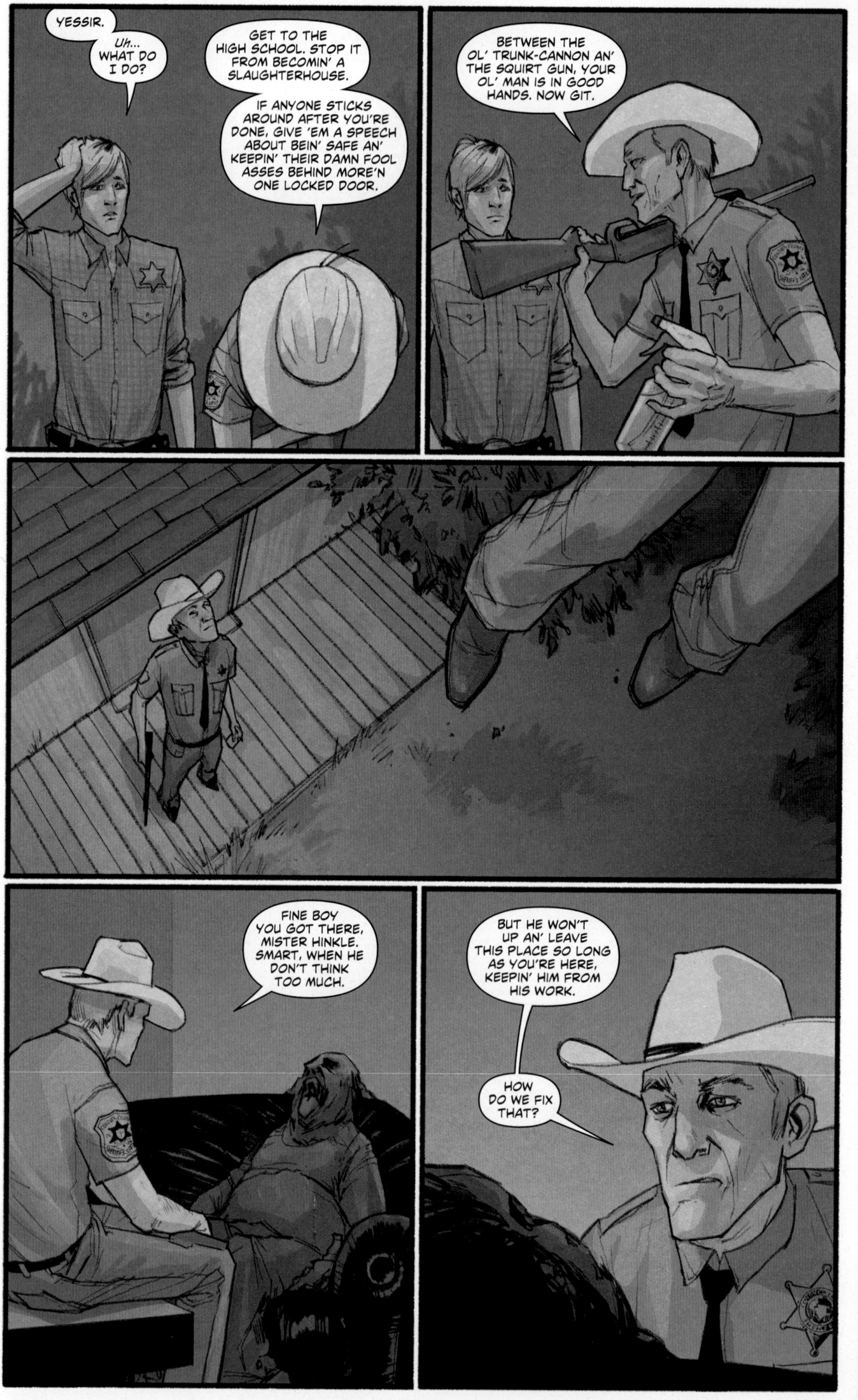
YESSIR.
Uh... WHAT DO I DO?
GET TO THE HIGH SCHOOL. STOP IT FROM BECOMIN' A SLAUGHTERHOUSE.
IF ANYONE STICKS AROUND AFTER YOU'RE DONE, GIVE 'EM A SPEECH ABOUT BEIN' SAFE AN' KEEPIN' THEIR DAMN FOOL ASSES BEHIND MORE'N ONE LOCKED DOOR.
BETWEEN THE OL' TRUNK-CANNON AN' THE SQUIRT GUN, YOUR OL' MAN IS IN GOOD HANDS. NOW GIT.
FINE BOY YOU GOT THERE, MISTER HINKLE. SMART, WHEN HE DON'T THINK TOO MUCH.
BUT HE WON'T UP AN' LEAVE THIS PLACE SO LONG AS YOU'RE HERE, KEEPIN' HIM FROM HIS WORK.
HOW DO WE FIX THAT?

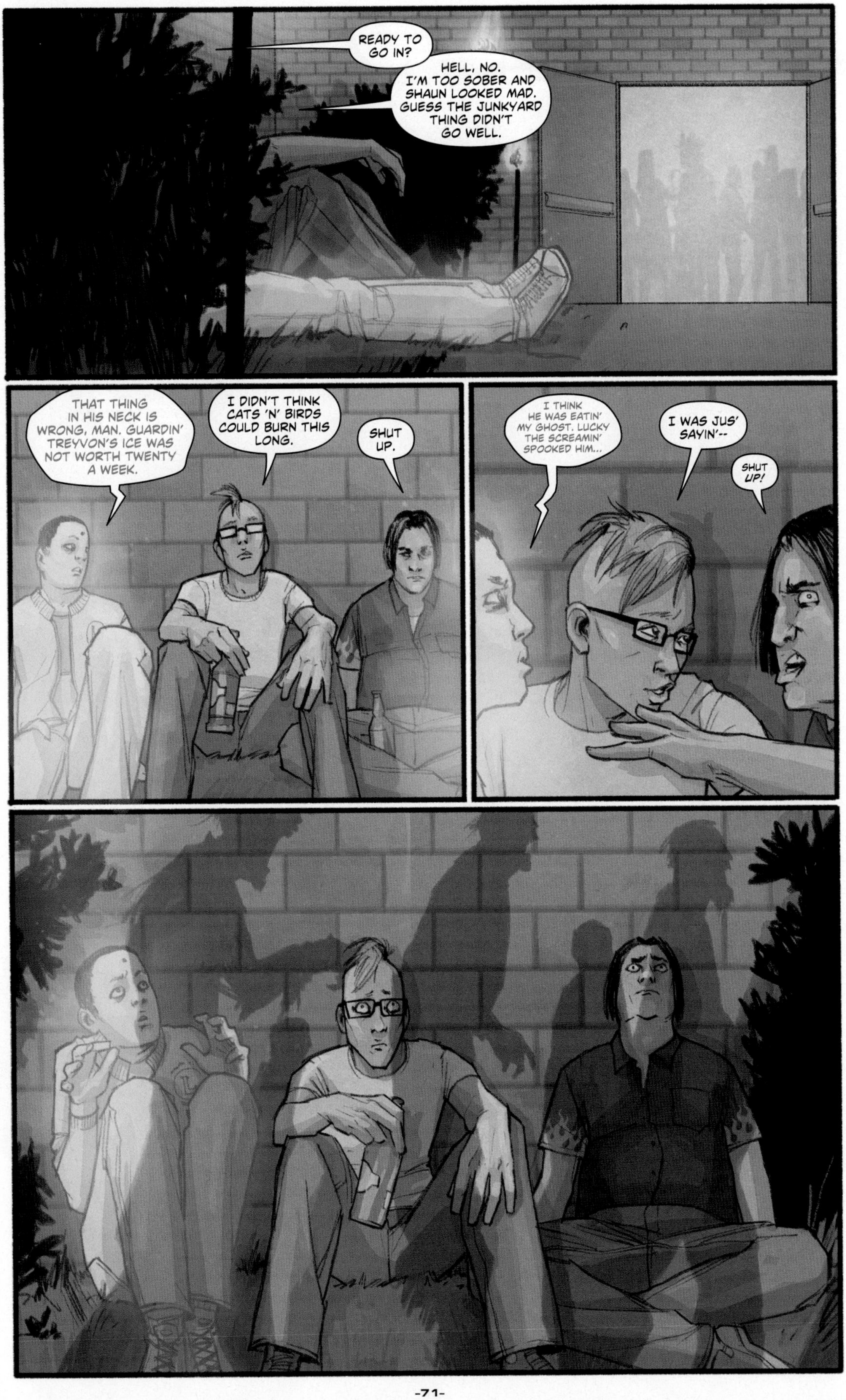
READY TO GO IN?
HELL, NO. I'M TOO SOBER AND SHAUN LOOKED MAD. GUESS THE JUNKYARD THING DIDN'T GO WELL.
THAT THING IN HIS NECK IS WRONG, MAN. GUARDIN' TREYVON'S ICE WAS NOT WORTH TWENTY A WEEK.
I DIDN'T THINK CATS 'N' BIRDS COULD BURN THIS LONG.
SHUT UP.
I THINK HE WAS EATIN' MY GHOST. LUCKY THE SCREAMIN' SPOOKED HIM...
I WAS JUS' SAYIN'--
SHUT *UP!*

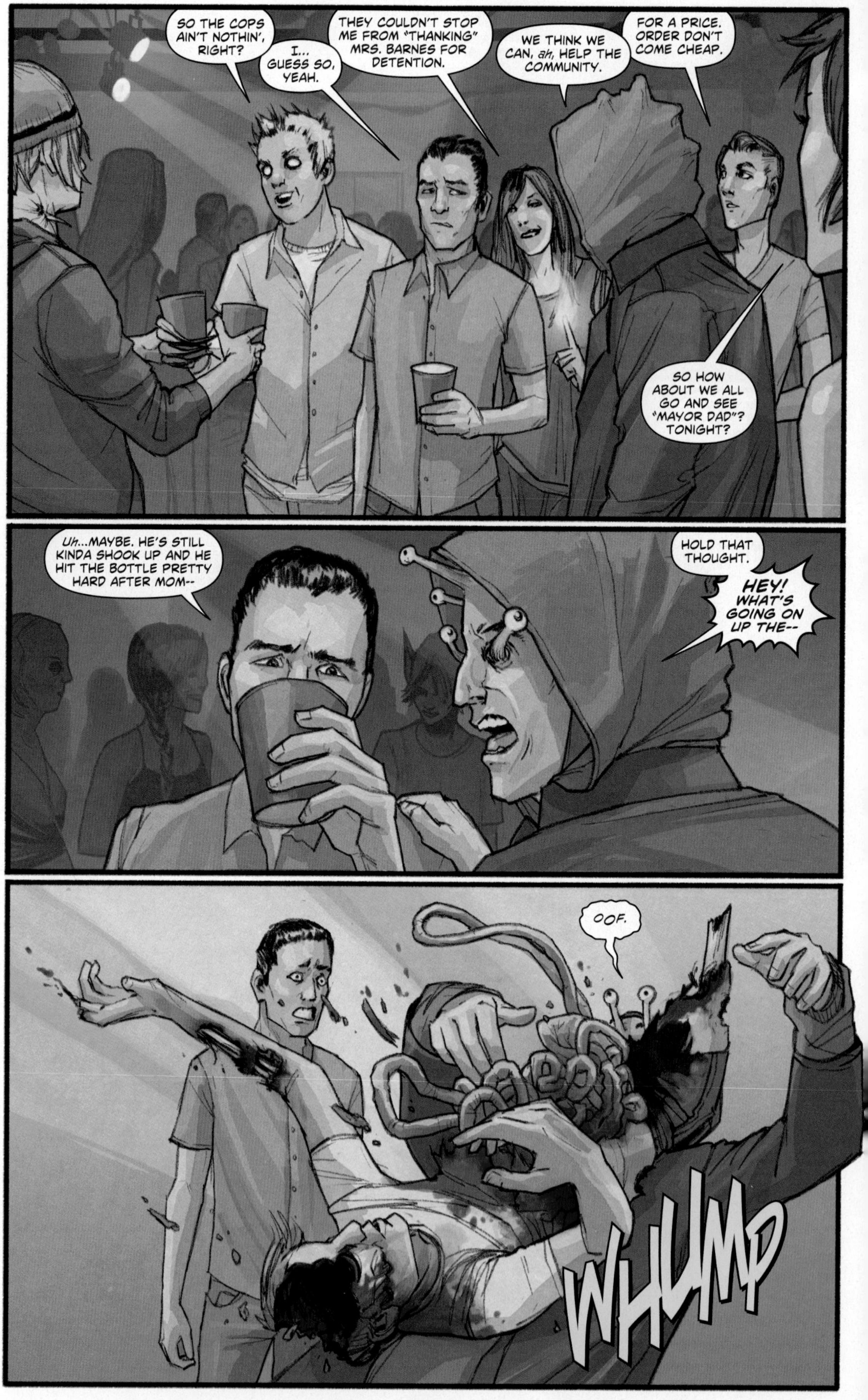
SO THE COPS AIN'T NOTHIN', RIGHT?
I... GUESS SO, YEAH.
THEY COULDN'T STOP ME FROM "THANKING" MRS. BARNES FOR DETENTION.
WE THINK WE CAN, *ah*, HELP THE COMMUNITY.
FOR A PRICE. ORDER DON'T COME CHEAP.
SO HOW ABOUT WE ALL GO AND SEE "MAYOR DAD"? TONIGHT?
Uh...MAYBE. HE'S STILL KINDA SHOOK UP AND HE HIT THE BOTTLE PRETTY HARD AFTER MOM--
HOLD THAT THOUGHT.
HEY! WHAT'S GOING ON UP THE--
OOF.
WHUMP

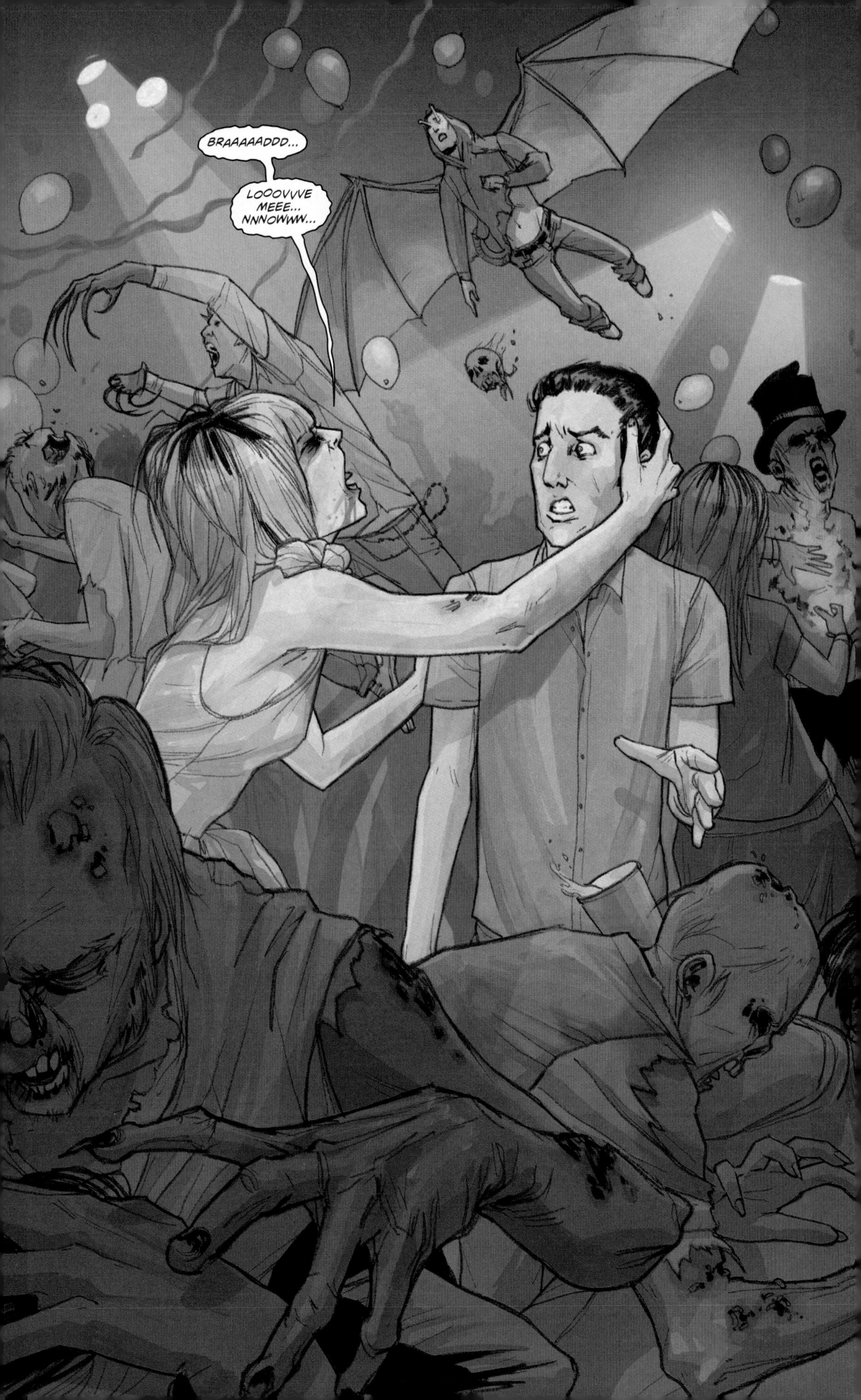
BRAAAAADDD...
LOOOVVVE MEEE... NNNOWWW...

CHAPTER FOUR

Tremblin' 'neath the Feet of Giants

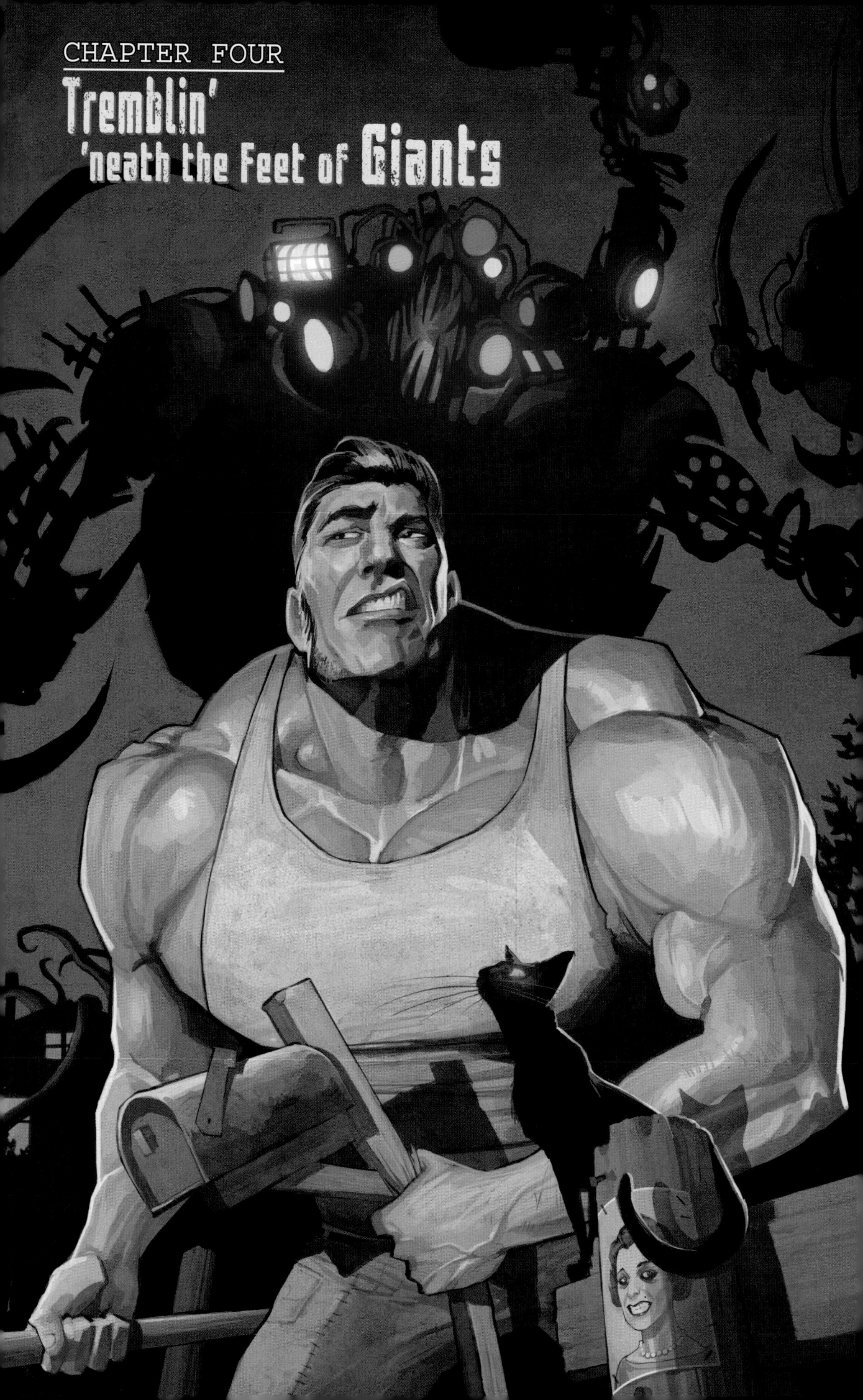

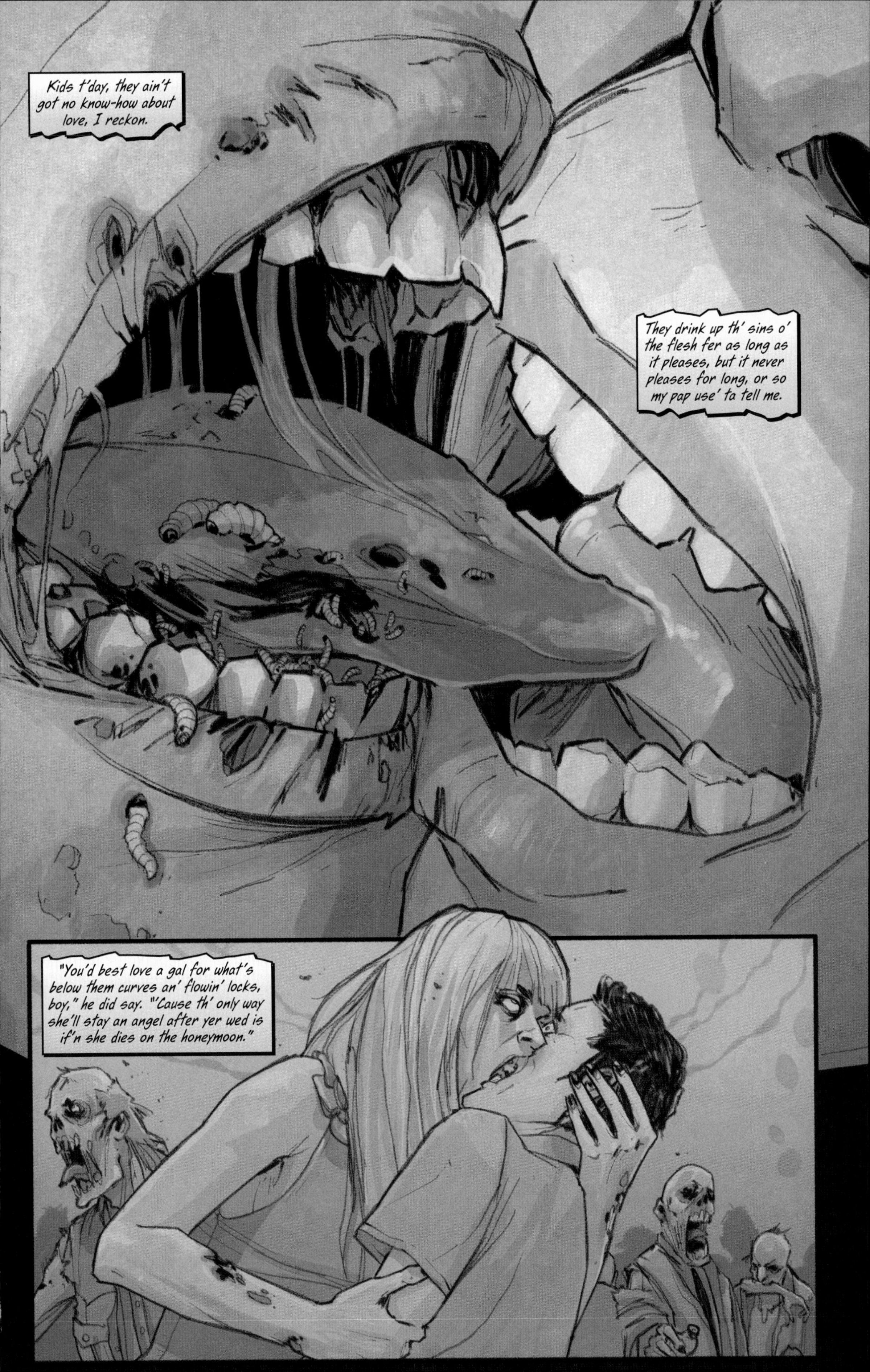
Kids t'day, they ain't got no know-how about love, I reckon.
They drink up th' sins o' the flesh fer as long as it pleases, but it never pleases for long, or so my pap use' ta tell me.
"You'd best love a gal for what's below them curves an' flowin' locks, boy," he did say. "'Cause th' only way she'll stay an angel after yer wed is if'n she dies on the honeymoon."

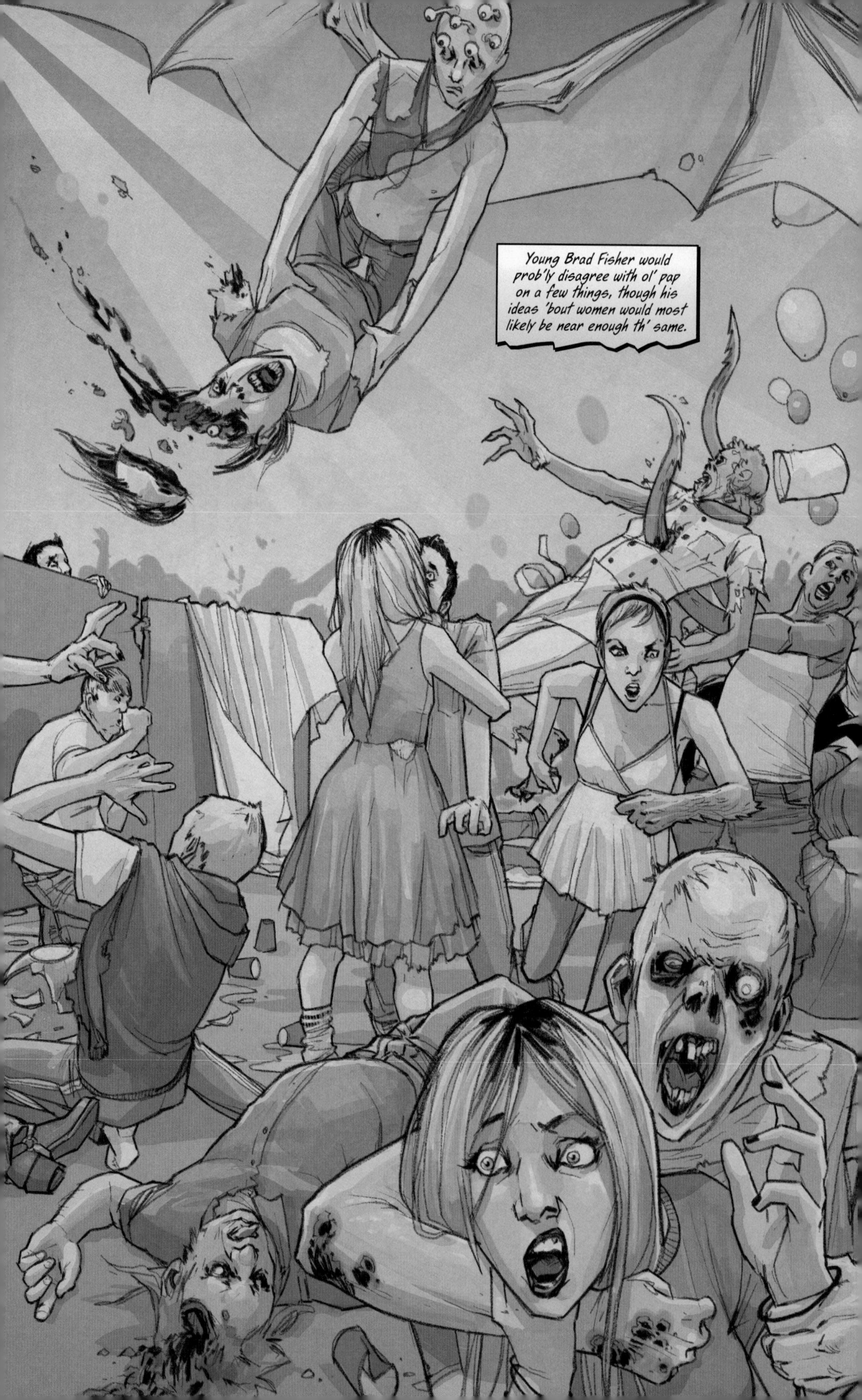
Young Brad Fisher would prob'ly disagree with ol' pap on a few things, though his ideas 'bout women would most likely be near enough th' same.

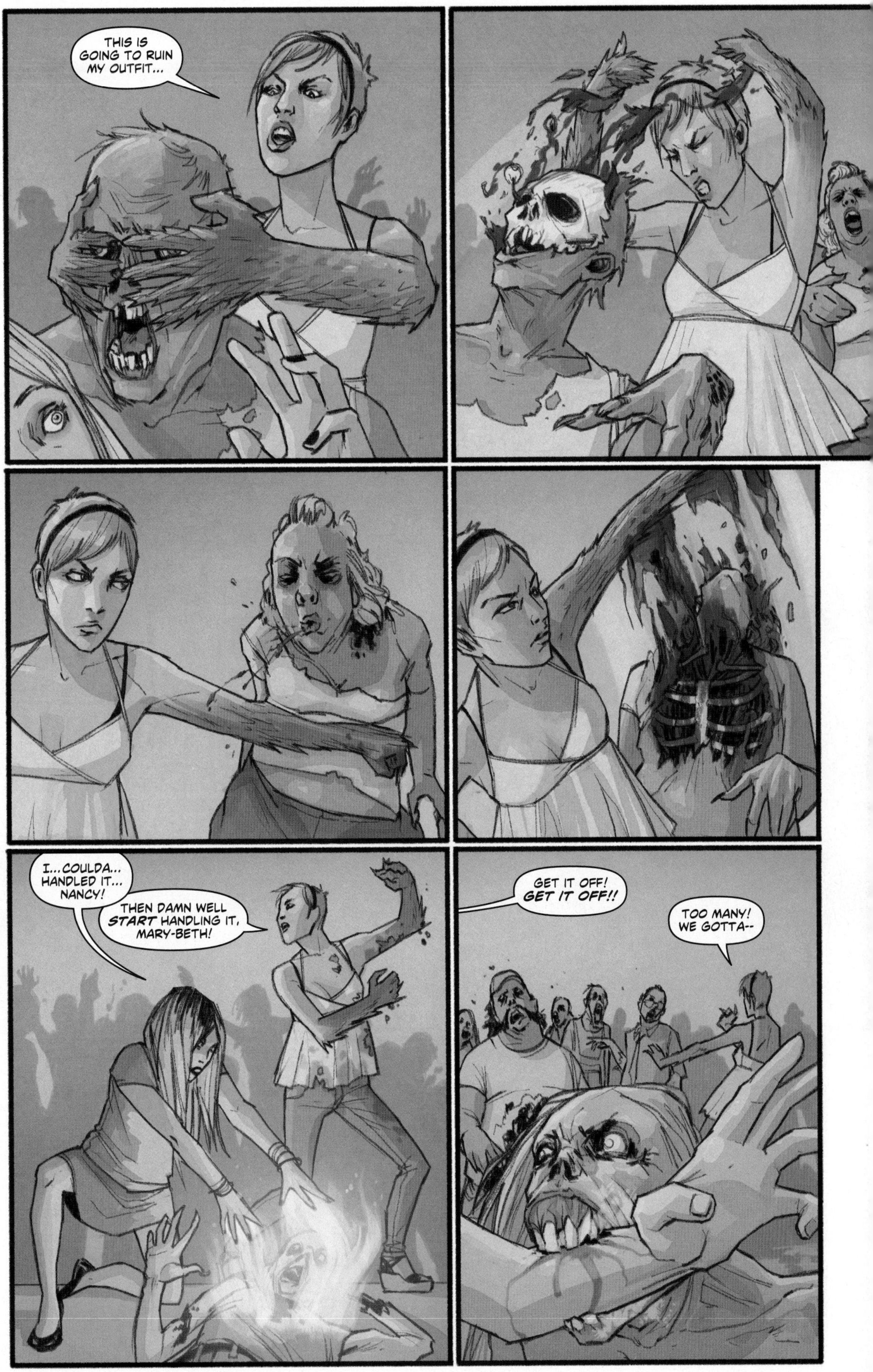
THIS IS GOING TO RUIN MY OUTFIT...
I...COULDA... HANDLED IT... NANCY!
THEN DAMN WELL *START* HANDLING IT, MARY-BETH!
GET IT OFF! ***GET IT OFF!!***
TOO MANY! WE GOTTA--

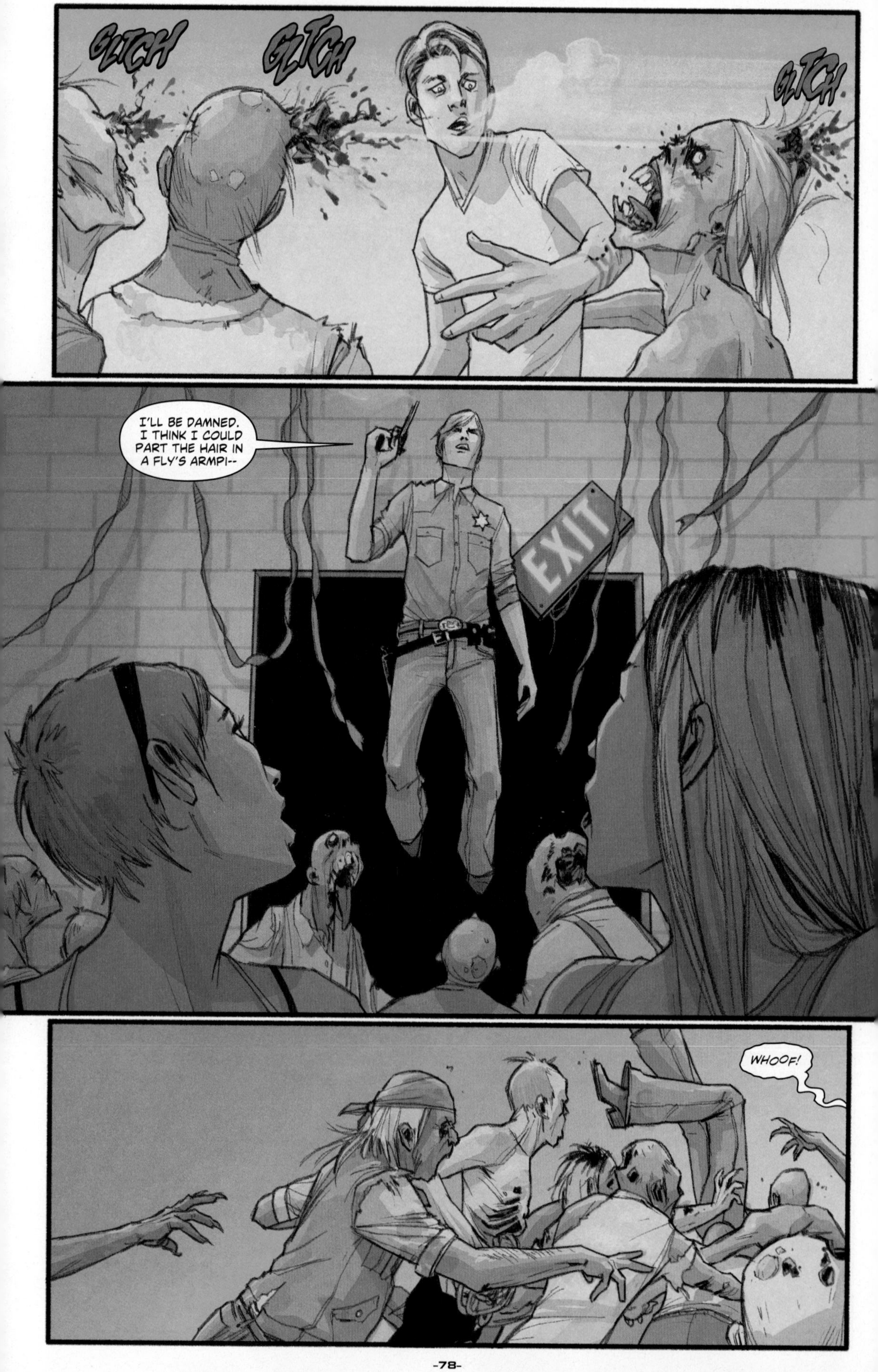
GLITCH
GLITCH
GLITCH
I'LL BE DAMNED. I THINK I COULD PART THE HAIR IN A FLY'S ARMPI--
EXIT
WHOOF!

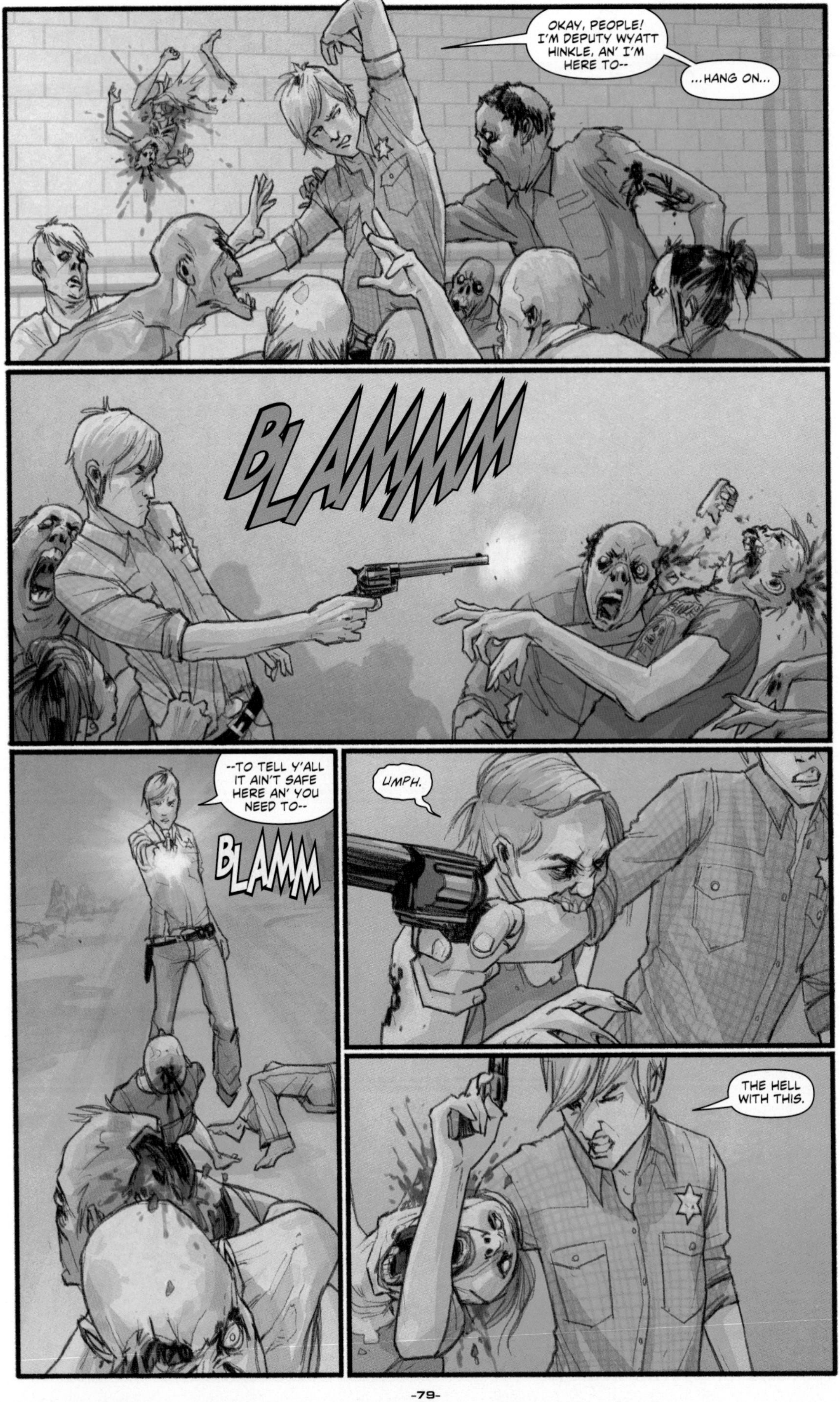
OKAY, PEOPLE! I'M DEPUTY WYATT HINKLE, AN' I'M HERE TO--
...HANG ON...
BLAMMM
--TO TELL Y'ALL IT AIN'T SAFE HERE AN' YOU NEED TO--
BLAMM
UMPH.
THE HELL WITH THIS.

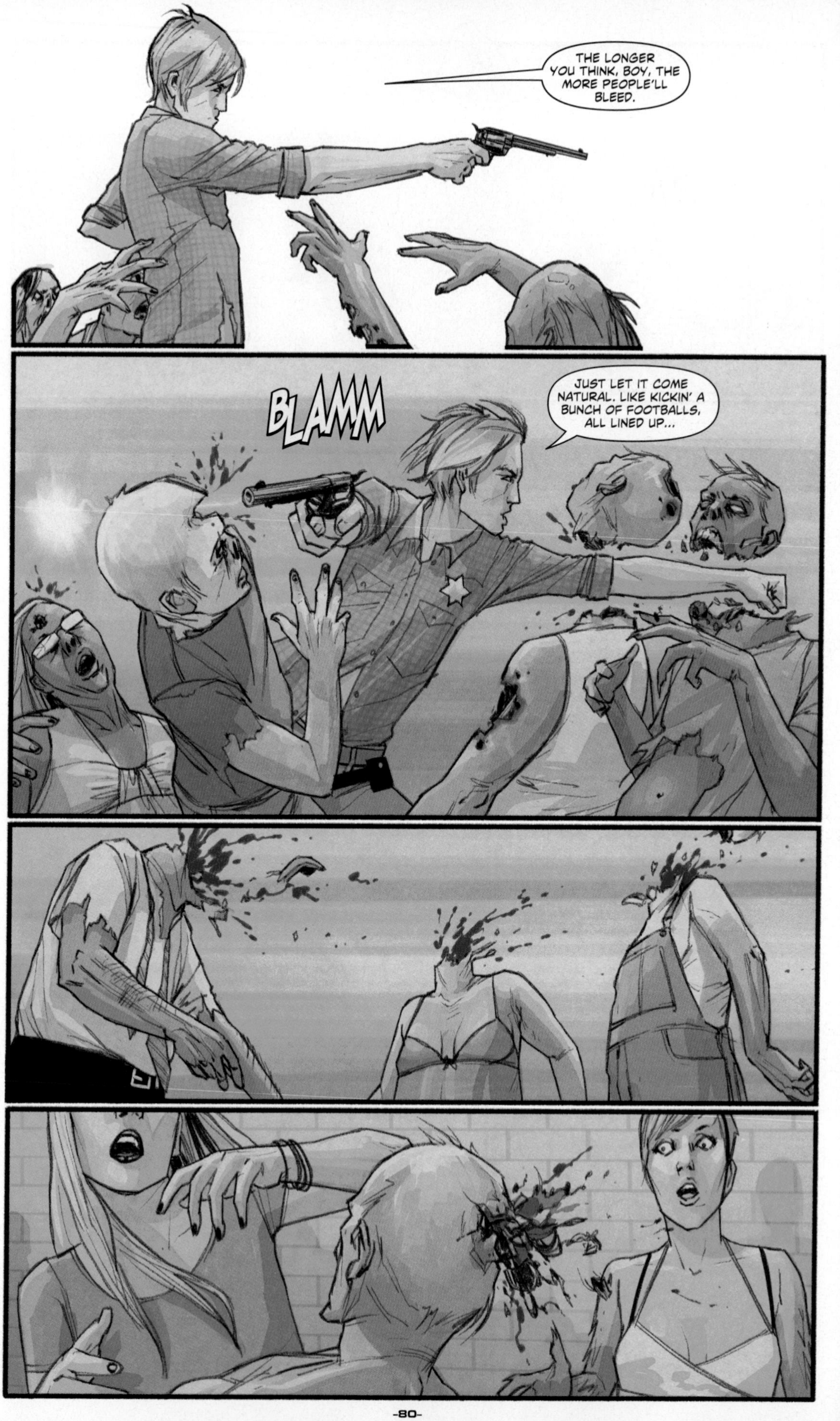
THE LONGER YOU THINK, BOY, THE MORE PEOPLE'LL BLEED.
BLAMM
JUST LET IT COME NATURAL. LIKE KICKIN' A BUNCH OF FOOTBALLS, ALL LINED UP...

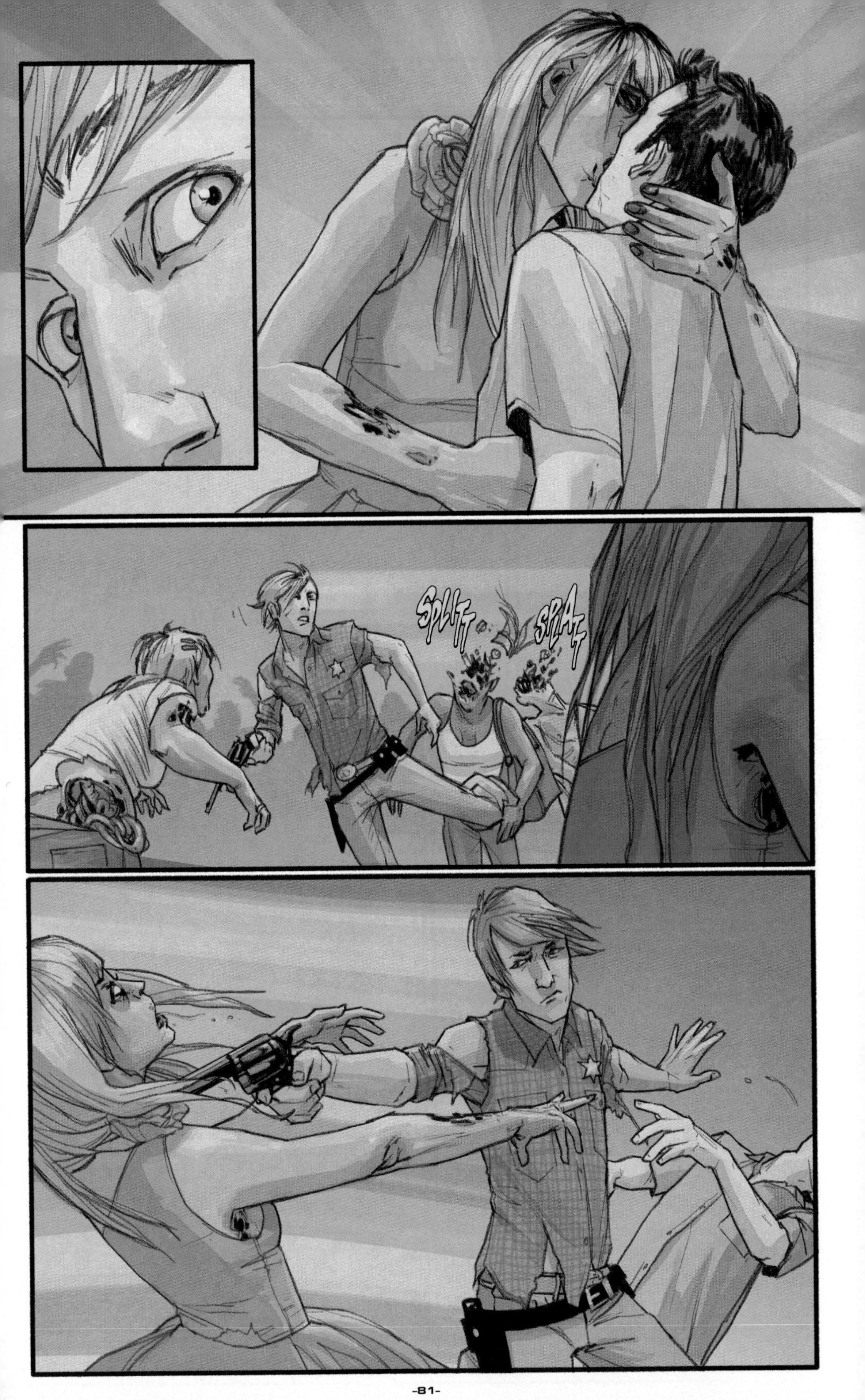
SPLITT
SPLATT

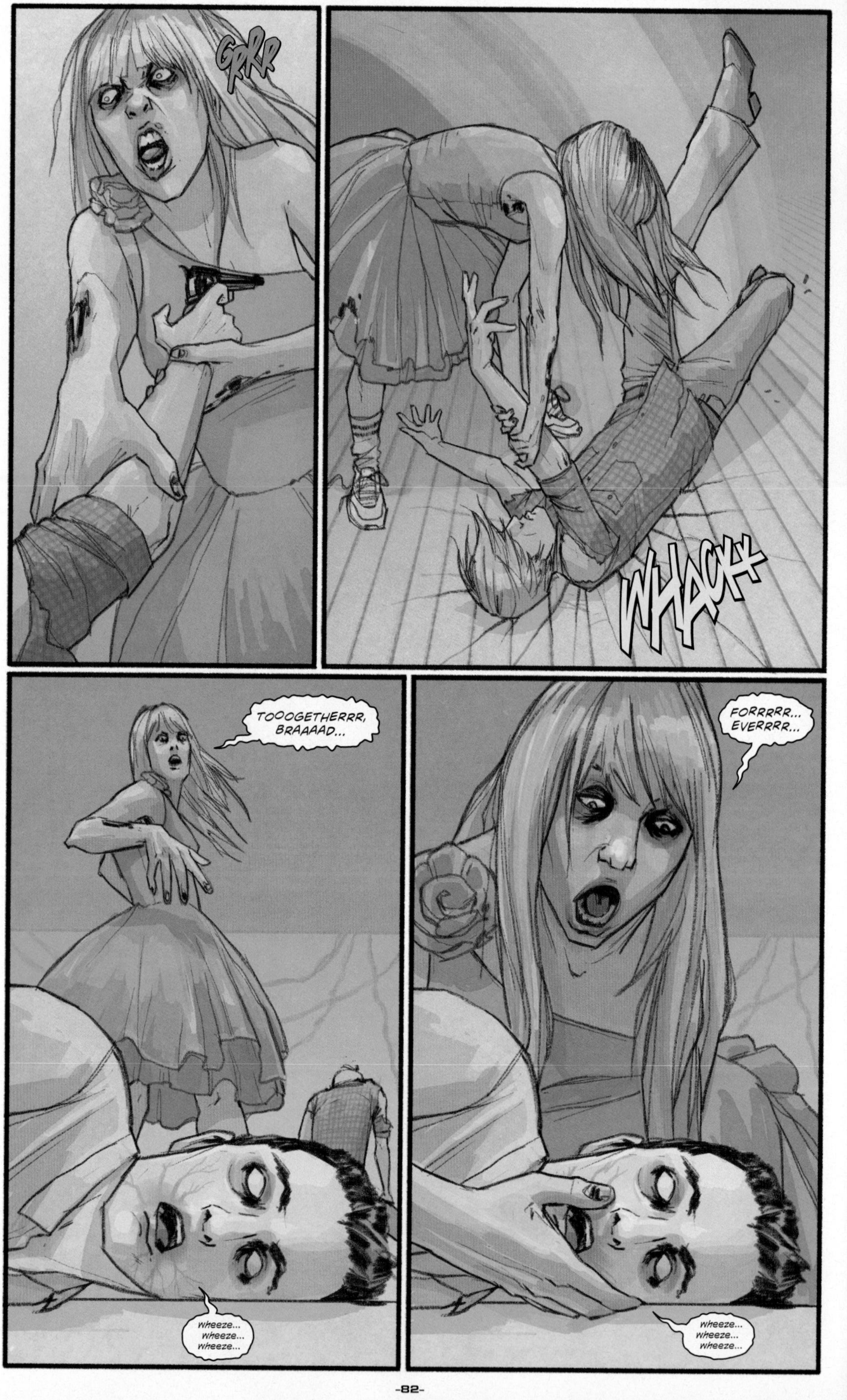
GRRR
WHACK
TOOOGETHERRR, BRAAAAD...
wheeze... wheeze... wheeze...
FORRRRR... EVERRRR...
wheeze... wheeze... wheeze...

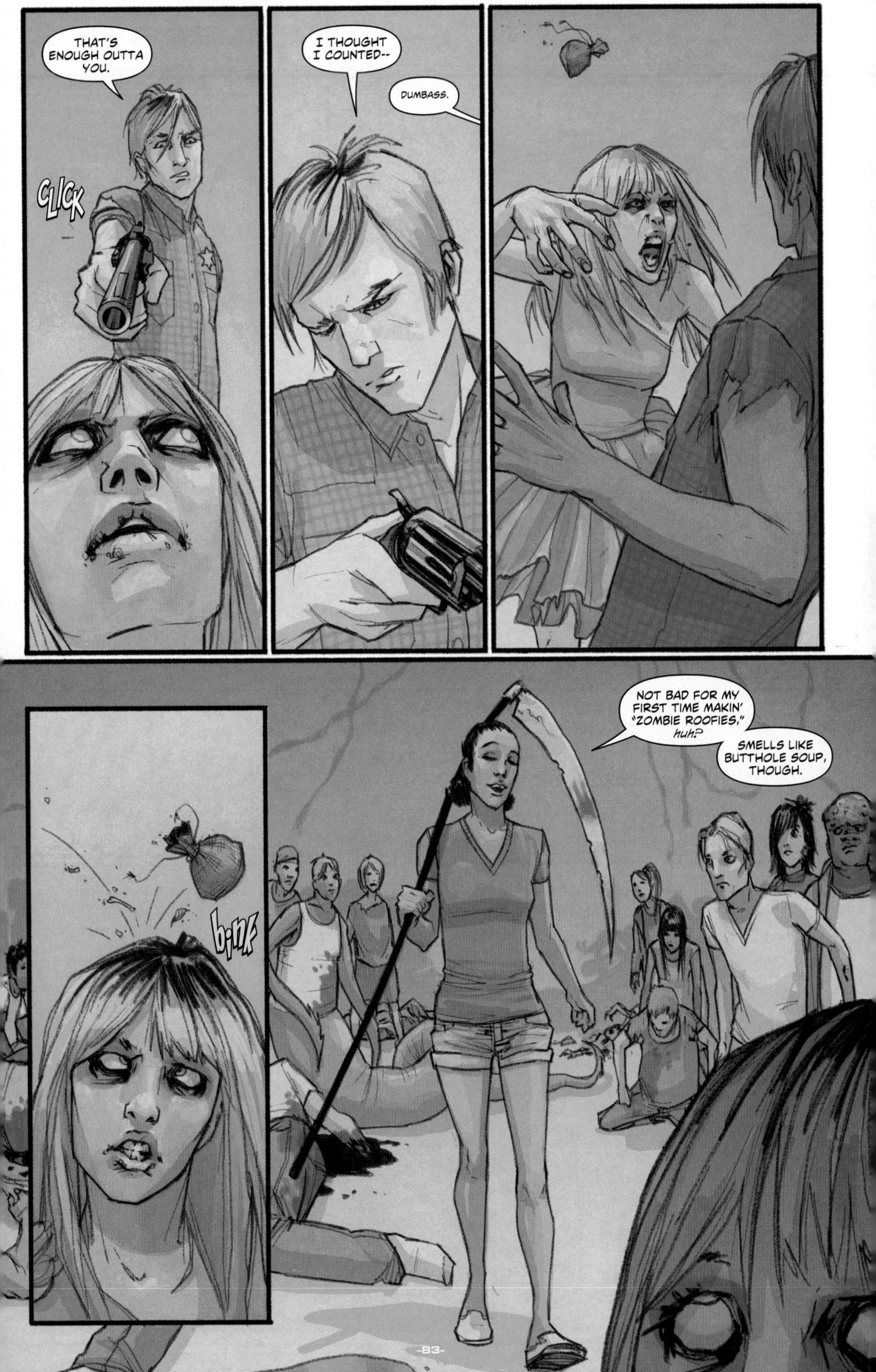
THAT'S ENOUGH OUTTA YOU.
CLICK
I THOUGHT I COUNTED--
DUMBASS.
bink
NOT BAD FOR MY FIRST TIME MAKIN' "ZOMBIE ROOFIES," huh?
SMELLS LIKE BUTTHOLE SOUP, THOUGH.

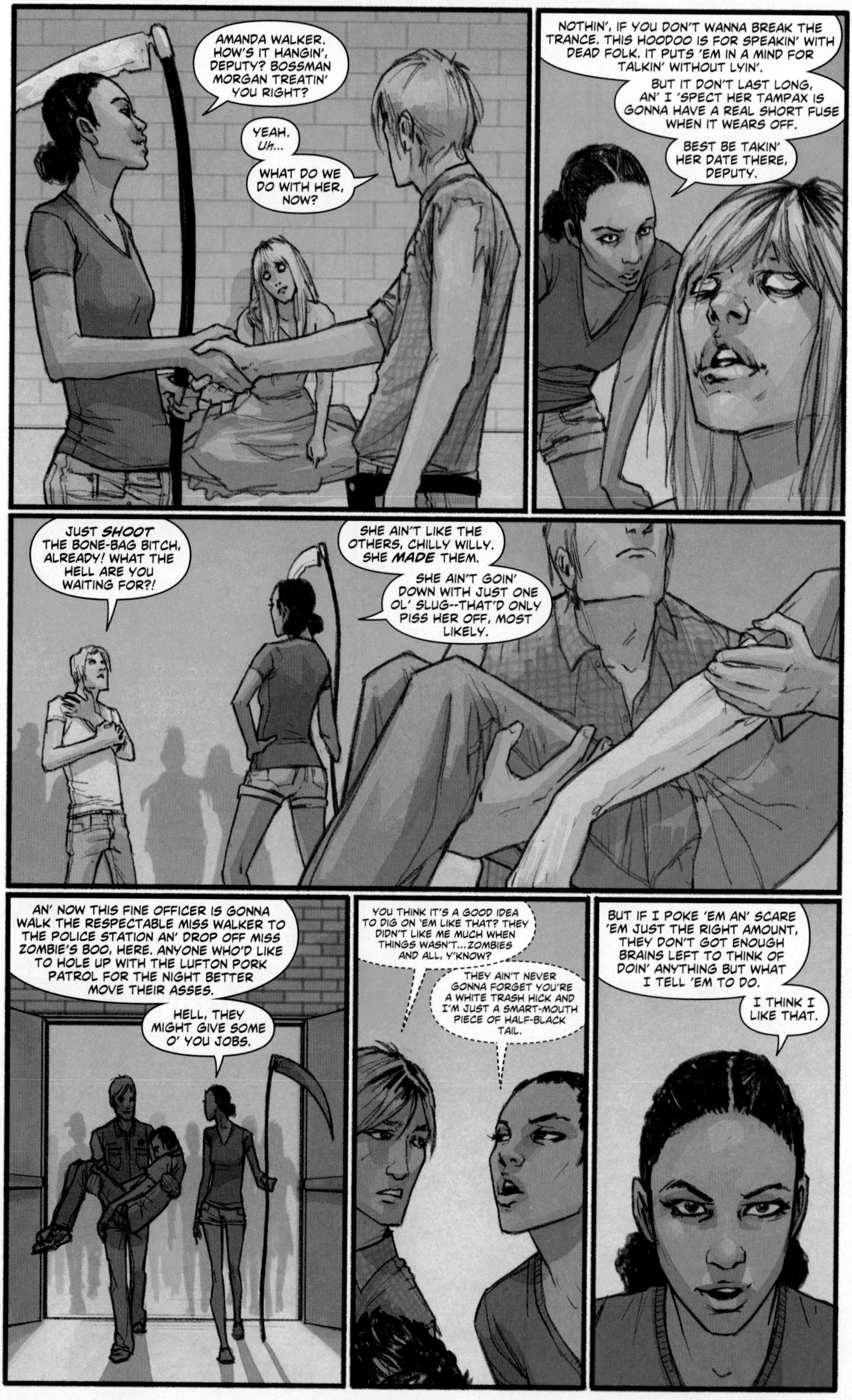
AMANDA WALKER. HOW'S IT HANGIN', DEPUTY? BOSSMAN MORGAN TREATIN' YOU RIGHT?
YEAH. Uh...
WHAT DO WE DO WITH HER, NOW?
NOTHIN', IF YOU DON'T WANNA BREAK THE TRANCE. THIS HOODOO IS FOR SPEAKIN' WITH DEAD FOLK. IT PUTS 'EM IN A MIND FOR TALKIN' WITHOUT LYIN'.
BUT IT DON'T LAST LONG, AN' I 'SPECT HER TAMPAX IS GONNA HAVE A REAL SHORT FUSE WHEN IT WEARS OFF.
BEST BE TAKIN' HER DATE THERE, DEPUTY.
JUST SHOOT THE BONE-BAG BITCH, ALREADY! WHAT THE HELL ARE YOU WAITING FOR?!
SHE AIN'T LIKE THE OTHERS, CHILLY WILLY. SHE MADE THEM.
SHE AIN'T GOIN' DOWN WITH JUST ONE OL' SLUG--THAT'D ONLY PISS HER OFF, MOST LIKELY.
AN' NOW THIS FINE OFFICER IS GONNA WALK THE RESPECTABLE MISS WALKER TO THE POLICE STATION AN' DROP OFF MISS ZOMBIE'S BOO, HERE. ANYONE WHO'D LIKE TO HOLE UP WITH THE LUFTON PORK PATROL FOR THE NIGHT BETTER MOVE THEIR ASSES.
HELL, THEY MIGHT GIVE SOME O' YOU JOBS.
YOU THINK IT'S A GOOD IDEA TO DIG ON 'EM LIKE THAT? THEY DIDN'T LIKE ME MUCH WHEN THINGS WASN'T...ZOMBIES AND ALL, Y'KNOW?
THEY AIN'T NEVER GONNA FORGET YOU'RE A WHITE TRASH HICK AND I'M JUST A SMART-MOUTH PIECE OF HALF-BLACK TAIL.
BUT IF I POKE 'EM AN' SCARE 'EM JUST THE RIGHT AMOUNT, THEY DON'T GOT ENOUGH BRAINS LEFT TO THINK OF DOIN' ANYTHING BUT WHAT I TELL 'EM TO DO.
I THINK I LIKE THAT.

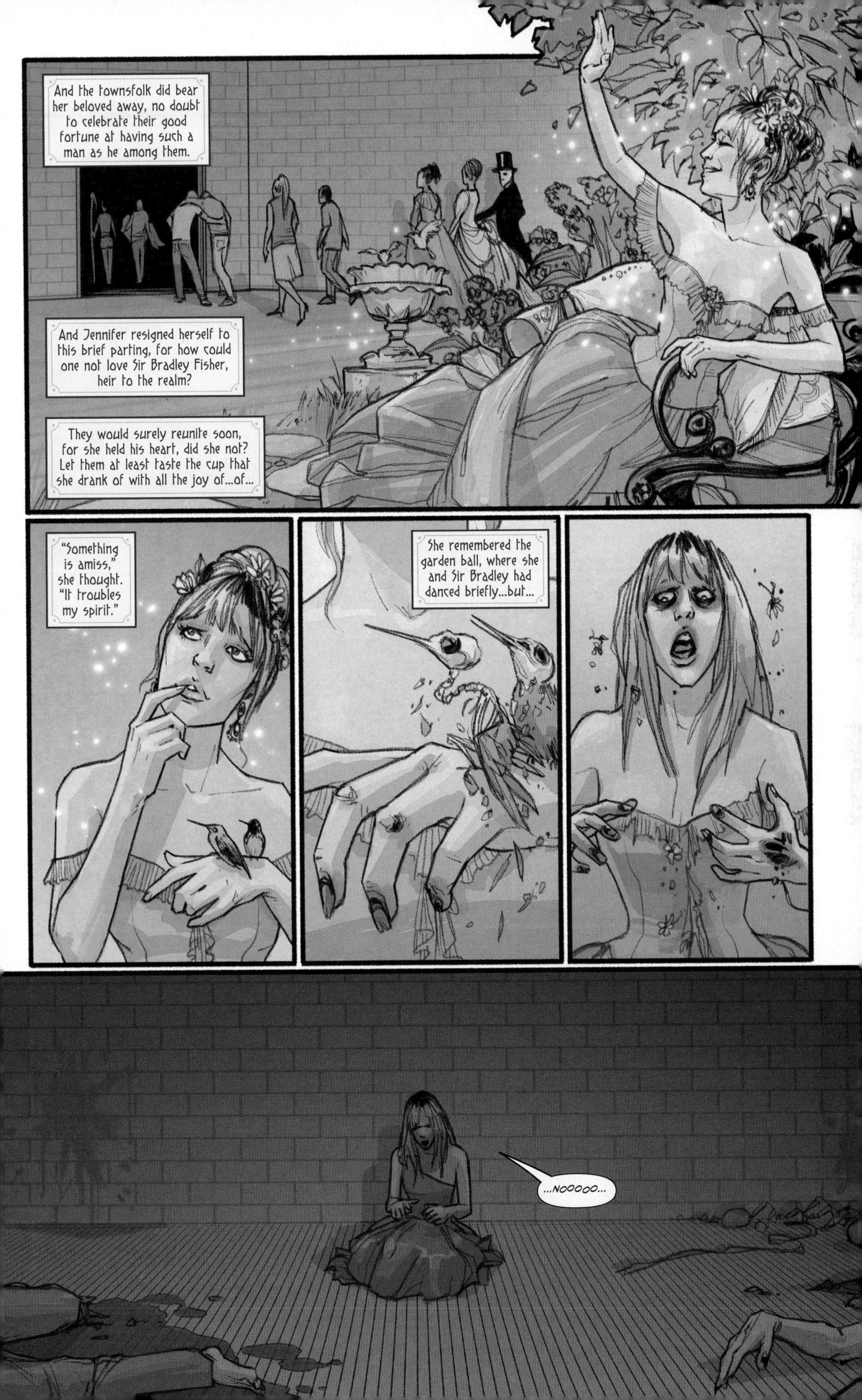

And the townsfolk did bear her beloved away, no doubt to celebrate their good fortune at having such a man as he among them.
And Jennifer resigned herself to this brief parting, for how could one not love Sir Bradley Fisher, heir to the realm?
They would surely reunite soon, for she held his heart, did she not? Let them at least taste the cup that she drank of with all the joy of...of...
"Something is amiss," she thought. "It troubles my spirit."
She remembered the garden ball, where she and Sir Bradley had danced briefly...but...
...NOOOOO...

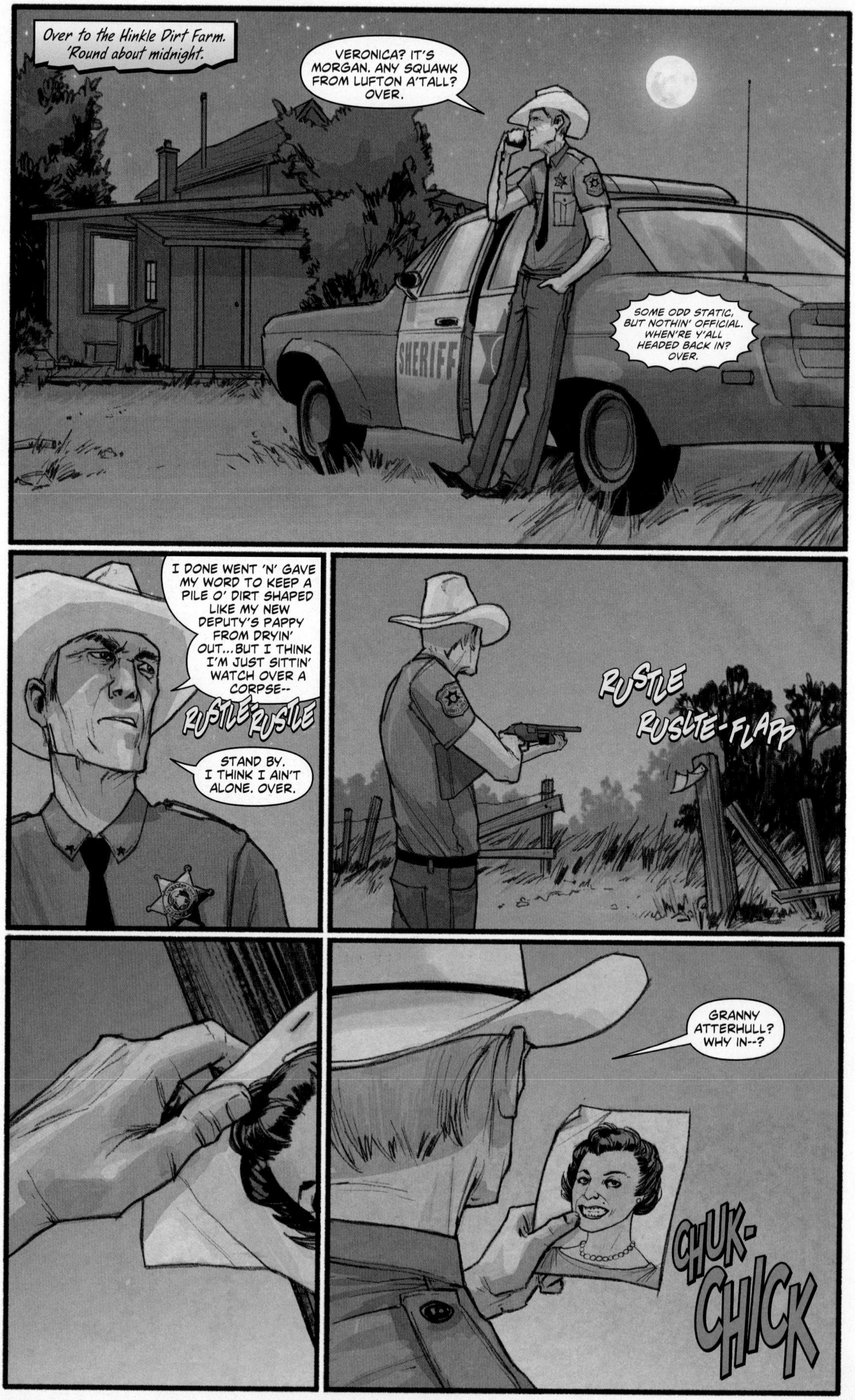

Over to the Hinkle Dirt Farm. 'Round about midnight.
VERONICA? IT'S MORGAN. ANY SQUAWK FROM LUFTON A'TALL? OVER.
SOME ODD STATIC, BUT NOTHIN' OFFICIAL. WHEN'RE Y'ALL HEADED BACK IN? OVER.
SHERIFF
I DONE WENT 'N' GAVE MY WORD TO KEEP A PILE O' DIRT SHAPED LIKE MY NEW DEPUTY'S PAPPY FROM DRYIN' OUT...BUT I THINK I'M JUST SITTIN' WATCH OVER A CORPSE--
RUSTLE-RUSTLE
STAND BY. I THINK I AIN'T ALONE. OVER.
RUSTLE
RUSLTE-FLAPP
GRANNY ATTERHULL? WHY IN--?
CHUK-CHICK

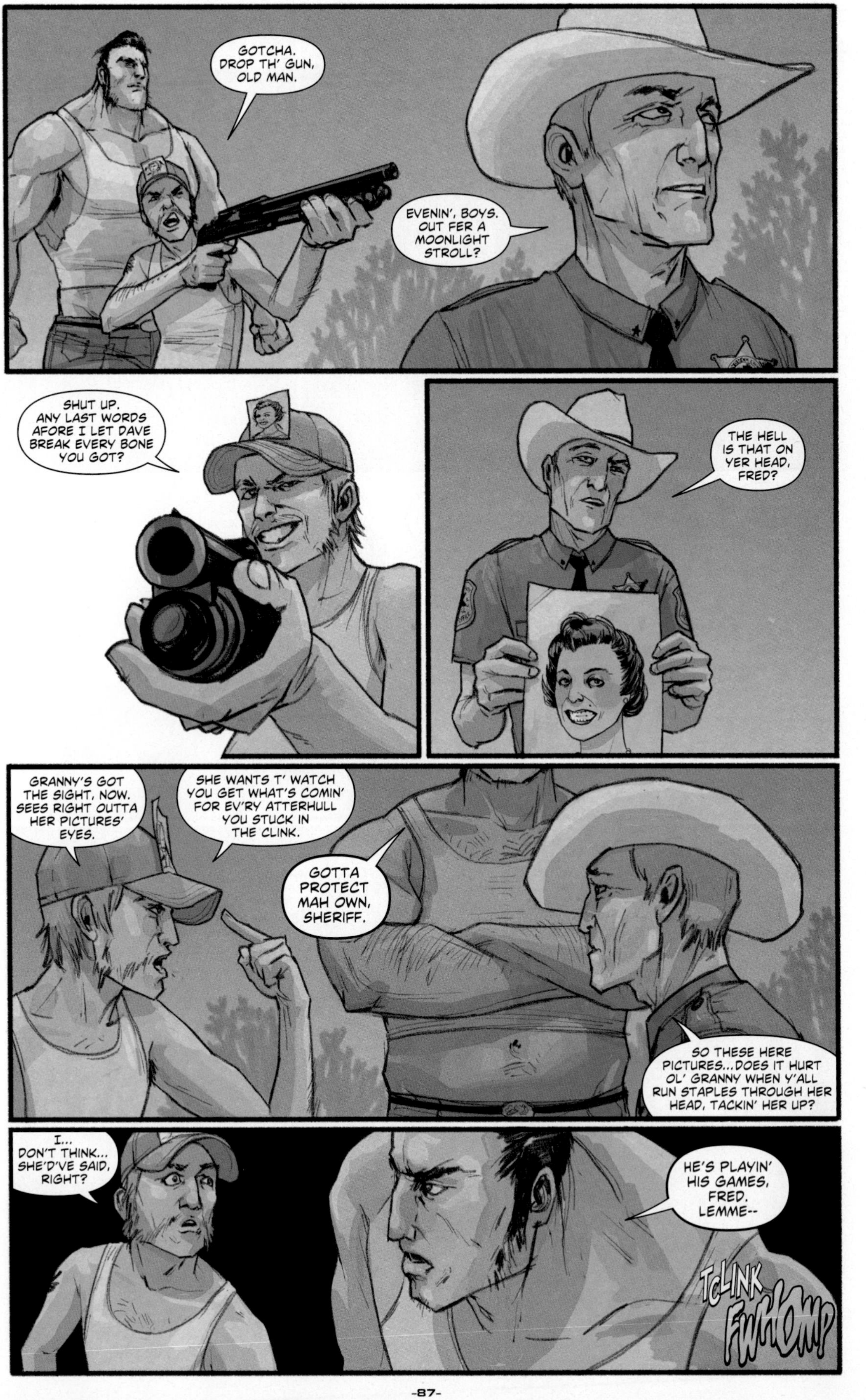
GOTCHA. DROP TH' GUN, OLD MAN.
EVENIN', BOYS. OUT FER A MOONLIGHT STROLL?
SHUT UP. ANY LAST WORDS AFORE I LET DAVE BREAK EVERY BONE YOU GOT?
THE HELL IS THAT ON YER HEAD, FRED?
GRANNY'S GOT THE SIGHT, NOW. SEES RIGHT OUTTA HER PICTURES' EYES.
SHE WANTS T' WATCH YOU GET WHAT'S COMIN' FOR EV'RY ATTERHULL YOU STUCK IN THE CLINK.
GOTTA PROTECT MAH OWN, SHERIFF.
SO THESE HERE PICTURES...DOES IT HURT OL' GRANNY WHEN Y'ALL RUN STAPLES THROUGH HER HEAD, TACKIN' HER UP?
I... DON'T THINK... SHE'D'VE SAID, RIGHT?
HE'S PLAYIN' HIS GAMES, FRED. LEMME--
TCLINK
FWHOMP

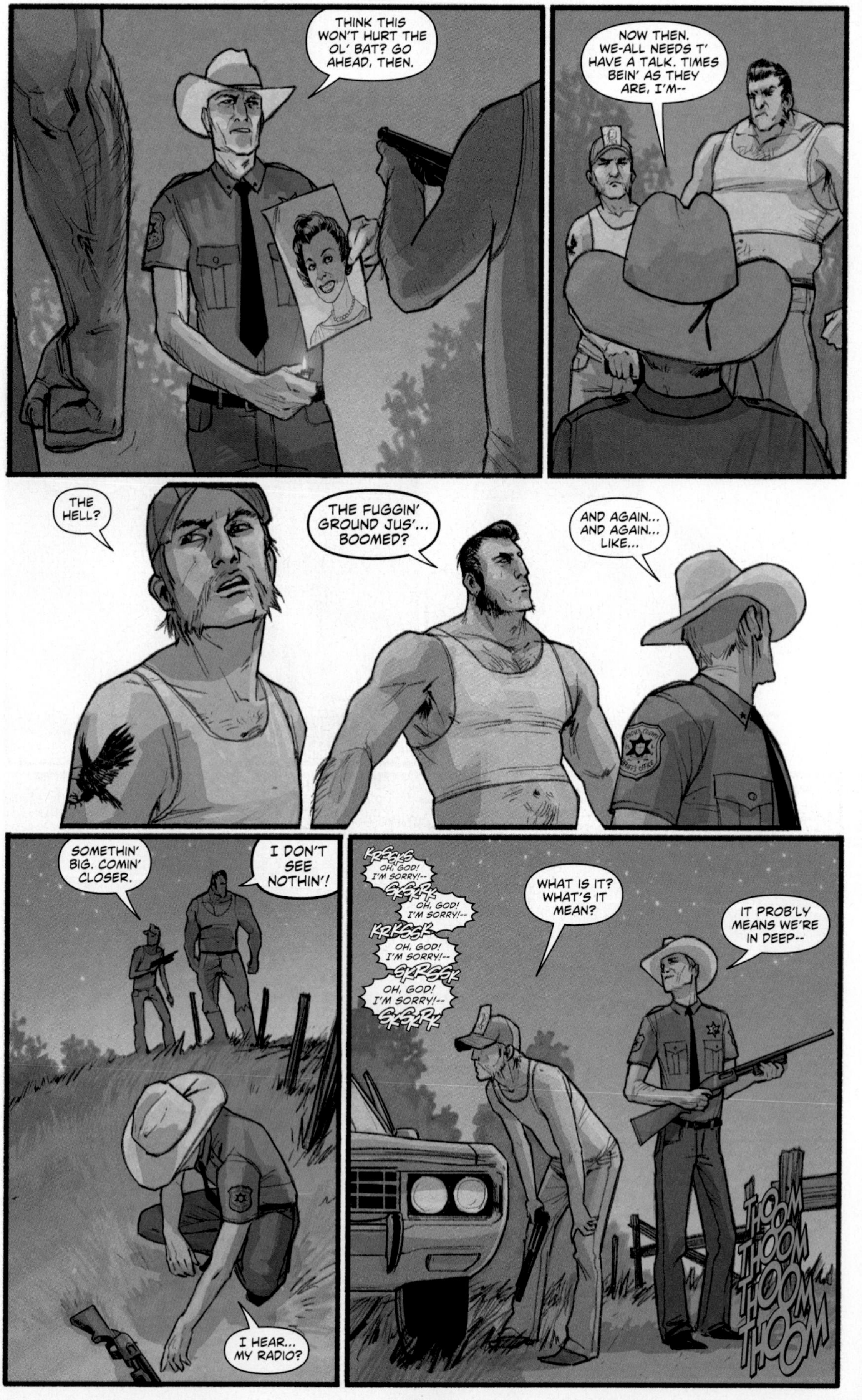
THINK THIS WON'T HURT THE OL' BAT? GO AHEAD, THEN.
NOW THEN. WE-ALL NEEDS T' HAVE A TALK. TIMES BEIN' AS THEY ARE, I'M--
THE HELL?
THE FUGGIN' GROUND JUS'... BOOMED?
AND AGAIN... AND AGAIN... LIKE...
SOMETHIN' BIG. COMIN' CLOSER.
I DON'T SEE NOTHIN'!
I HEAR... MY RADIO?
OH, GOD! I'M SORRY!--
OH, GOD! I'M SORRY!--
OH, GOD! I'M SORRY!--
OH, GOD! I'M SORRY!--
WHAT IS IT? WHAT'S IT MEAN?
IT PROB'LY MEANS WE'RE IN DEEP--
THOOM THOOM THOOM THOOM

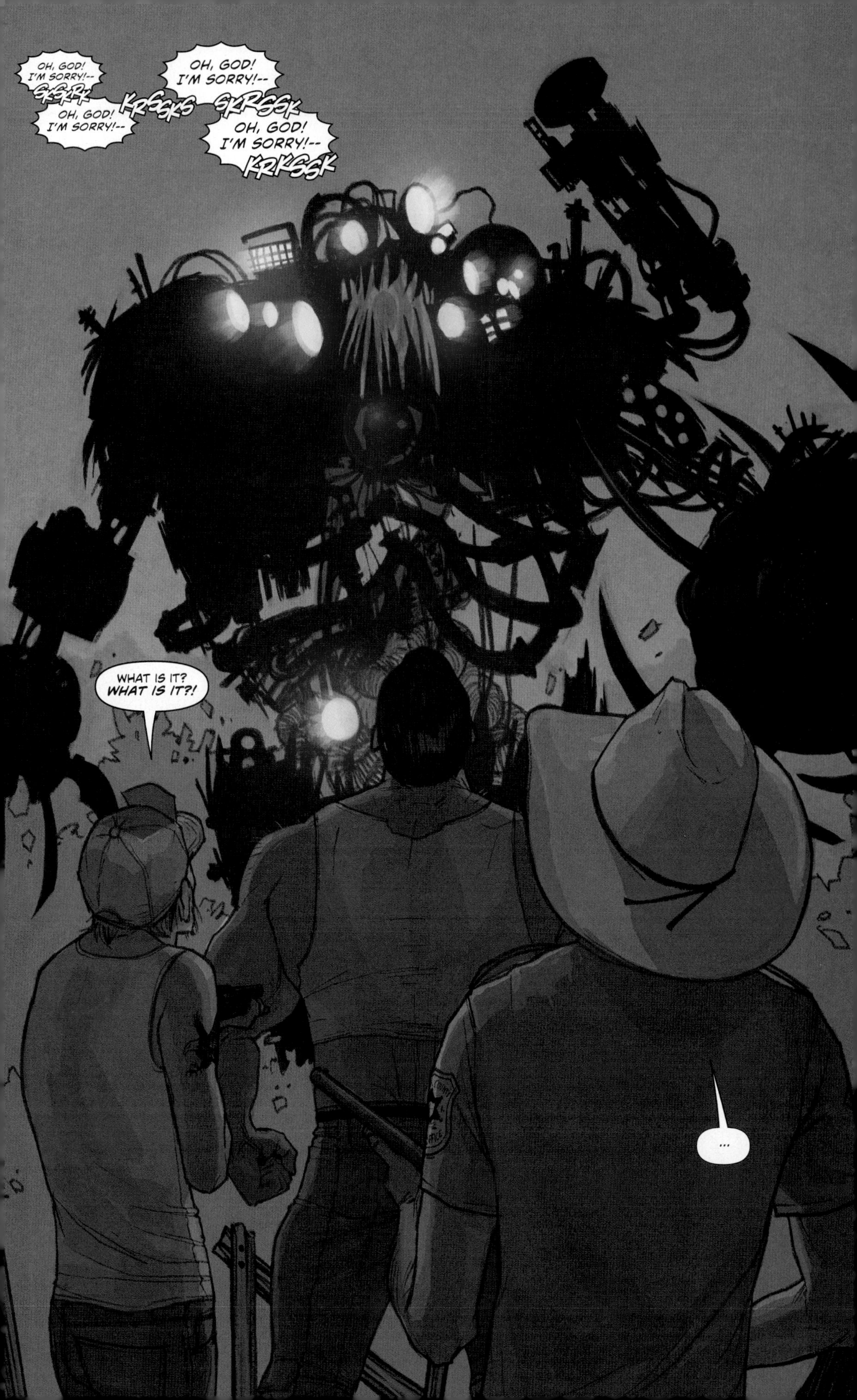
OH, GOD! I'M SORRY!--
SKSKRK
OH, GOD! I'M SORRY!--
KRSSKS
OH, GOD! I'M SORRY!--
SKRSSK
OH, GOD! I'M SORRY!--
KRKSSK
WHAT IS IT? WHAT IS IT?!
...

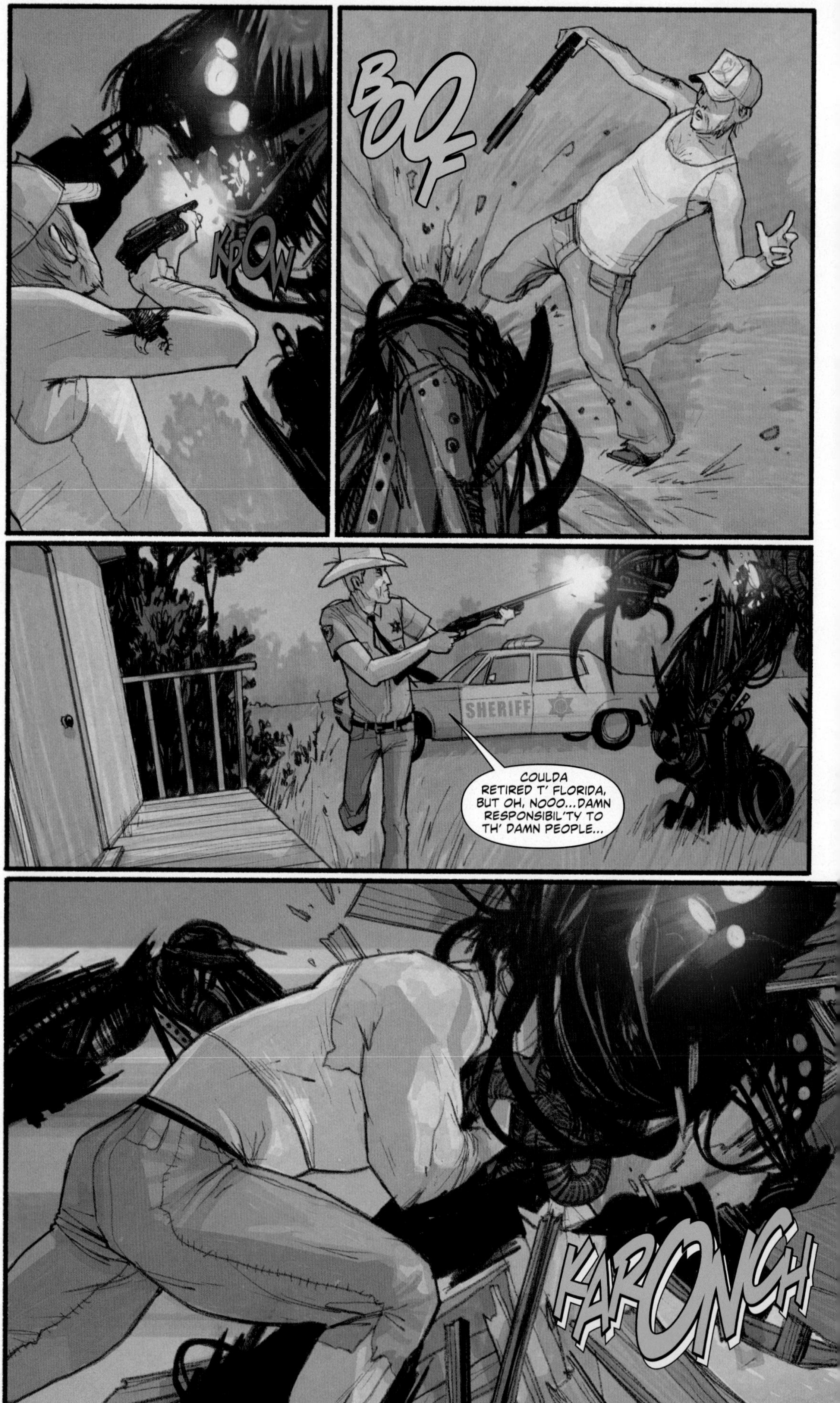
KPOW
BOOF
SHERIFF
COULDA RETIRED T' FLORIDA, BUT OH, NOOO...DAMN RESPONSIBIL'TY TO TH' DAMN PEOPLE...
KARONCH

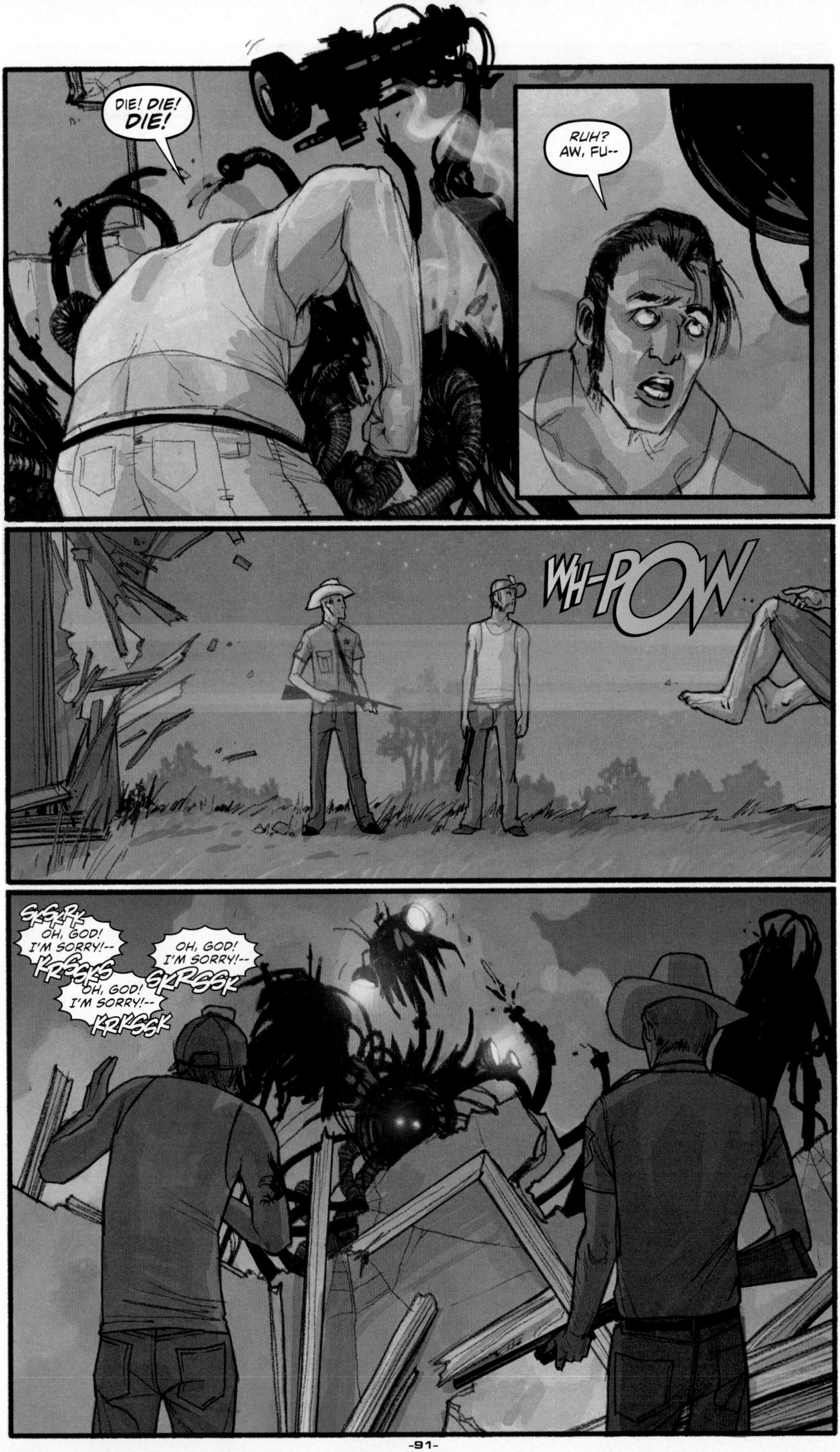
DIE! DIE! DIE!
RUH? AW, FU--
WH-POW
SKSKRK
OH, GOD! I'M SORRY!--
KRSSKS
OH, GOD! I'M SORRY!--
KRKSSK
OH, GOD! I'M SORRY!--
SKRSSK

SKRSSK
OH, GOD!
I'M SORRY!--

KRSSK
OH, GOD!
I'M SORRY!--

KRSSK

SKRSSK
OH, GOD!
I'M SORRY!--

KKGRRAACKKLE

BLAMM

IZZIT DEAD?

RECKON SO.

THINK DAVE IS?

I AIN'T THAT LUCKY...

Meanwhiles, at that very moment, over to Pittman Auto...

DENNY? THE LIGHT YOU TOLD ME TO WATCH JUST WENT OUT.

CAN YOU STOP NOW, JUST FOR A REST? PLEASE?

NO. KINKS. GOTTA WORK 'EM OUT. SIX MONTHS OR THREE THOUSAN' MILES, YOU BET!

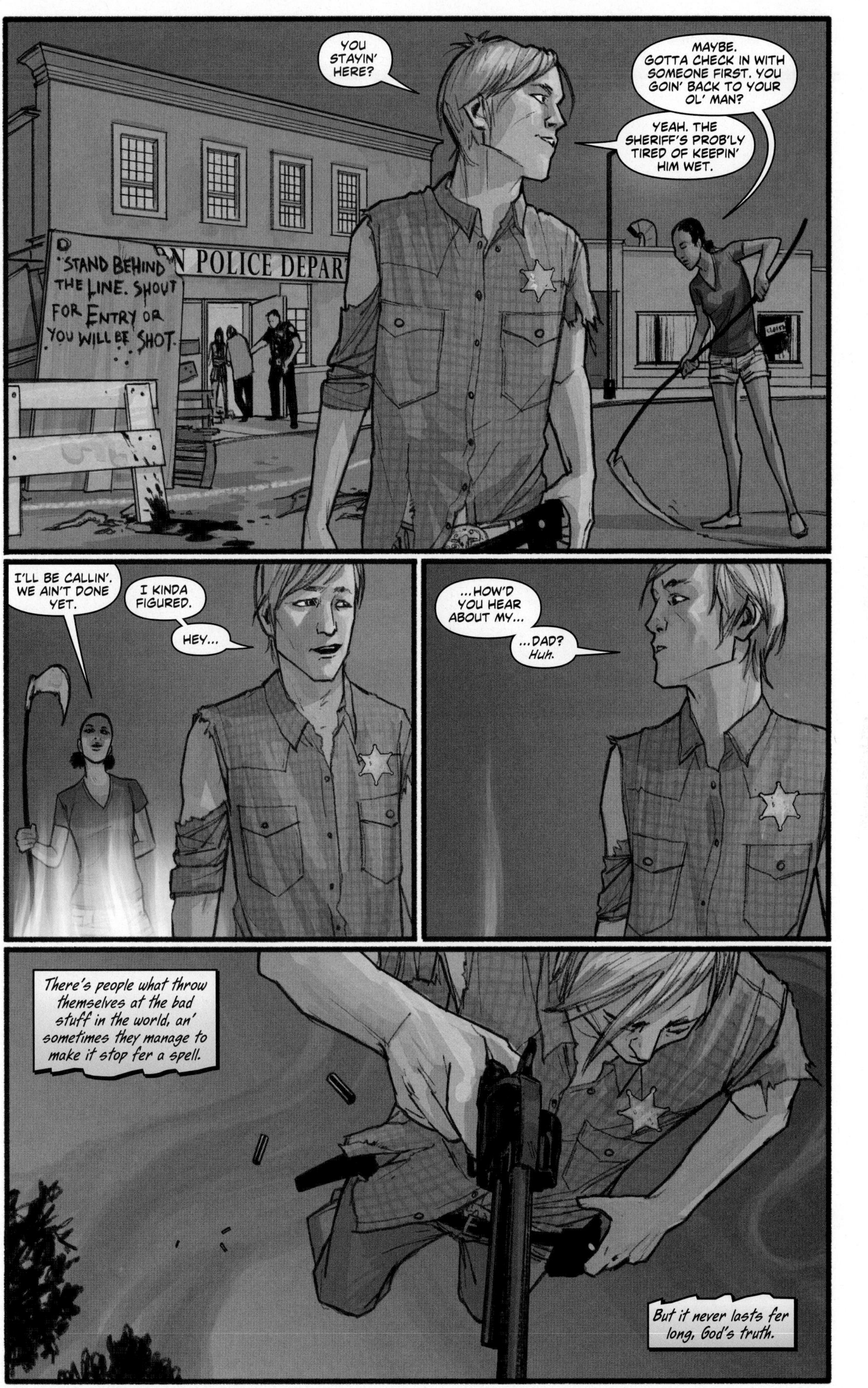
STAND BEHIND THE LINE. SHOUT FOR ENTRY OR YOU WILL BE SHOT.
N POLICE DEPART
YOU STAYIN' HERE?
MAYBE. GOTTA CHECK IN WITH SOMEONE FIRST. YOU GOIN' BACK TO YOUR OL' MAN?
YEAH. THE SHERIFF'S PROB'LY TIRED OF KEEPIN' HIM WET.
I'LL BE CALLIN'. WE AIN'T DONE YET.
I KINDA FIGURED.
HEY...
...HOW'D YOU HEAR ABOUT MY...
...DAD? *Huh.*
There's people what throw themselves at the bad stuff in the world, an' sometimes they manage to make it stop fer a spell.
But it never lasts fer long, God's truth.

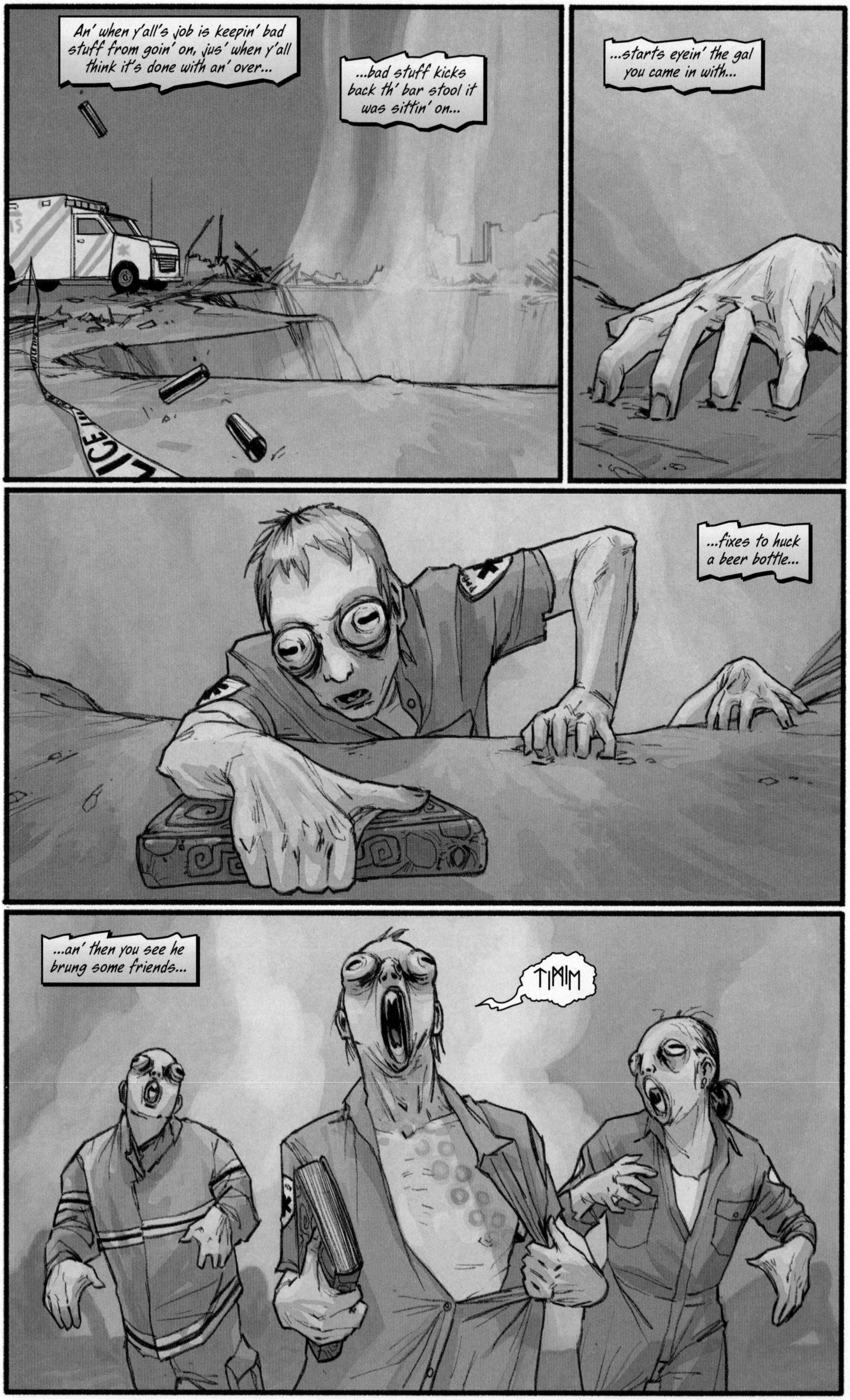

An' when y'all's job is keepin' bad stuff from goin' on, jus' when y'all think it's done with an' over...
...bad stuff kicks back th' bar stool it was sittin' on...
...starts eyein' the gal you came in with...
...fixes to huck a beer bottle...
...an' then you see he brung some friends...

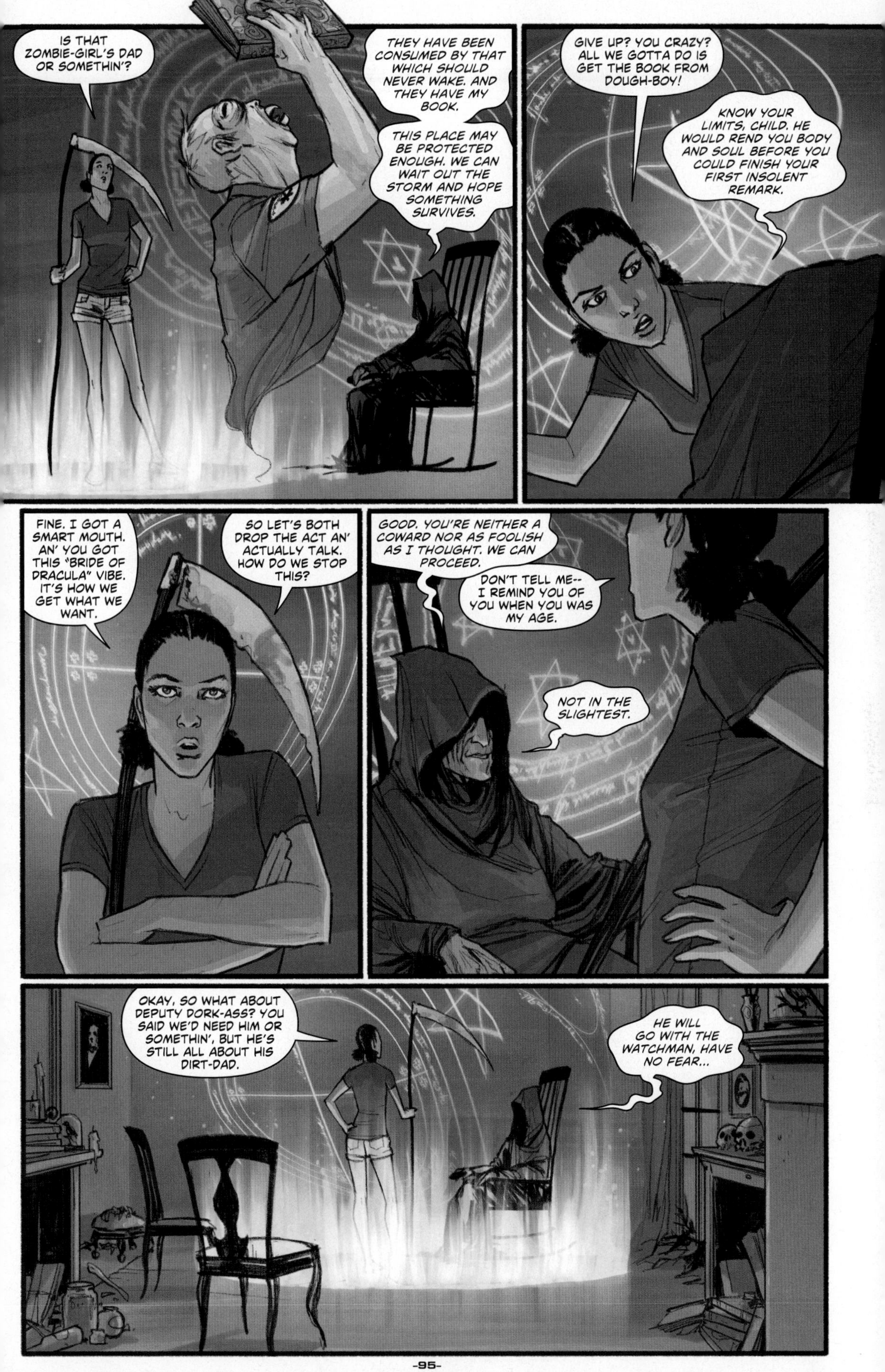
IS THAT ZOMBIE-GIRL'S DAD OR SOMETHIN'?
THEY HAVE BEEN CONSUMED BY THAT WHICH SHOULD NEVER WAKE. AND THEY HAVE MY BOOK.
THIS PLACE MAY BE PROTECTED ENOUGH. WE CAN WAIT OUT THE STORM AND HOPE SOMETHING SURVIVES.
GIVE UP? YOU CRAZY? ALL WE GOTTA DO IS GET THE BOOK FROM DOUGH-BOY!
KNOW YOUR LIMITS, CHILD. HE WOULD REND YOU BODY AND SOUL BEFORE YOU COULD FINISH YOUR FIRST INSOLENT REMARK.
FINE. I GOT A SMART MOUTH. AN' YOU GOT THIS "BRIDE OF DRACULA" VIBE. IT'S HOW WE GET WHAT WE WANT.
SO LET'S BOTH DROP THE ACT AN' ACTUALLY TALK. HOW DO WE STOP THIS?
GOOD. YOU'RE NEITHER A COWARD NOR AS FOOLISH AS I THOUGHT. WE CAN PROCEED.
DON'T TELL ME-- I REMIND YOU OF YOU WHEN YOU WAS MY AGE.
NOT IN THE SLIGHTEST.
OKAY, SO WHAT ABOUT DEPUTY DORK-ASS? YOU SAID WE'D NEED HIM OR SOMETHIN', BUT HE'S STILL ALL ABOUT HIS DIRT-DAD.
HE WILL GO WITH THE WATCHMAN, HAVE NO FEAR...

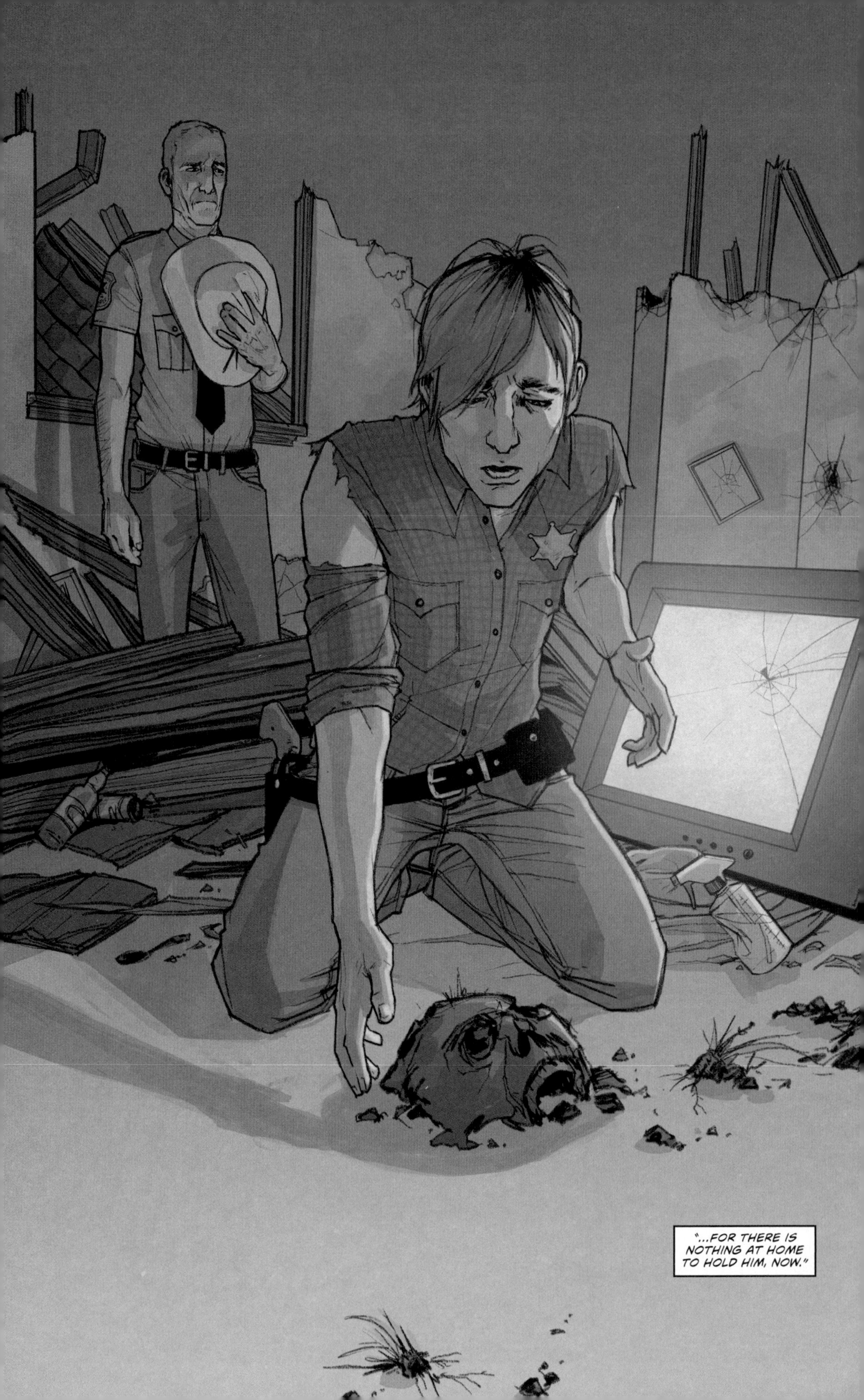
"...FOR THERE IS NOTHING AT HOME TO HOLD HIM, NOW."

CHAPTER FIVE

Gather Ye Strength, For Reapin' Is Nigh.

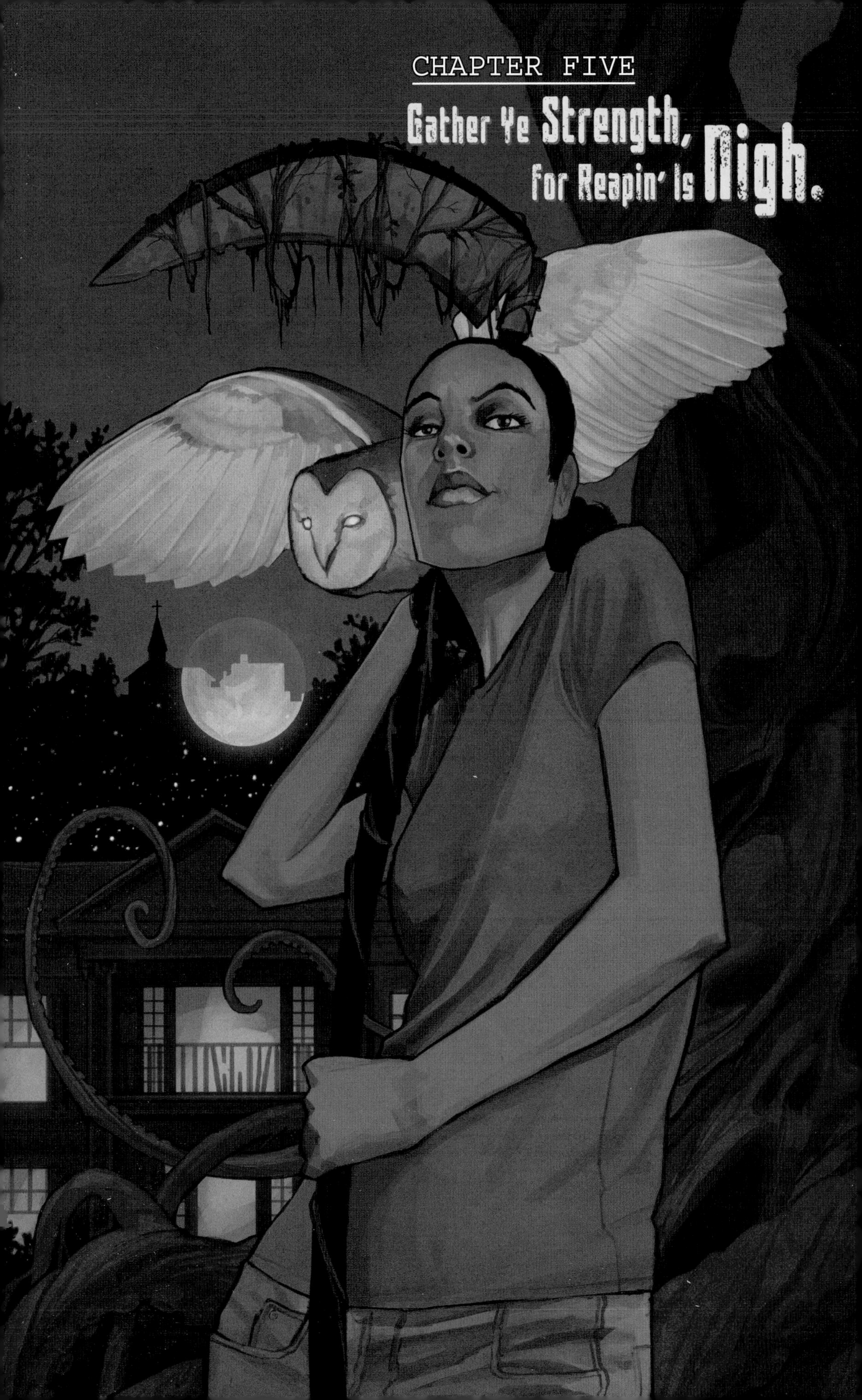

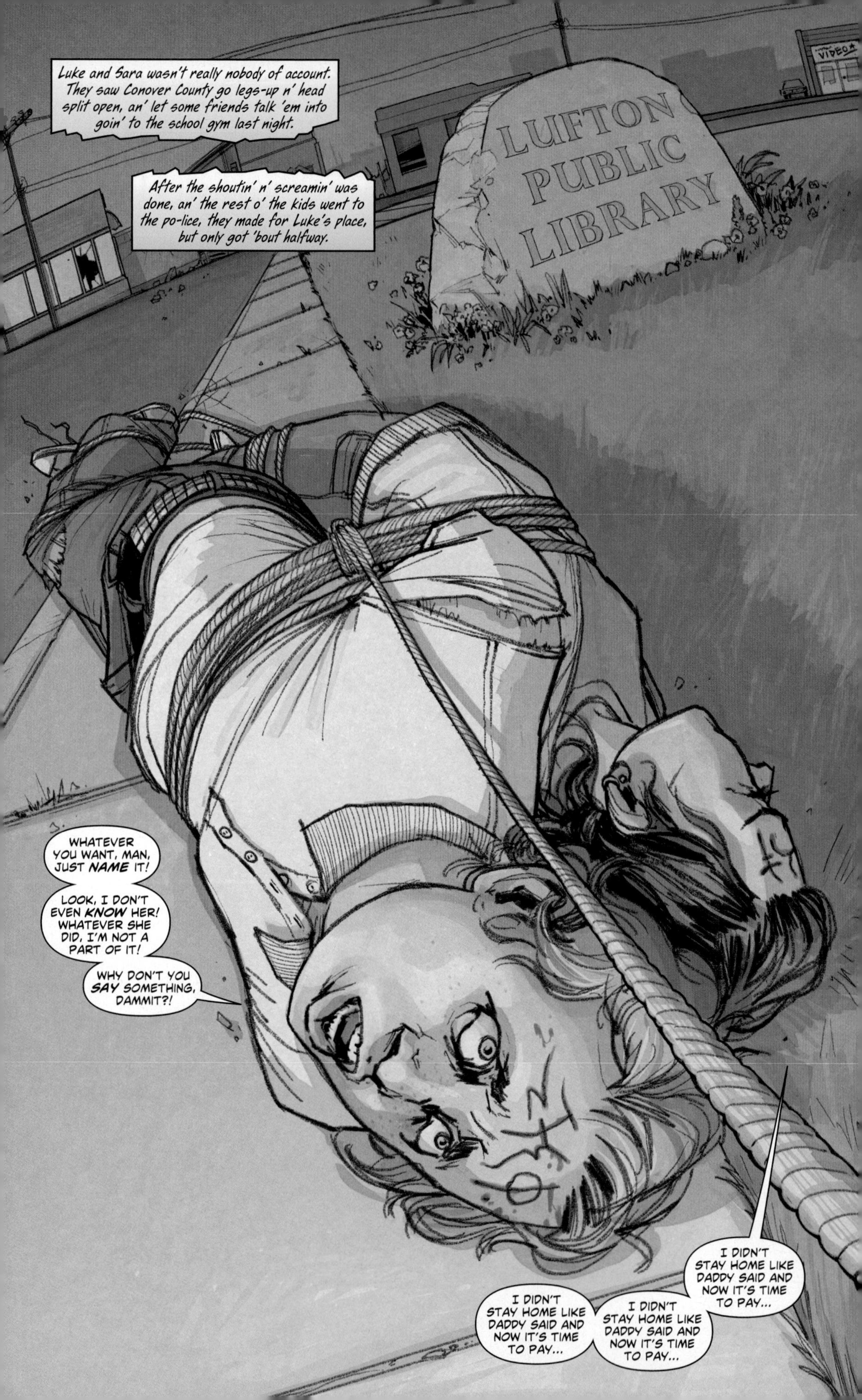
Luke and Sara wasn't really nobody of account. They saw Conover County go legs-up n' head split open, an' let some friends talk 'em into goin' to the school gym last night.
After the shoutin' n' screamin' was done, an' the rest o' the kids went to the po-lice, they made for Luke's place, but only got 'bout halfway.
LUFTON PUBLIC LIBRARY
VIDEO
WHATEVER YOU WANT, MAN, JUST **NAME** IT!
LOOK, I DON'T EVEN **KNOW** HER! WHATEVER SHE DID, I'M NOT A PART OF IT!
WHY DON'T YOU **SAY** SOMETHING, DAMMIT?!
I DIDN'T STAY HOME LIKE DADDY SAID AND NOW IT'S TIME TO PAY...
I DIDN'T STAY HOME LIKE DADDY SAID AND NOW IT'S TIME TO PAY...
I DIDN'T STAY HOME LIKE DADDY SAID AND NOW IT'S TIME TO PAY...

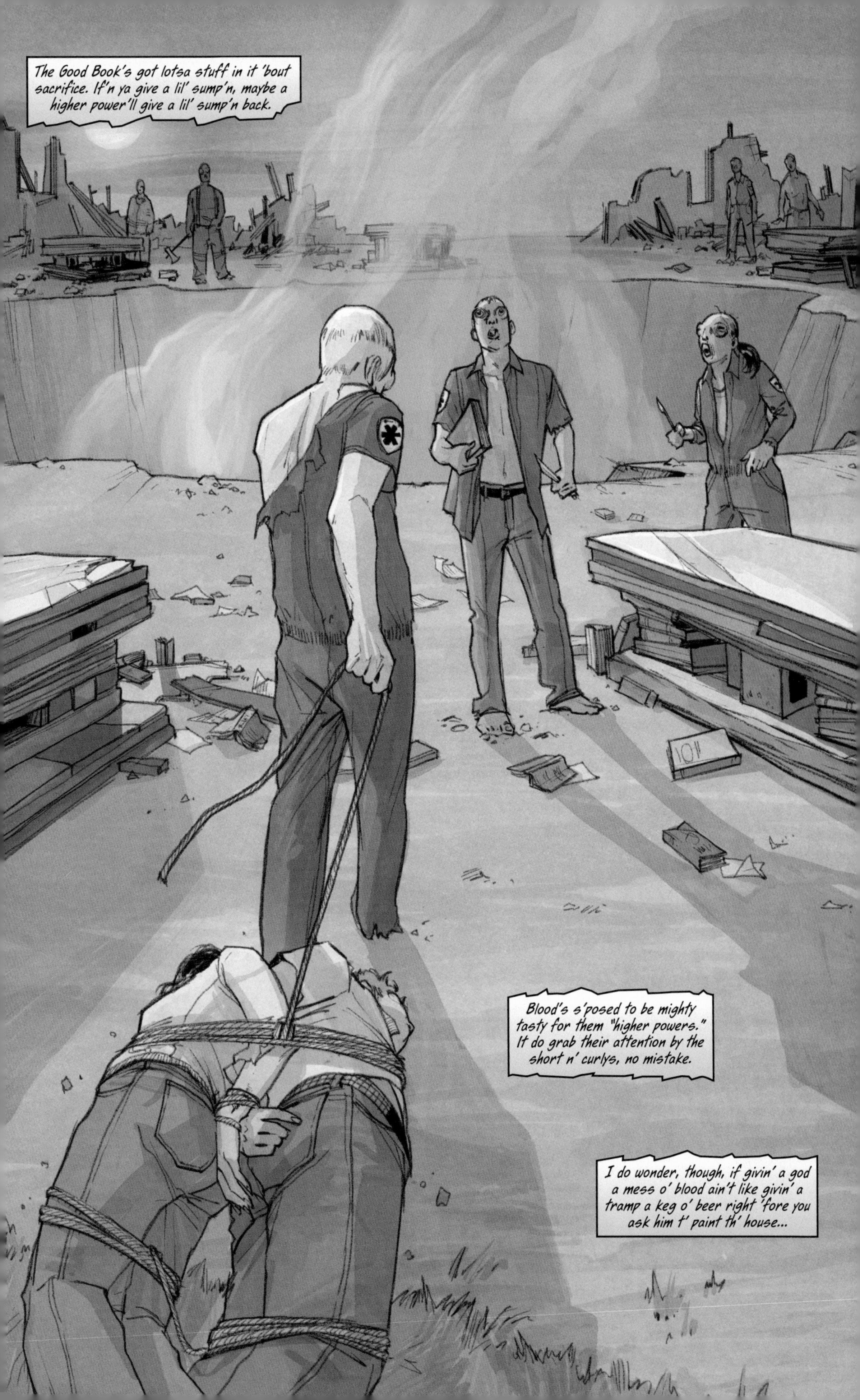
The Good Book's got lotsa stuff in it 'bout sacrifice. If'n ya give a lil' sump'n, maybe a higher power'll give a lil' sump'n back.
Blood's s'posed to be mighty tasty for them "higher powers." It do grab their attention by the short n' curlys, no mistake.
I do wonder, though, if givin' a god a mess o' blood ain't like givin' a tramp a keg o' beer right 'fore you ask him t' paint th' house...

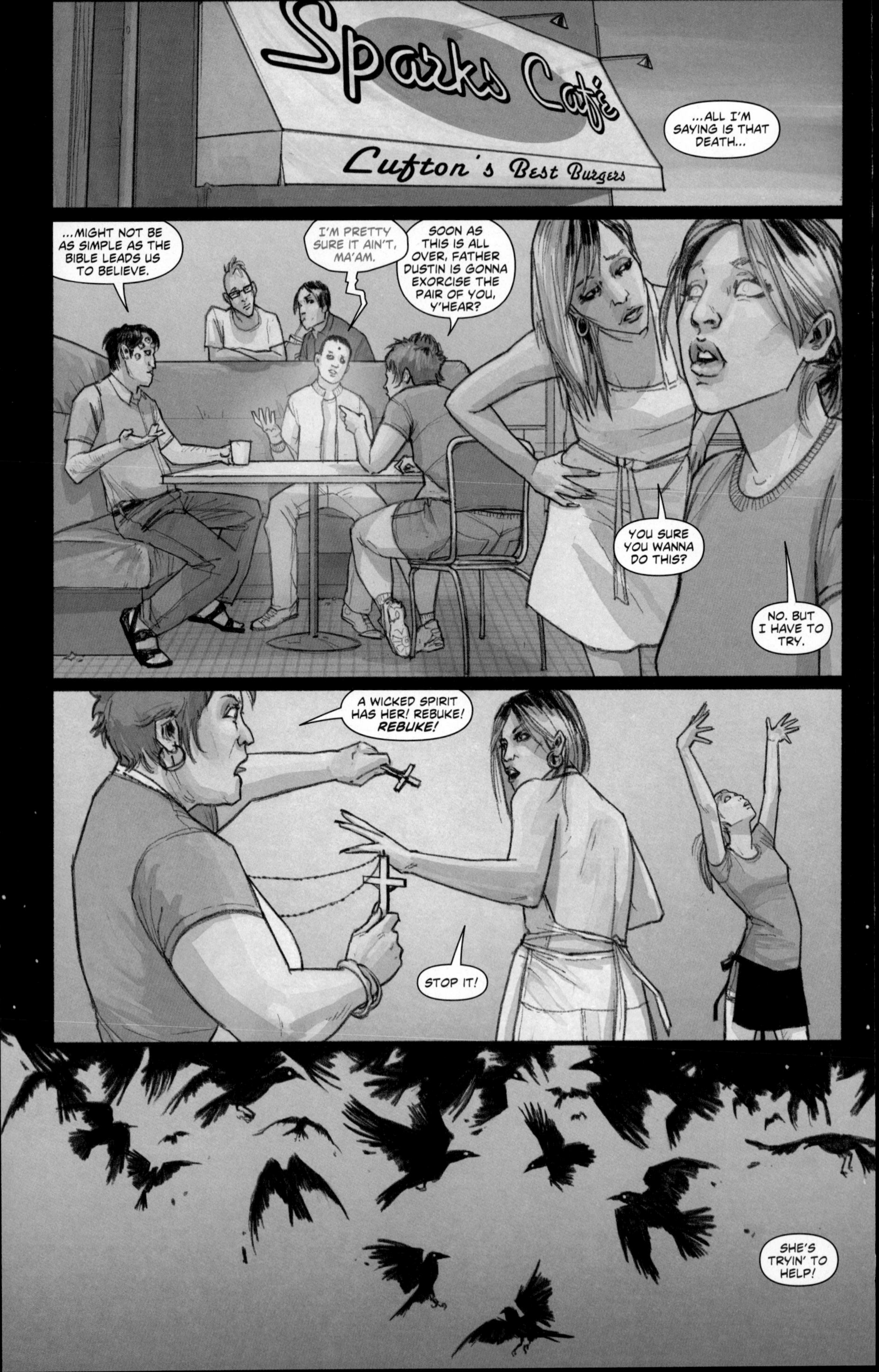
Sparks Café
Lufton's Best Burgers
...ALL I'M SAYING IS THAT DEATH...
...MIGHT NOT BE AS SIMPLE AS THE BIBLE LEADS US TO BELIEVE.
I'M PRETTY SURE IT AIN'T, MA'AM.
SOON AS THIS IS ALL OVER, FATHER DUSTIN IS GONNA EXORCISE THE PAIR OF YOU, Y'HEAR?
YOU SURE YOU WANNA DO THIS?
NO. BUT I HAVE TO TRY.
A WICKED SPIRIT HAS HER! REBUKE! ***REBUKE!***
STOP IT!
SHE'S TRYIN' TO HELP!

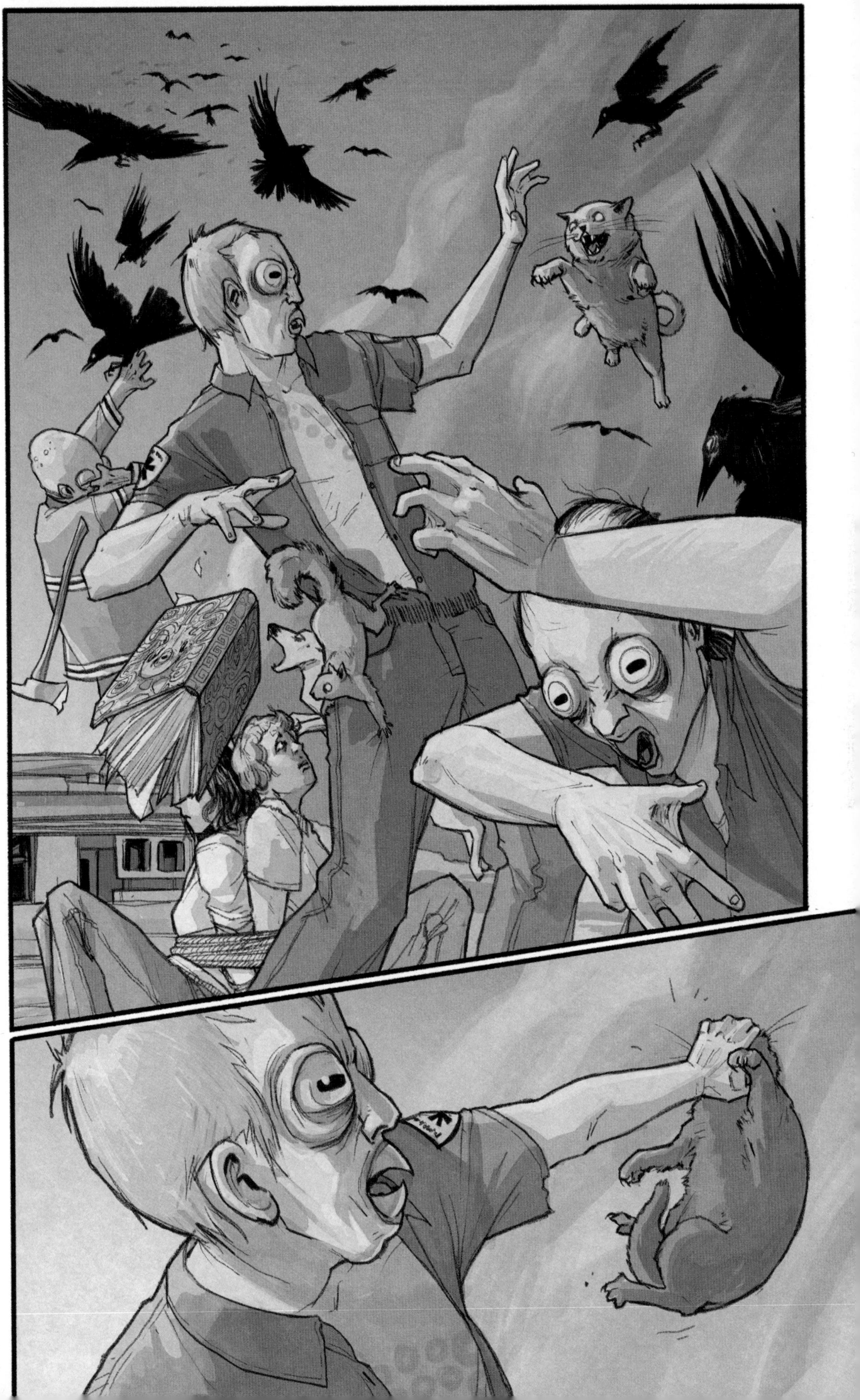

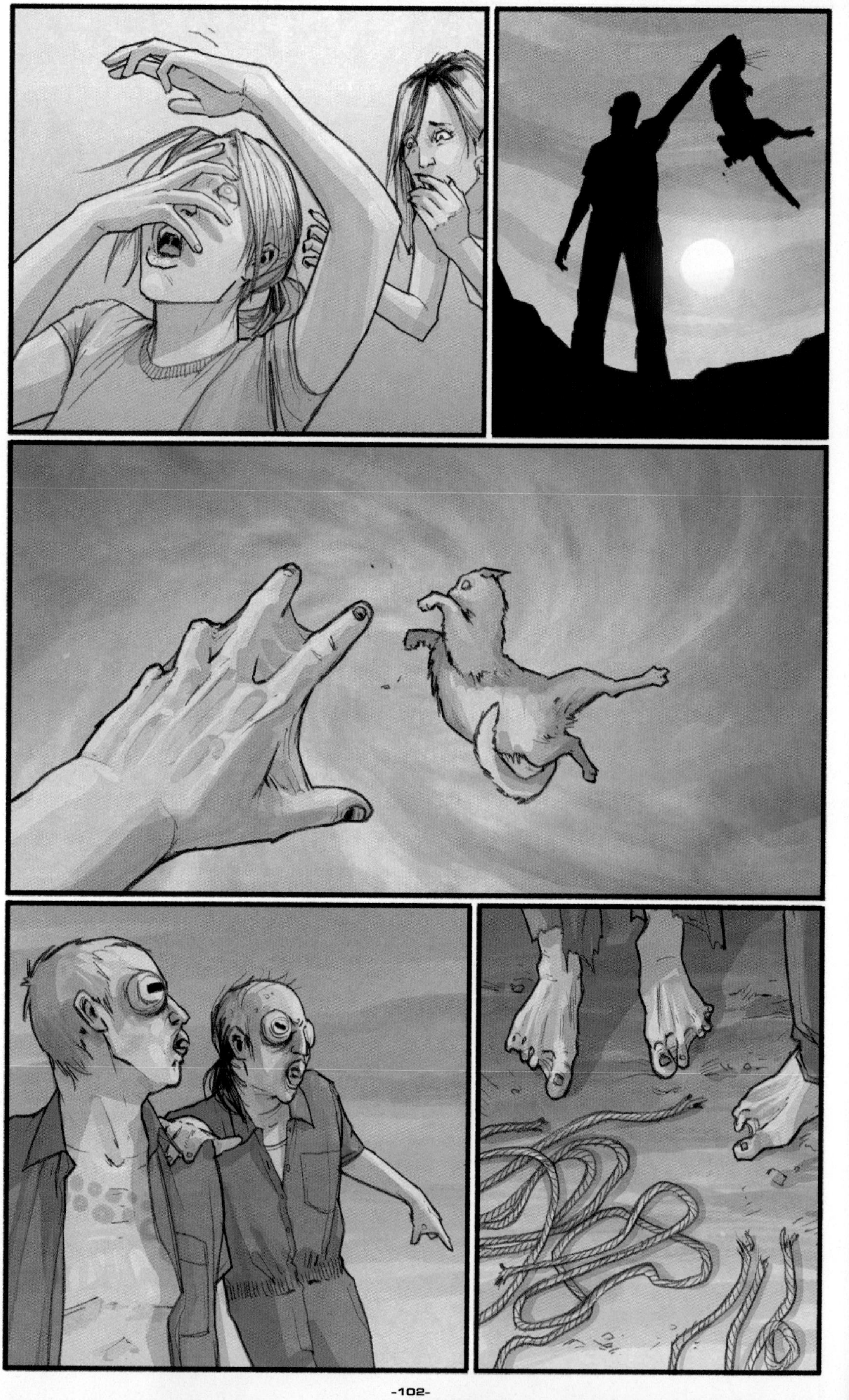

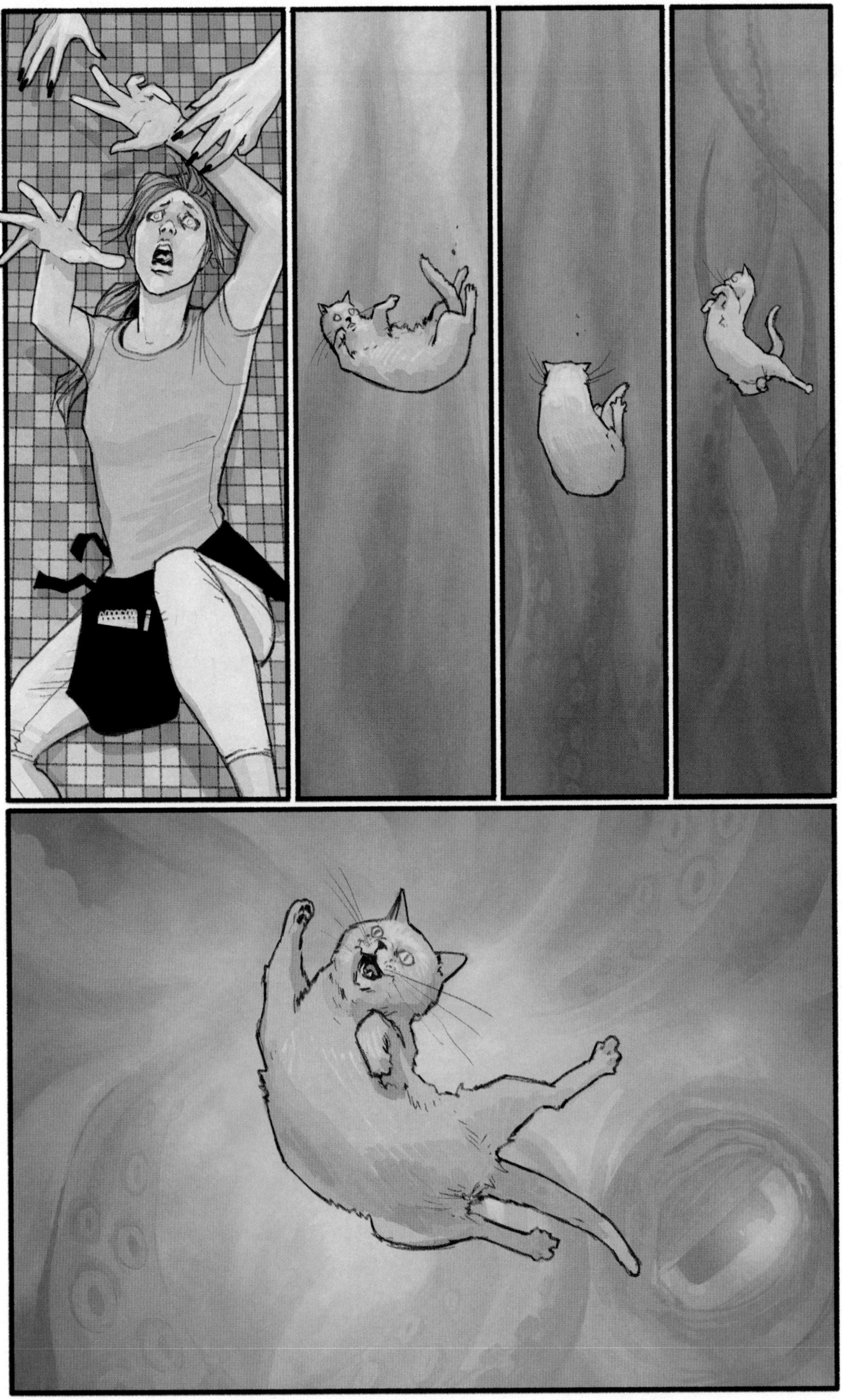

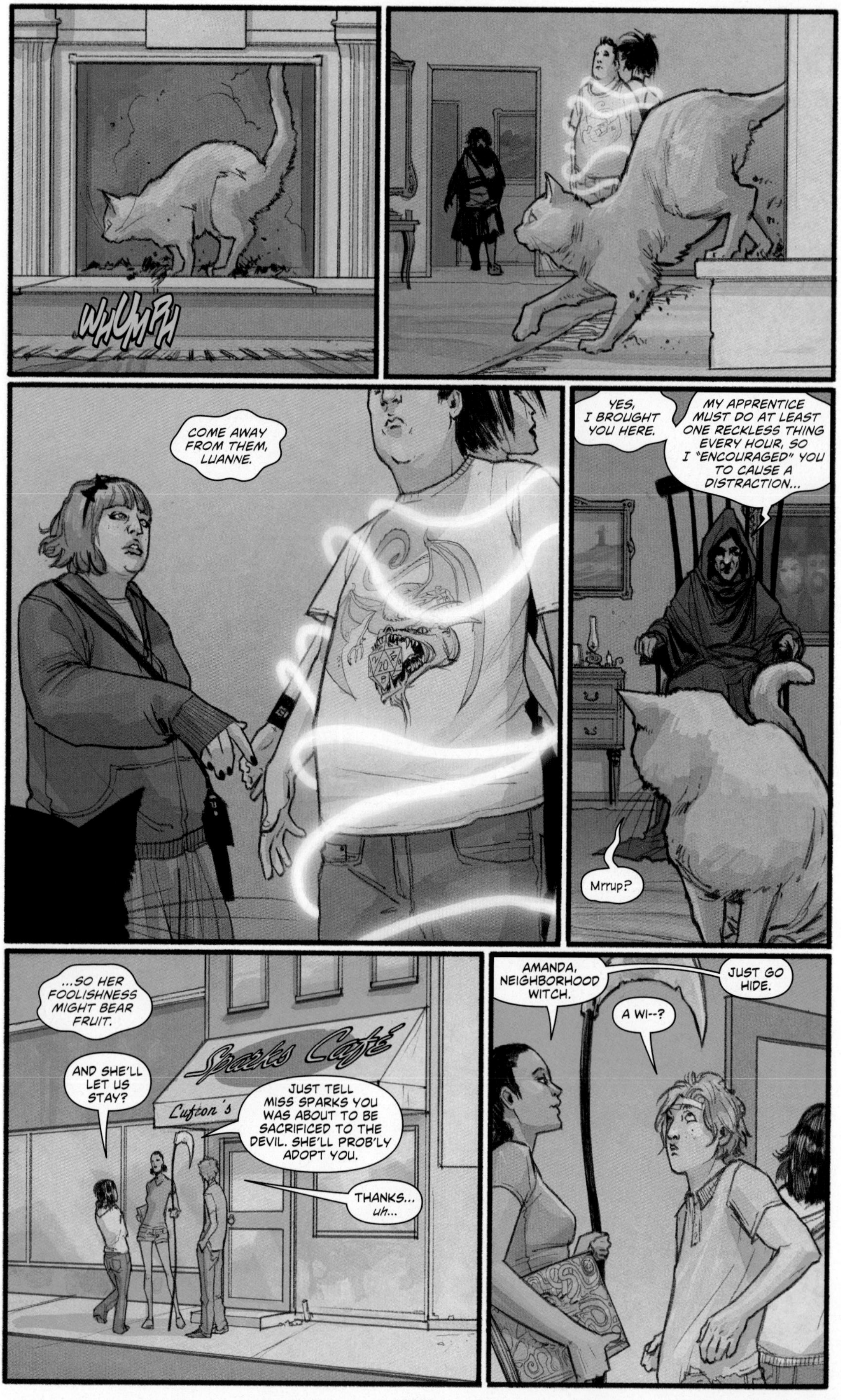
WHUMPH
COME AWAY FROM THEM, LUANNE.
YES, I BROUGHT YOU HERE.
MY APPRENTICE MUST DO AT LEAST ONE RECKLESS THING EVERY HOUR, SO I "ENCOURAGED" YOU TO CAUSE A DISTRACTION...
Mrrup?
...SO HER FOOLISHNESS MIGHT BEAR FRUIT.
AND SHE'LL LET US STAY?
JUST TELL MISS SPARKS YOU WAS ABOUT TO BE SACRIFICED TO THE DEVIL. SHE'LL PROB'LY ADOPT YOU.
THANKS... uh...
Sparks Café
Cufton's
AMANDA, NEIGHBORHOOD WITCH.
JUST GO HIDE.
A WI--?

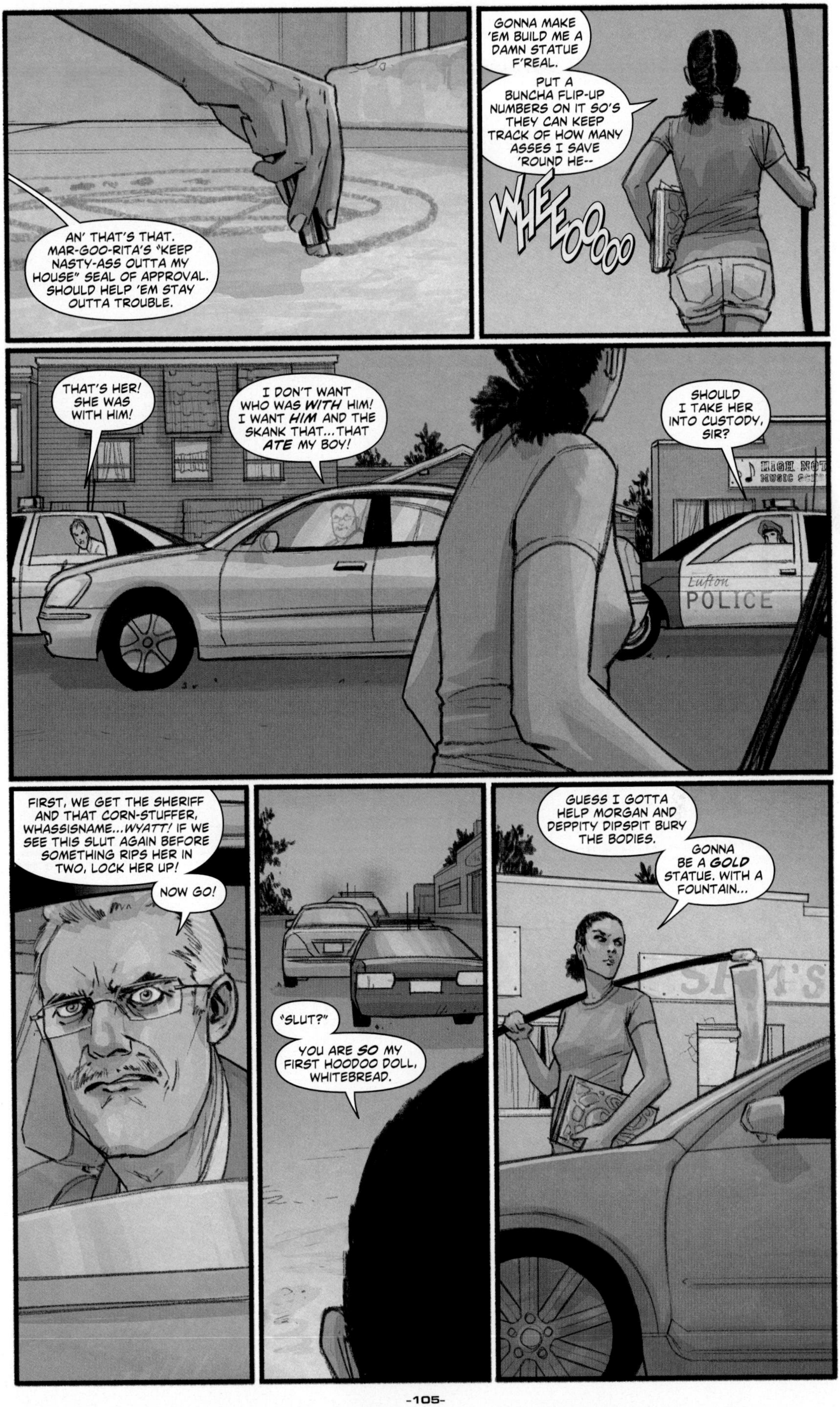
AN' THAT'S THAT. MAR-GOO-RITA'S "KEEP NASTY-ASS OUTTA MY HOUSE" SEAL OF APPROVAL. SHOULD HELP 'EM STAY OUTTA TROUBLE.
GONNA MAKE 'EM BUILD ME A DAMN STATUE F'REAL.
PUT A BUNCHA FLIP-UP NUMBERS ON IT SO'S THEY CAN KEEP TRACK OF HOW MANY ASSES I SAVE 'ROUND HE--
WHEEOOOOO
THAT'S HER! SHE WAS WITH HIM!
I DON'T WANT WHO WAS WITH HIM! I WANT HIM AND THE SKANK THAT...THAT ATE MY BOY!
SHOULD I TAKE HER INTO CUSTODY, SIR?
Lufton
POLICE
FIRST, WE GET THE SHERIFF AND THAT CORN-STUFFER, WHASSISNAME...WYATT! IF WE SEE THIS SLUT AGAIN BEFORE SOMETHING RIPS HER IN TWO, LOCK HER UP!
NOW GO!
"SLUT?"
YOU ARE SO MY FIRST HOODOO DOLL, WHITEBREAD.
GUESS I GOTTA HELP MORGAN AND DEPPITY DIPSPIT BURY THE BODIES.
GONNA BE A GOLD STATUE. WITH A FOUNTAIN...

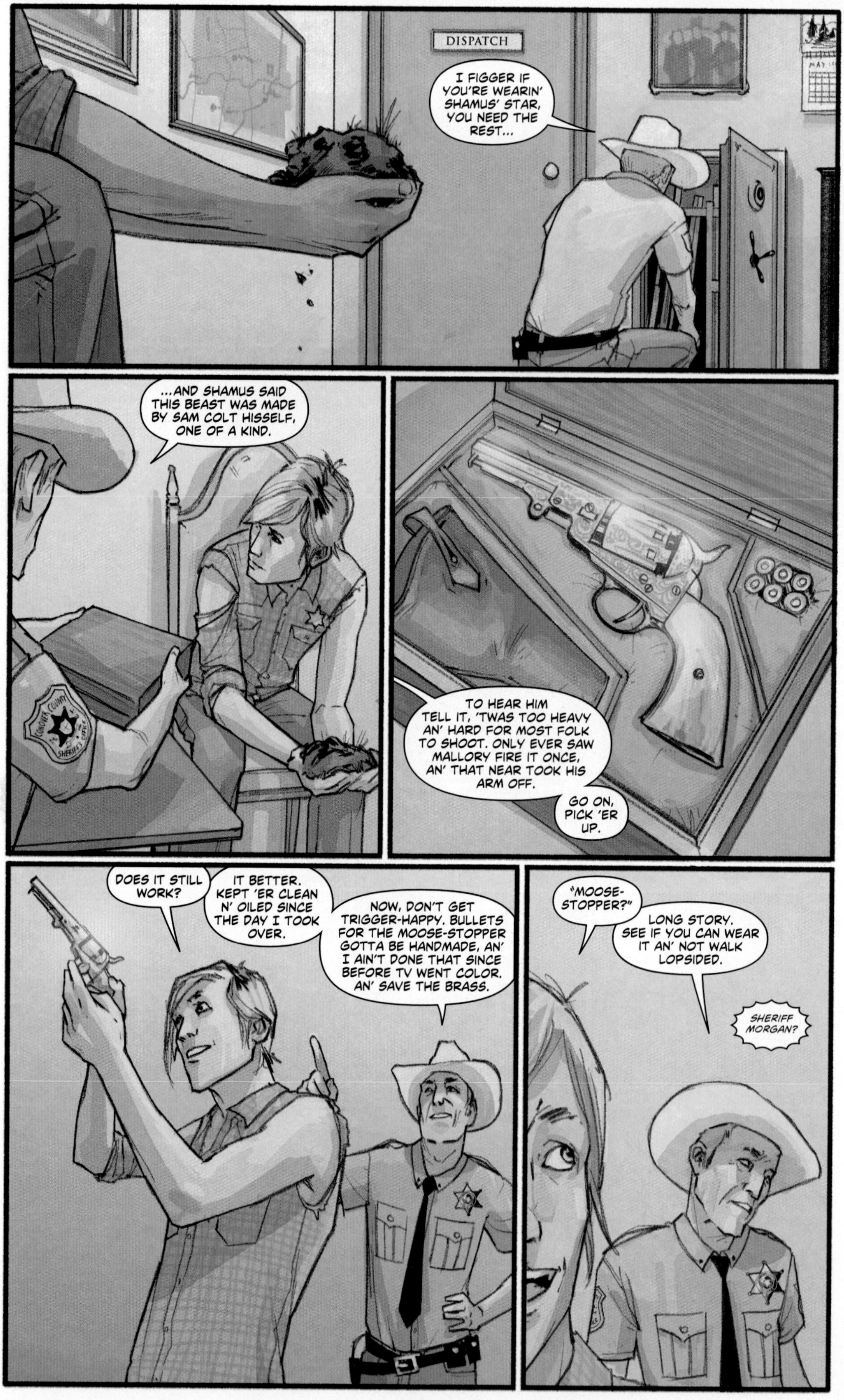
DISPATCH
I FIGGER IF YOU'RE WEARIN' SHAMUS' STAR, YOU NEED THE REST...
...AND SHAMUS SAID THIS BEAST WAS MADE BY SAM COLT HISSELF, ONE OF A KIND.
TO HEAR HIM TELL IT, 'TWAS TOO HEAVY AN' HARD FOR MOST FOLK TO SHOOT. ONLY EVER SAW MALLORY FIRE IT ONCE, AN' THAT NEAR TOOK HIS ARM OFF.
GO ON, PICK 'ER UP.
DOES IT STILL WORK?
IT BETTER. KEPT 'ER CLEAN N' OILED SINCE THE DAY I TOOK OVER.
NOW, DON'T GET TRIGGER-HAPPY. BULLETS FOR THE MOOSE-STOPPER GOTTA BE HANDMADE, AN' I AIN'T DONE THAT SINCE BEFORE TV WENT COLOR. AN' SAVE THE BRASS.
"MOOSE-STOPPER?"
LONG STORY. SEE IF YOU CAN WEAR IT AN' NOT WALK LOPSIDED.
SHERIFF MORGAN?

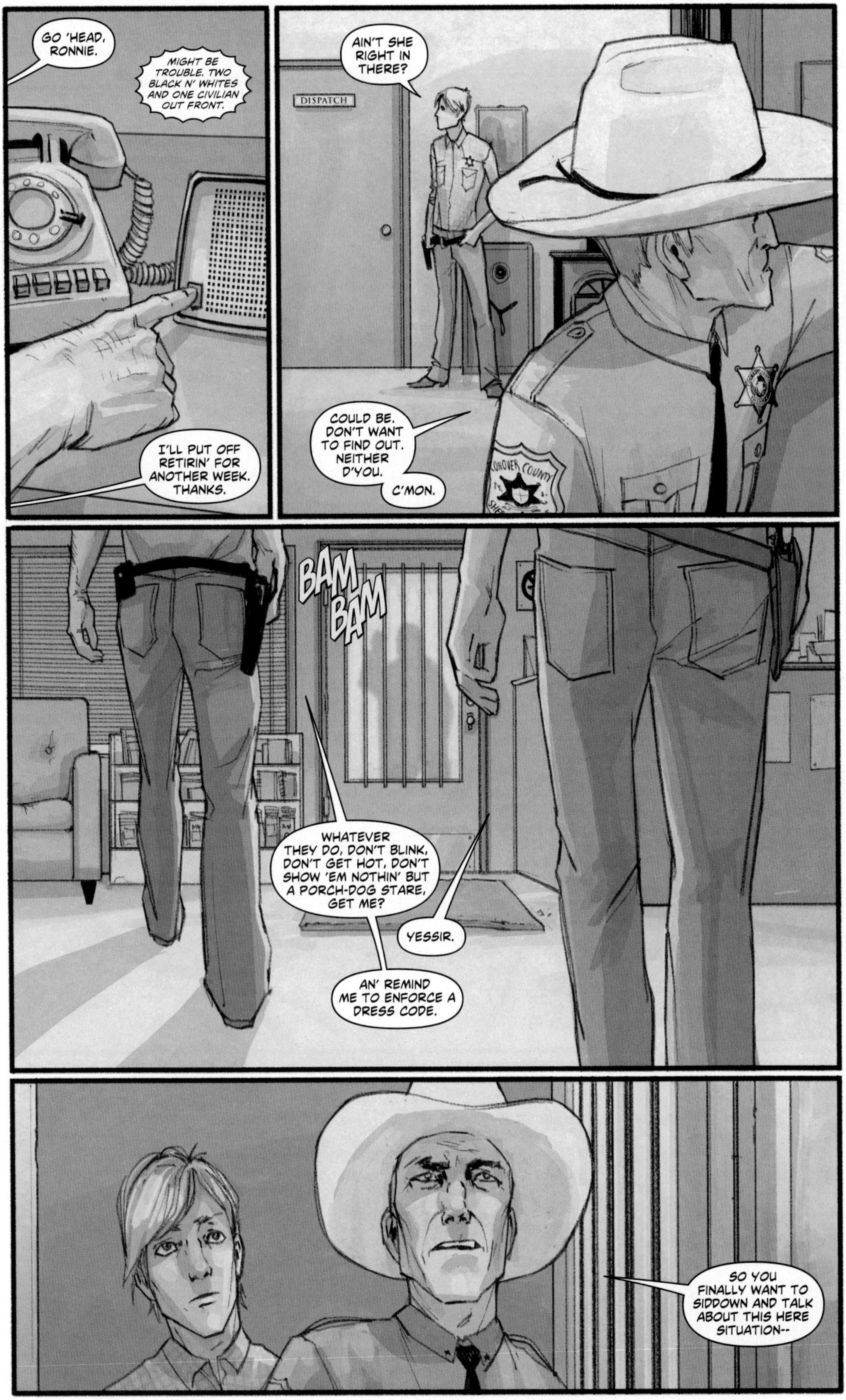

GO 'HEAD, RONNIE.
MIGHT BE TROUBLE. TWO BLACK N' WHITES AND ONE CIVILIAN OUT FRONT.
I'LL PUT OFF RETIRIN' FOR ANOTHER WEEK. THANKS.
DISPATCH
AIN'T SHE RIGHT IN THERE?
COULD BE. DON'T WANT TO FIND OUT. NEITHER D'YOU.
C'MON.
CONOVER COUNTY
BAM BAM
WHATEVER THEY DO, DON'T BLINK, DON'T GET HOT, DON'T SHOW 'EM NOTHIN' BUT A PORCH-DOG STARE, GET ME?
YESSIR.
AN' REMIND ME TO ENFORCE A DRESS CODE.
SO YOU FINALLY WANT TO SIDDOWN AND TALK ABOUT THIS HERE SITUATION--

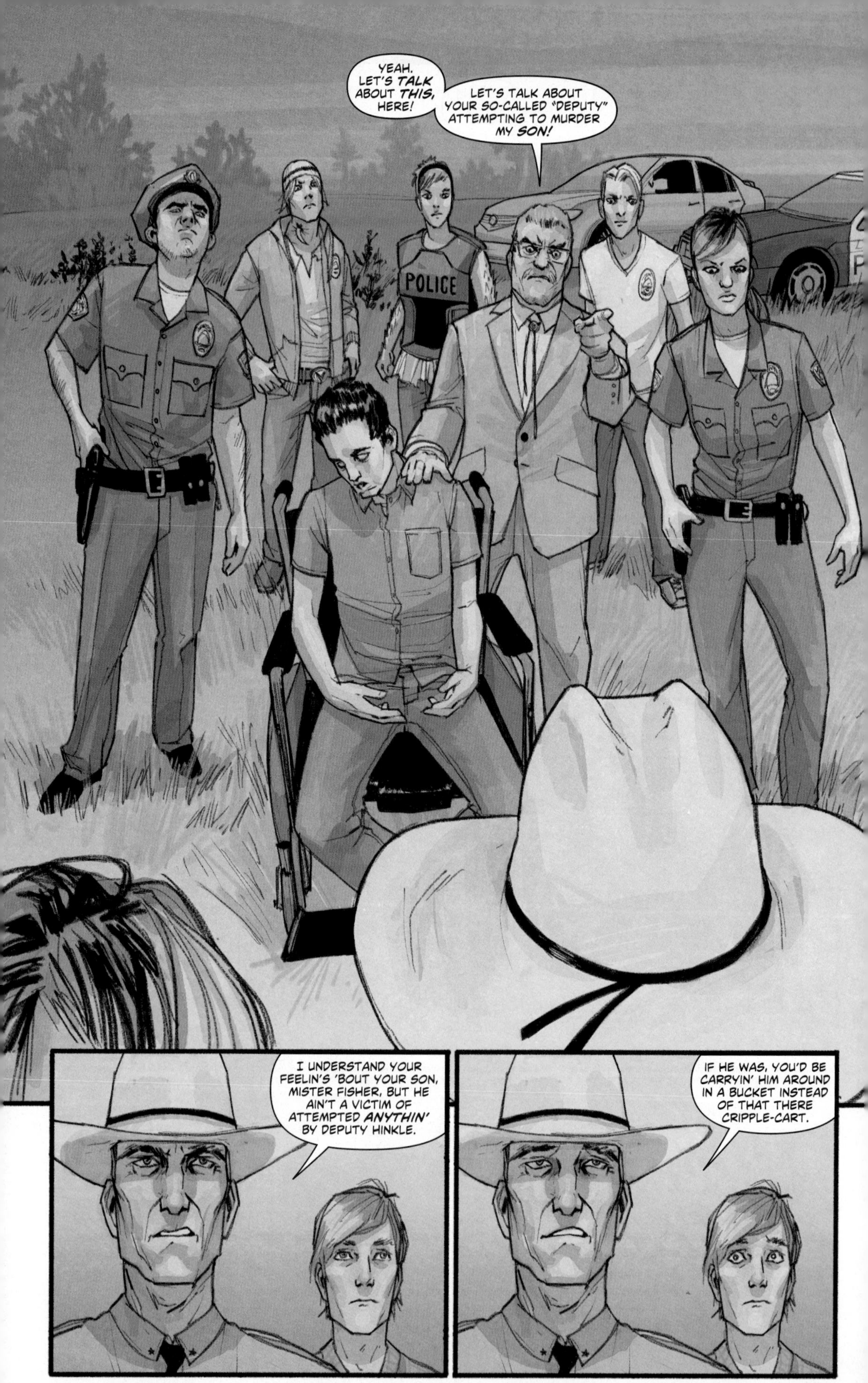

YEAH. LET'S TALK ABOUT THIS, HERE!
LET'S TALK ABOUT YOUR SO-CALLED "DEPUTY" ATTEMPTING TO MURDER MY SON!
POLICE
I UNDERSTAND YOUR FEELIN'S 'BOUT YOUR SON, MISTER FISHER, BUT HE AIN'T A VICTIM OF ATTEMPTED ANYTHIN' BY DEPUTY HINKLE.
IF HE WAS, YOU'D BE CARRYIN' HIM AROUND IN A BUCKET INSTEAD OF THAT THERE CRIPPLE-CART.

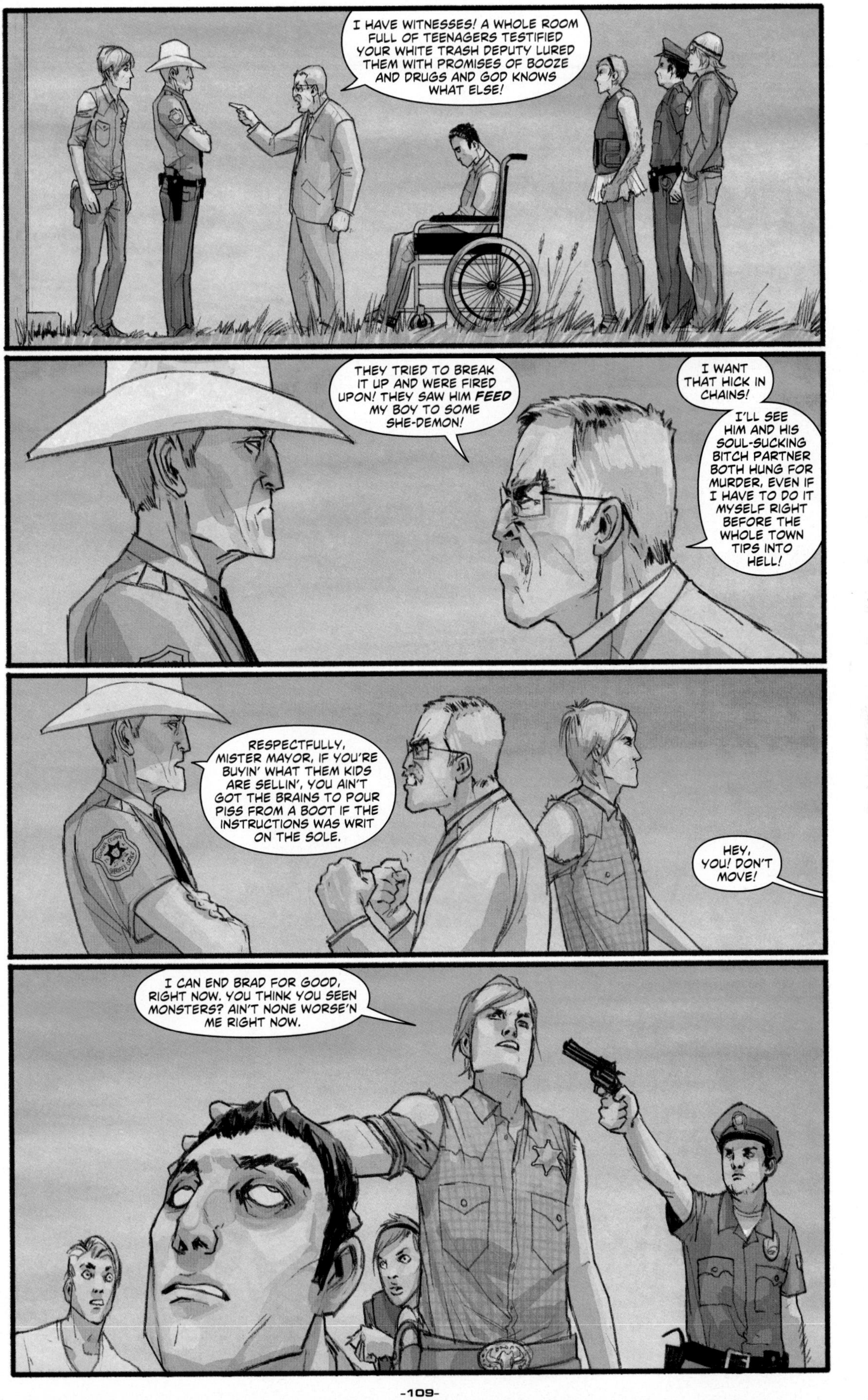
I HAVE WITNESSES! A WHOLE ROOM FULL OF TEENAGERS TESTIFIED YOUR WHITE TRASH DEPUTY LURED THEM WITH PROMISES OF BOOZE AND DRUGS AND GOD KNOWS WHAT ELSE!
THEY TRIED TO BREAK IT UP AND WERE FIRED UPON! THEY SAW HIM FEED MY BOY TO SOME SHE-DEMON!
I WANT THAT HICK IN CHAINS!
I'LL SEE HIM AND HIS SOUL-SUCKING BITCH PARTNER BOTH HUNG FOR MURDER, EVEN IF I HAVE TO DO IT MYSELF RIGHT BEFORE THE WHOLE TOWN TIPS INTO HELL!
RESPECTFULLY, MISTER MAYOR, IF YOU'RE BUYIN' WHAT THEM KIDS ARE SELLIN', YOU AIN'T GOT THE BRAINS TO POUR PISS FROM A BOOT IF THE INSTRUCTIONS WAS WRIT ON THE SOLE.
HEY, YOU! DON'T MOVE!
I CAN END BRAD FOR GOOD, RIGHT NOW. YOU THINK YOU SEEN MONSTERS? AIN'T NONE WORSE'N ME RIGHT NOW.

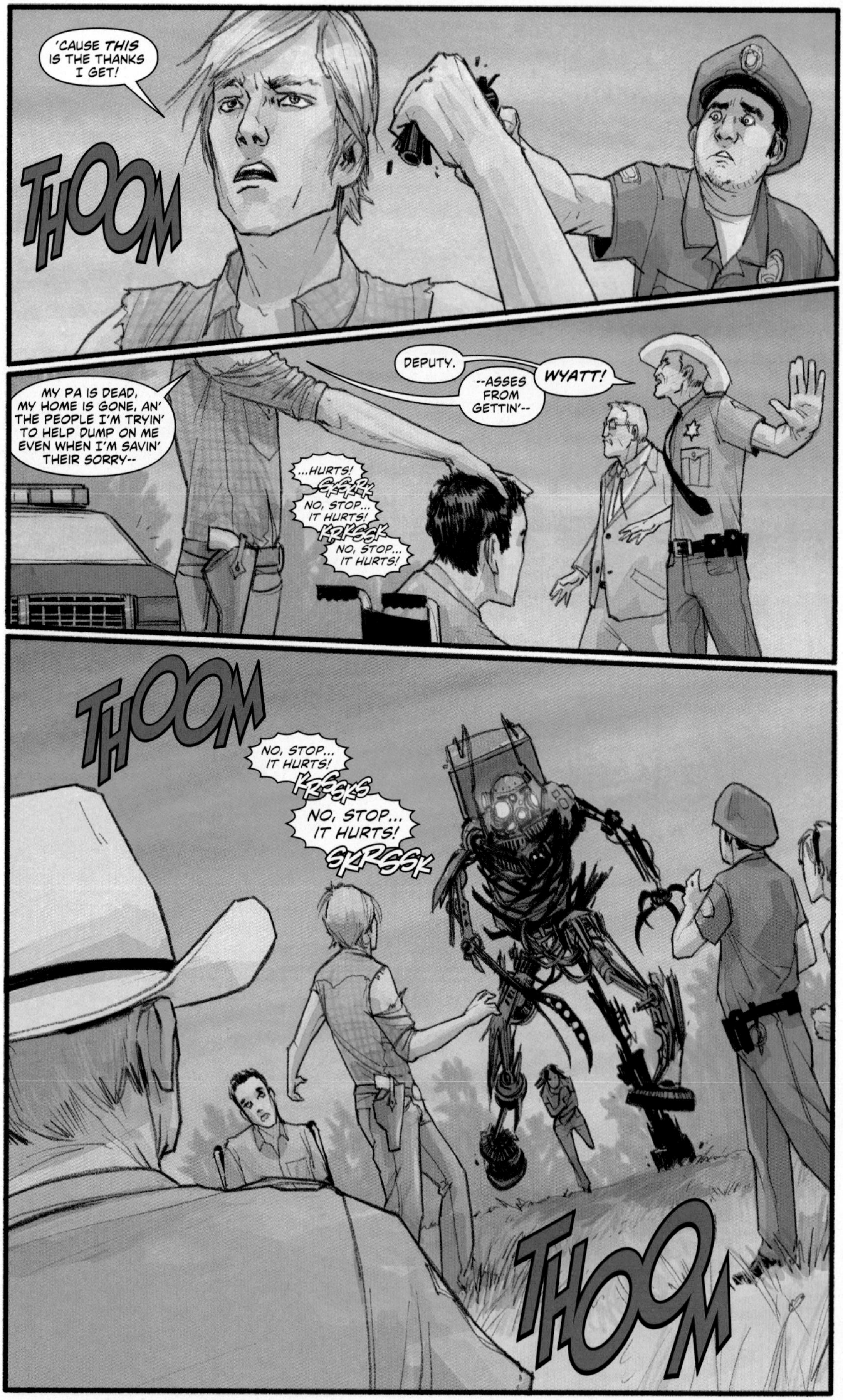
'CAUSE THIS IS THE THANKS I GET!
THOOM
MY PA IS DEAD, MY HOME IS GONE, AN' THE PEOPLE I'M TRYIN' TO HELP DUMP ON ME EVEN WHEN I'M SAVIN' THEIR SORRY--
--ASSES FROM GETTIN'--
DEPUTY.
WYATT!
...HURTS!
SKRRK
NO, STOP... IT HURTS!
KRKSSK
NO, STOP... IT HURTS!
THOOM
NO, STOP... IT HURTS!
KRSSKS
NO, STOP... IT HURTS!
SKRSSK
THOOM

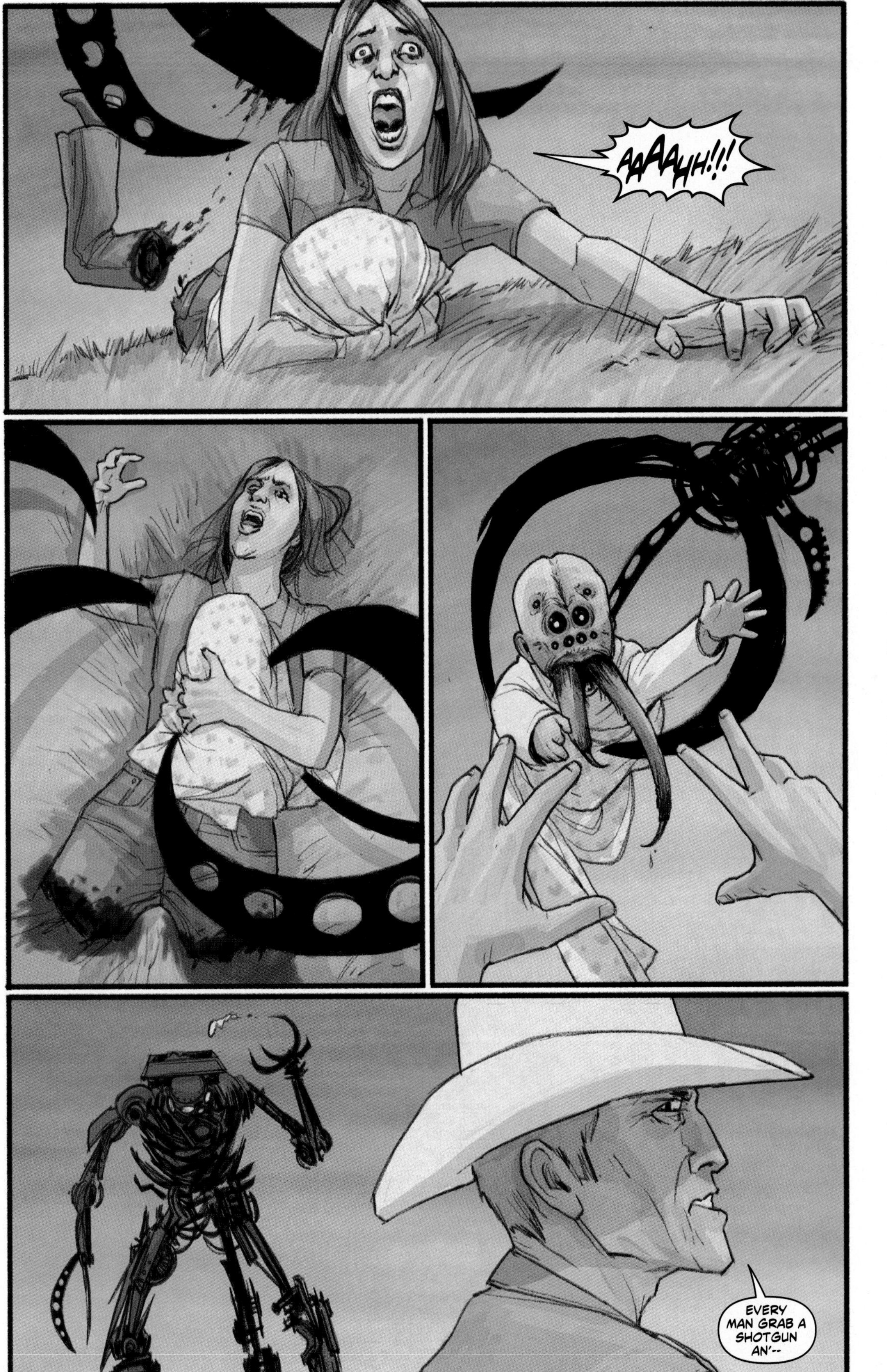
AAAAHH!!!
EVERY MAN GRAB A SHOTGUN AN'--

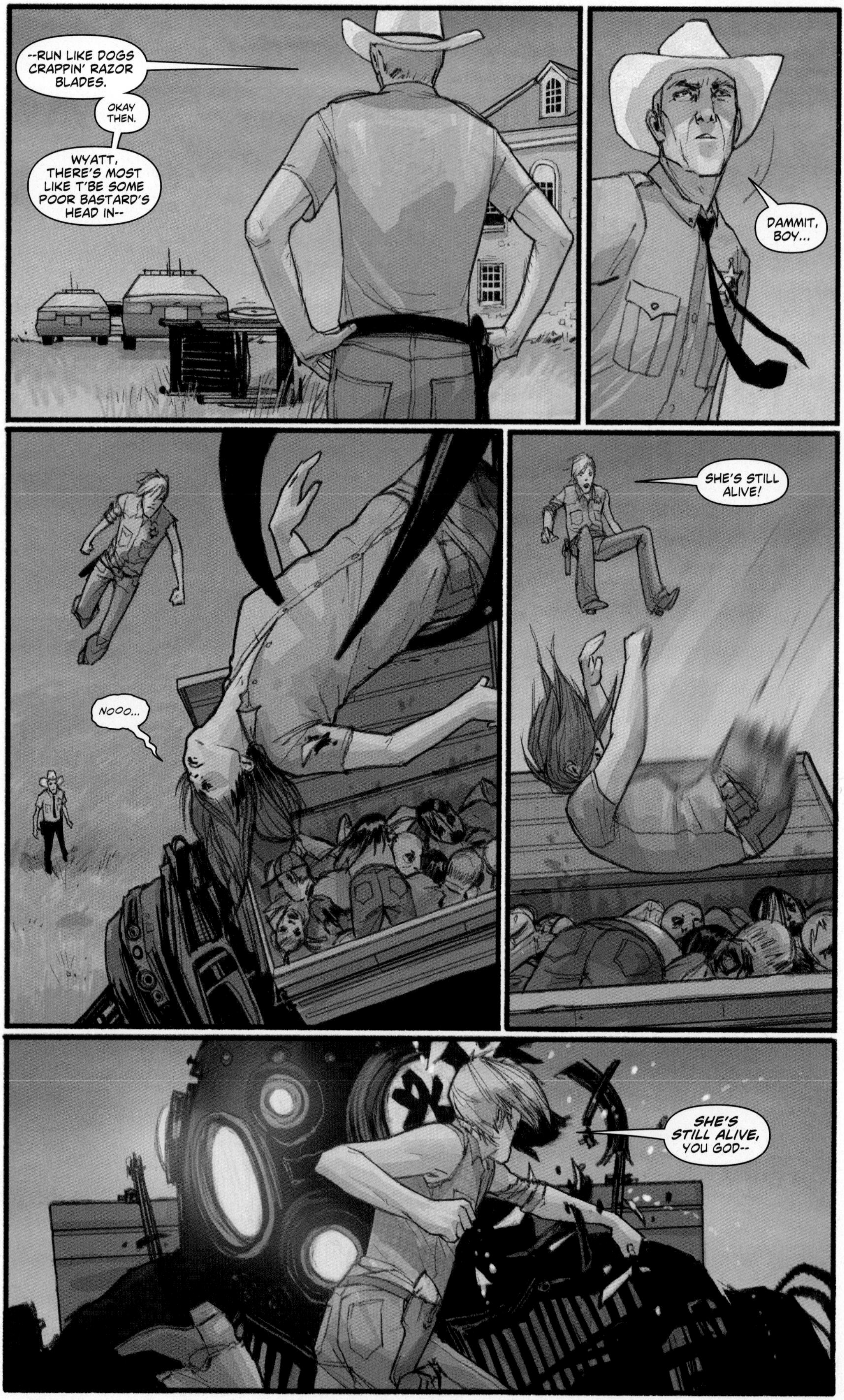
--RUN LIKE DOGS CRAPPIN' RAZOR BLADES.
OKAY THEN.
WYATT, THERE'S MOST LIKE T'BE SOME POOR BASTARD'S HEAD IN--
DAMMIT, BOY...
NOOO...
SHE'S STILL ALIVE!
SHE'S STILL ALIVE, YOU GOD--

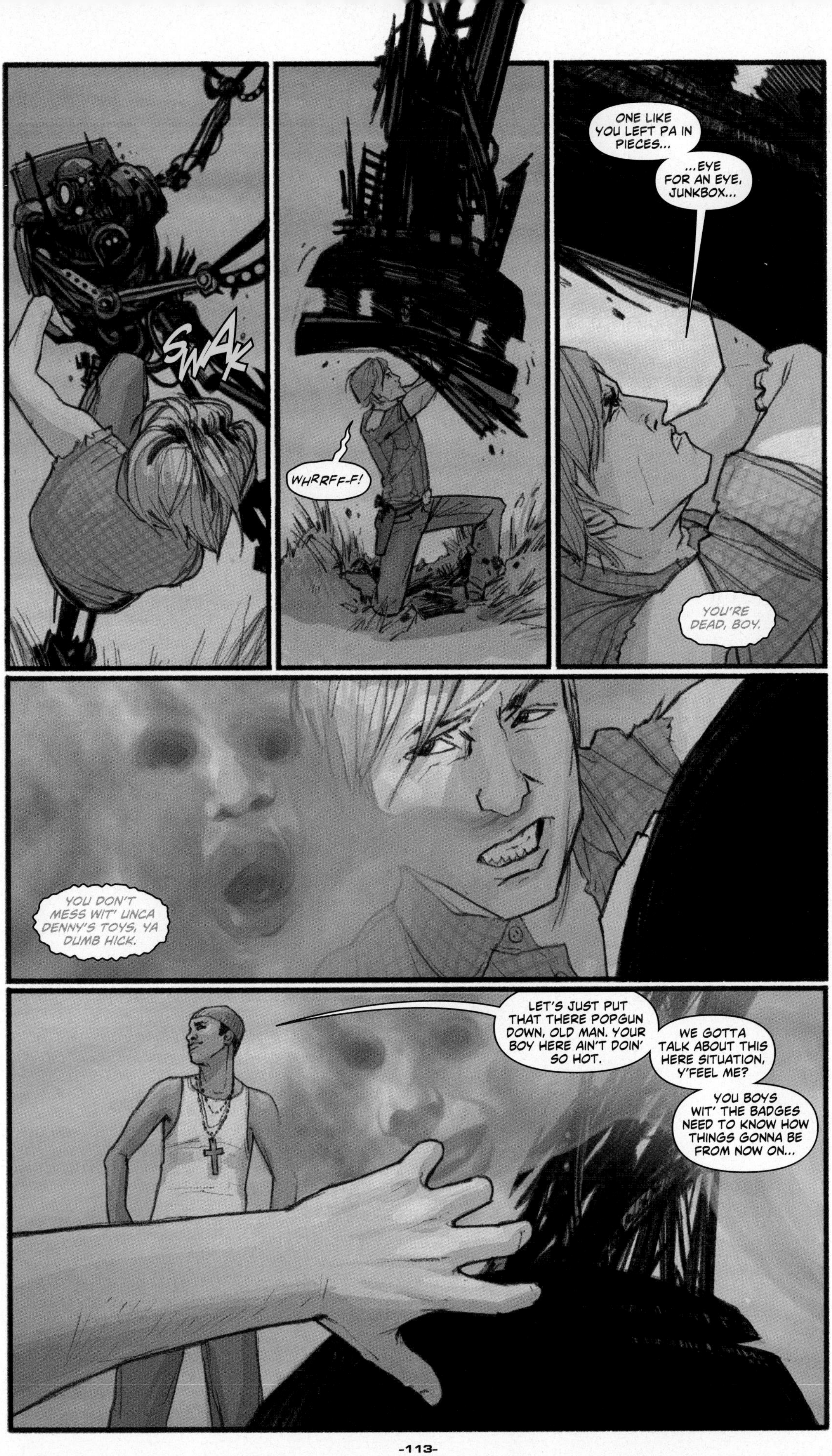
SWAK
WHRRFF-F!
ONE LIKE YOU LEFT PA IN PIECES...
...EYE FOR AN EYE, JUNKBOX...
YOU'RE DEAD, BOY.
YOU DON'T MESS WIT' UNCA DENNY'S TOYS, YA DUMB HICK.
LET'S JUST PUT THAT THERE POPGUN DOWN, OLD MAN. YOUR BOY HERE AIN'T DOIN' SO HOT.
WE GOTTA TALK ABOUT THIS HERE SITUATION, Y'FEEL ME?
YOU BOYS WIT' THE BADGES NEED TO KNOW HOW THINGS GONNA BE FROM NOW ON...

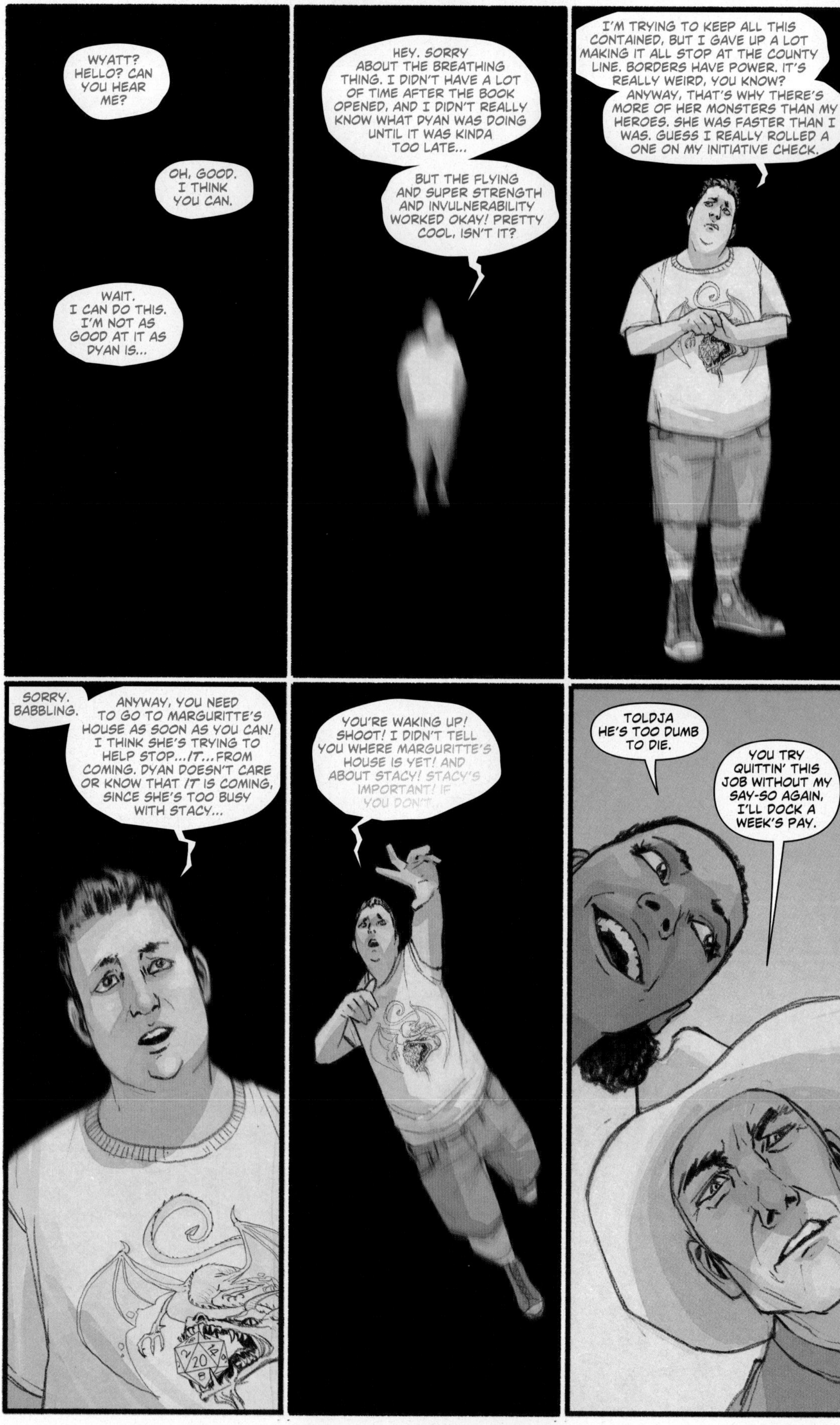
WYATT? HELLO? CAN YOU HEAR ME?
OH, GOOD. I THINK YOU CAN.
WAIT. I CAN DO THIS. I'M NOT AS GOOD AT IT AS DYAN IS...
HEY. SORRY ABOUT THE BREATHING THING. I DIDN'T HAVE A LOT OF TIME AFTER THE BOOK OPENED, AND I DIDN'T REALLY KNOW WHAT DYAN WAS DOING UNTIL IT WAS KINDA TOO LATE...
BUT THE FLYING AND SUPER STRENGTH AND INVULNERABILITY WORKED OKAY! PRETTY COOL, ISN'T IT?
I'M TRYING TO KEEP ALL THIS CONTAINED, BUT I GAVE UP A LOT MAKING IT ALL STOP AT THE COUNTY LINE. BORDERS HAVE POWER. IT'S REALLY WEIRD, YOU KNOW?
ANYWAY, THAT'S WHY THERE'S MORE OF HER MONSTERS THAN MY HEROES. SHE WAS FASTER THAN I WAS. GUESS I REALLY ROLLED A ONE ON MY INITIATIVE CHECK.
SORRY. BABBLING.
ANYWAY, YOU NEED TO GO TO MARGURITTE'S HOUSE AS SOON AS YOU CAN! I THINK SHE'S TRYING TO HELP STOP...*IT*...FROM COMING. DYAN DOESN'T CARE OR KNOW THAT *IT* IS COMING, SINCE SHE'S TOO BUSY WITH STACY...
YOU'RE WAKING UP! SHOOT! I DIDN'T TELL YOU WHERE MARGURITTE'S HOUSE IS YET! AND ABOUT STACY! STACY'S IMPORTANT! IF YOU DON'T...
TOLDJA HE'S TOO DUMB TO DIE.
YOU TRY QUITTIN' THIS JOB WITHOUT MY SAY-SO AGAIN, I'LL DOCK A WEEK'S PAY.

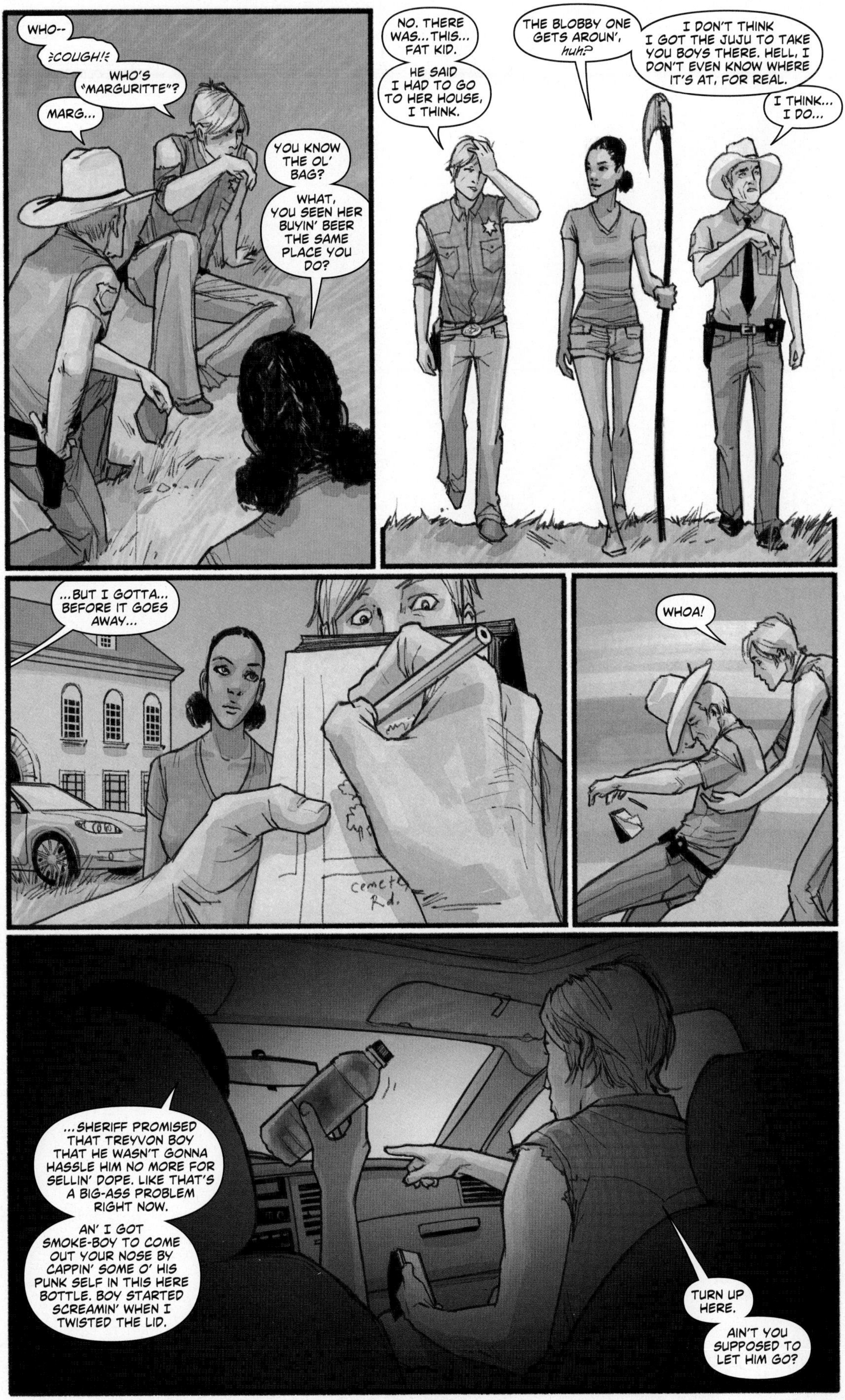
WHO--
COUGH!
WHO'S "MARGURITTE"?
MARG...
YOU KNOW THE OL' BAG?
WHAT, YOU SEEN HER BUYIN' BEER THE SAME PLACE YOU DO?
NO. THERE WAS... THIS... FAT KID.
HE SAID I HAD TO GO TO HER HOUSE, I THINK.
THE BLOBBY ONE GETS AROUN', huh?
I DON'T THINK I GOT THE JUJU TO TAKE YOU BOYS THERE. HELL, I DON'T EVEN KNOW WHERE IT'S AT, FOR REAL.
I THINK... I DO...
...BUT I GOTTA... BEFORE IT GOES AWAY...
Cemet Rd.
WHOA!
...SHERIFF PROMISED THAT TREYVON BOY THAT HE WASN'T GONNA HASSLE HIM NO MORE FOR SELLIN' DOPE. LIKE THAT'S A BIG-ASS PROBLEM RIGHT NOW.
AN' I GOT SMOKE-BOY TO COME OUT YOUR NOSE BY CAPPIN' SOME O' HIS PUNK SELF IN THIS HERE BOTTLE. BOY STARTED SCREAMIN' WHEN I TWISTED THE LID.
TURN UP HERE.
AIN'T YOU SUPPOSED TO LET HIM GO?

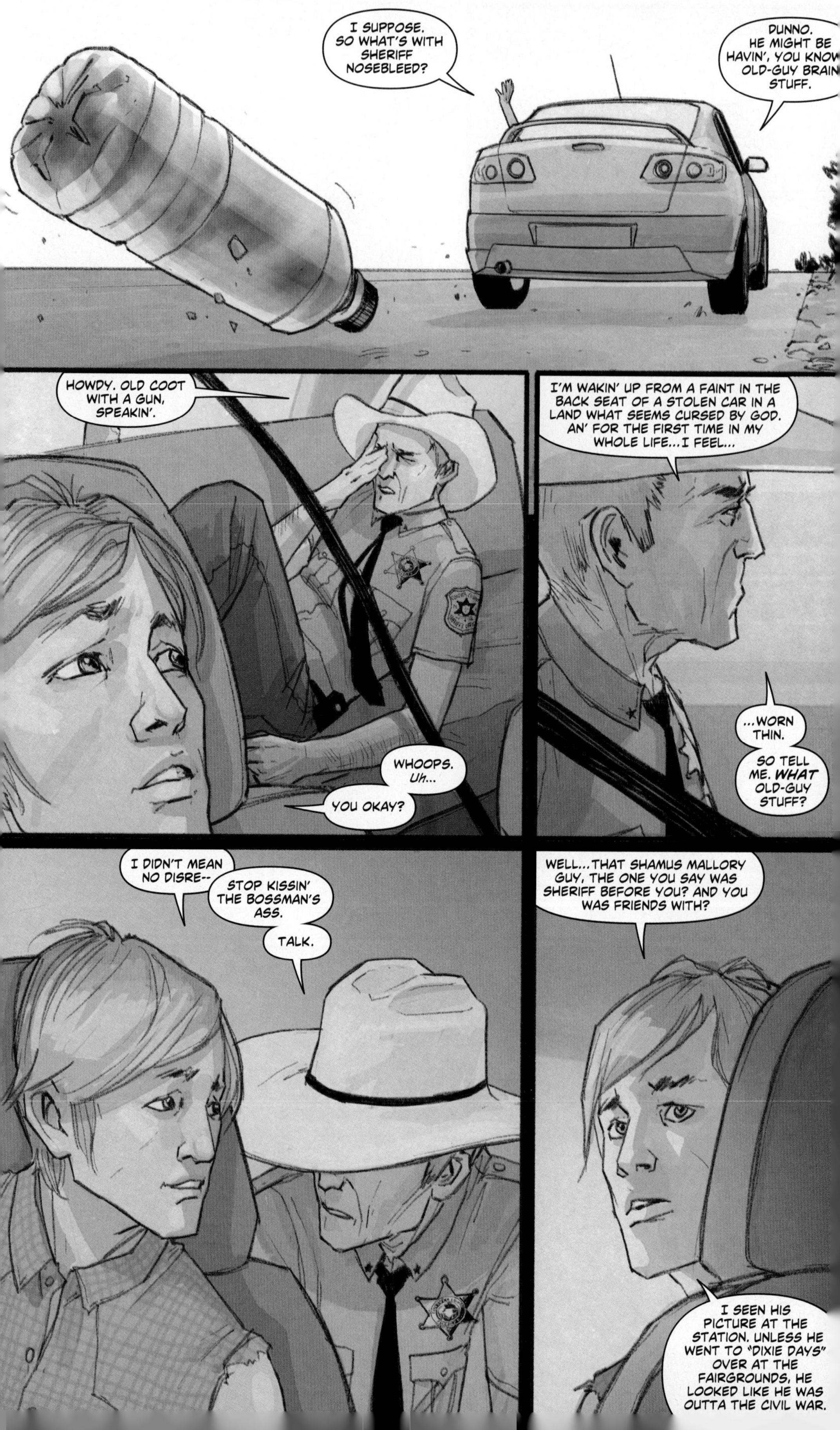
I SUPPOSE. SO WHAT'S WITH SHERIFF NOSEBLEED?
DUNNO. HE MIGHT BE HAVIN', YOU KNOW OLD-GUY BRAIN STUFF.
HOWDY. OLD COOT WITH A GUN, SPEAKIN'.
WHOOPS. Uh...
YOU OKAY?
I'M WAKIN' UP FROM A FAINT IN THE BACK SEAT OF A STOLEN CAR IN A LAND WHAT SEEMS CURSED BY GOD. AN' FOR THE FIRST TIME IN MY WHOLE LIFE... I FEEL...
...WORN THIN.
SO TELL ME. WHAT OLD-GUY STUFF?
I DIDN'T MEAN NO DISRE--
STOP KISSIN' THE BOSSMAN'S ASS.
TALK.
WELL... THAT SHAMUS MALLORY GUY, THE ONE YOU SAY WAS SHERIFF BEFORE YOU? AND YOU WAS FRIENDS WITH?
I SEEN HIS PICTURE AT THE STATION. UNLESS HE WENT TO "DIXIE DAYS" OVER AT THE FAIRGROUNDS, HE LOOKED LIKE HE WAS OUTTA THE CIVIL WAR.

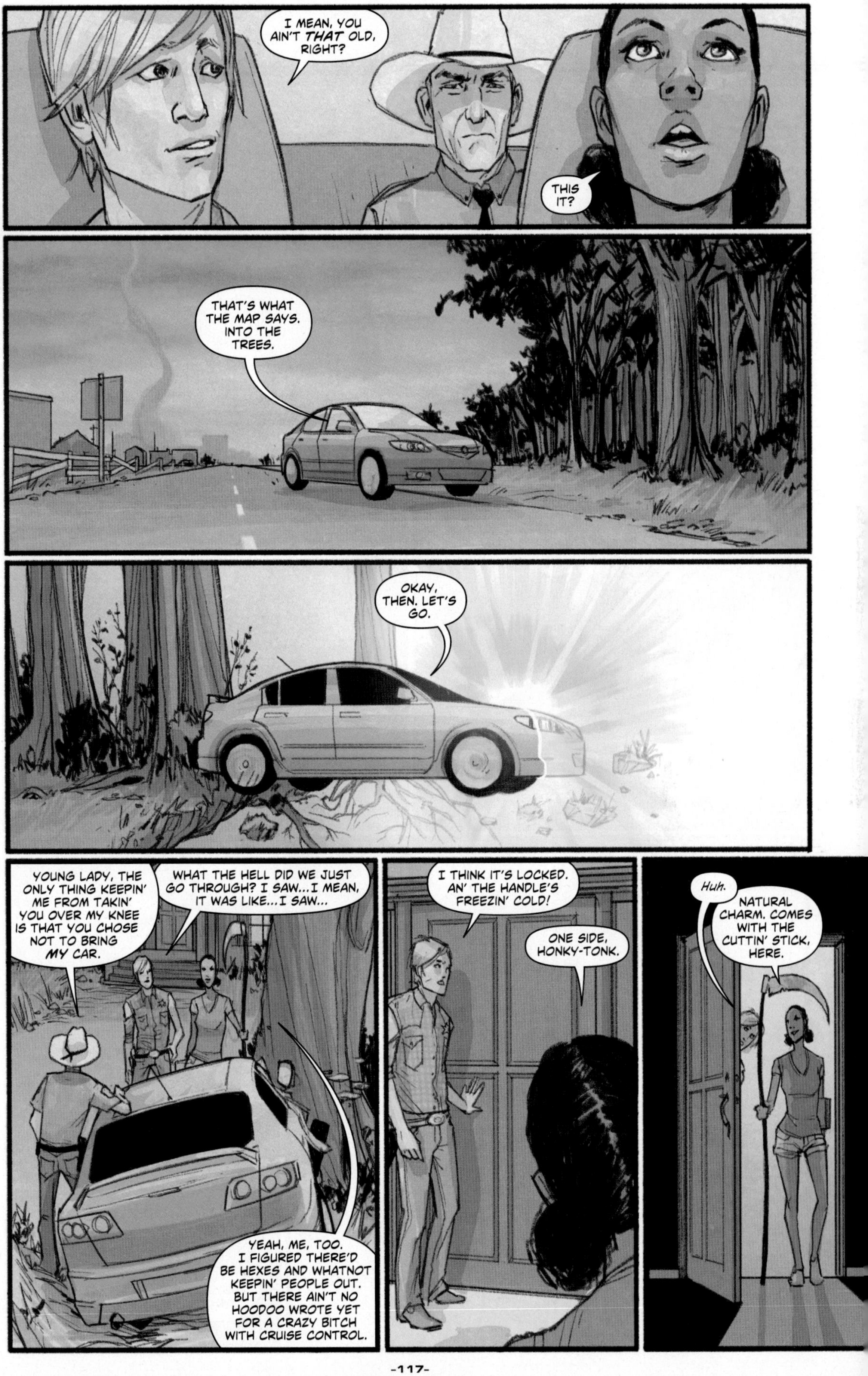
I MEAN, YOU AIN'T THAT OLD, RIGHT?
THIS IT?
THAT'S WHAT THE MAP SAYS. INTO THE TREES.
OKAY, THEN. LET'S GO.
YOUNG LADY, THE ONLY THING KEEPIN' ME FROM TAKIN' YOU OVER MY KNEE IS THAT YOU CHOSE NOT TO BRING MY CAR.
WHAT THE HELL DID WE JUST GO THROUGH? I SAW... I MEAN, IT WAS LIKE... I SAW...
YEAH, ME, TOO. I FIGURED THERE'D BE HEXES AND WHATNOT KEEPIN' PEOPLE OUT. BUT THERE AIN'T NO HOODOO WROTE YET FOR A CRAZY BITCH WITH CRUISE CONTROL.
I THINK IT'S LOCKED. AN' THE HANDLE'S FREEZIN' COLD!
ONE SIDE, HONKY-TONK.
Huh.
NATURAL CHARM. COMES WITH THE CUTTIN' STICK, HERE.

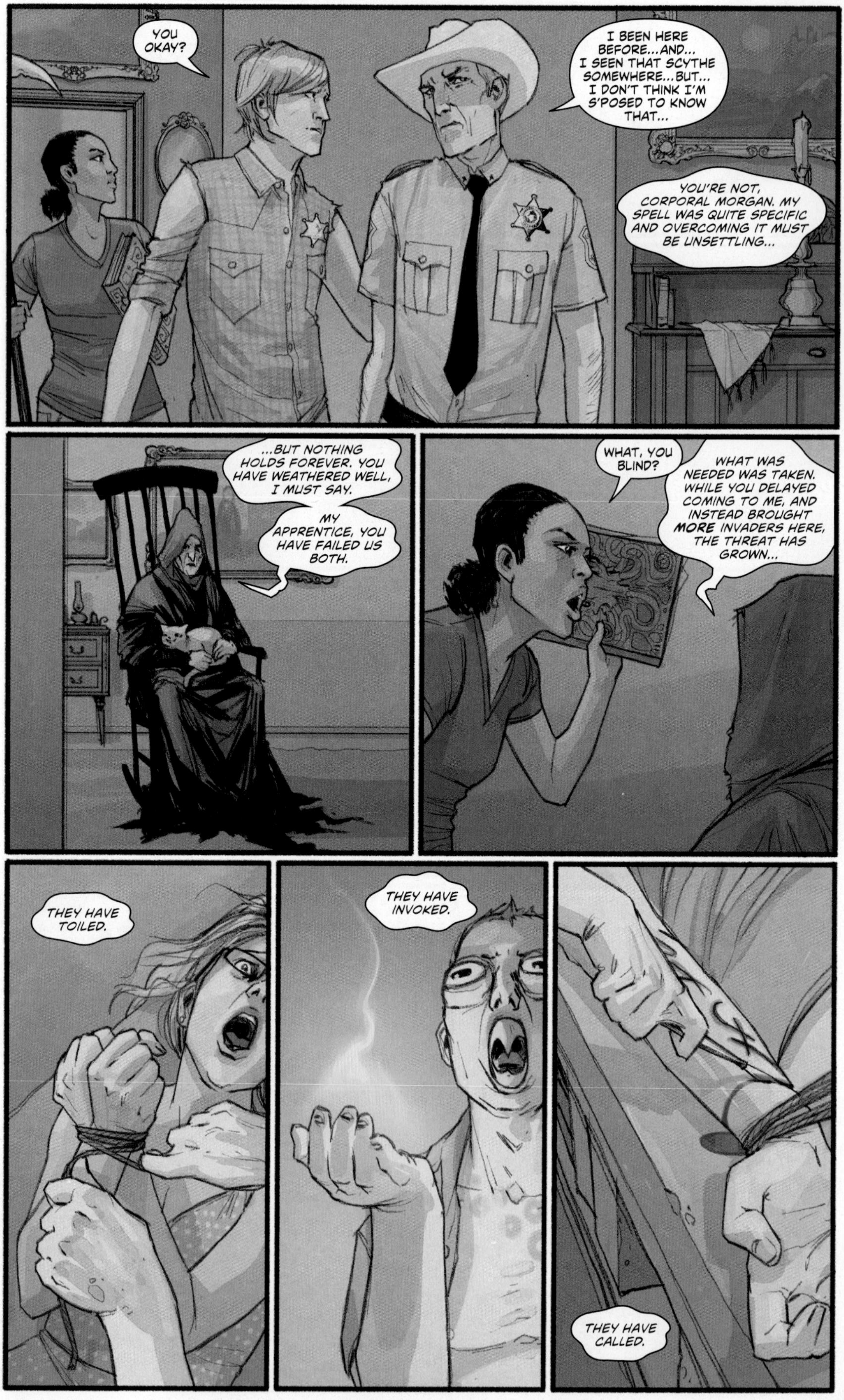
YOU OKAY?
I BEEN HERE BEFORE...AND... I SEEN THAT SCYTHE SOMEWHERE...BUT... I DON'T THINK I'M S'POSED TO KNOW THAT...
YOU'RE NOT, CORPORAL MORGAN. MY SPELL WAS QUITE SPECIFIC AND OVERCOMING IT MUST BE UNSETTLING...
...BUT NOTHING HOLDS FOREVER. YOU HAVE WEATHERED WELL, I MUST SAY.
MY APPRENTICE, YOU HAVE FAILED US BOTH.
WHAT, YOU BLIND?
WHAT WAS NEEDED WAS TAKEN. WHILE YOU DELAYED COMING TO ME, AND INSTEAD BROUGHT MORE INVADERS HERE, THE THREAT HAS GROWN...
THEY HAVE TOILED.
THEY HAVE INVOKED.
THEY HAVE CALLED.

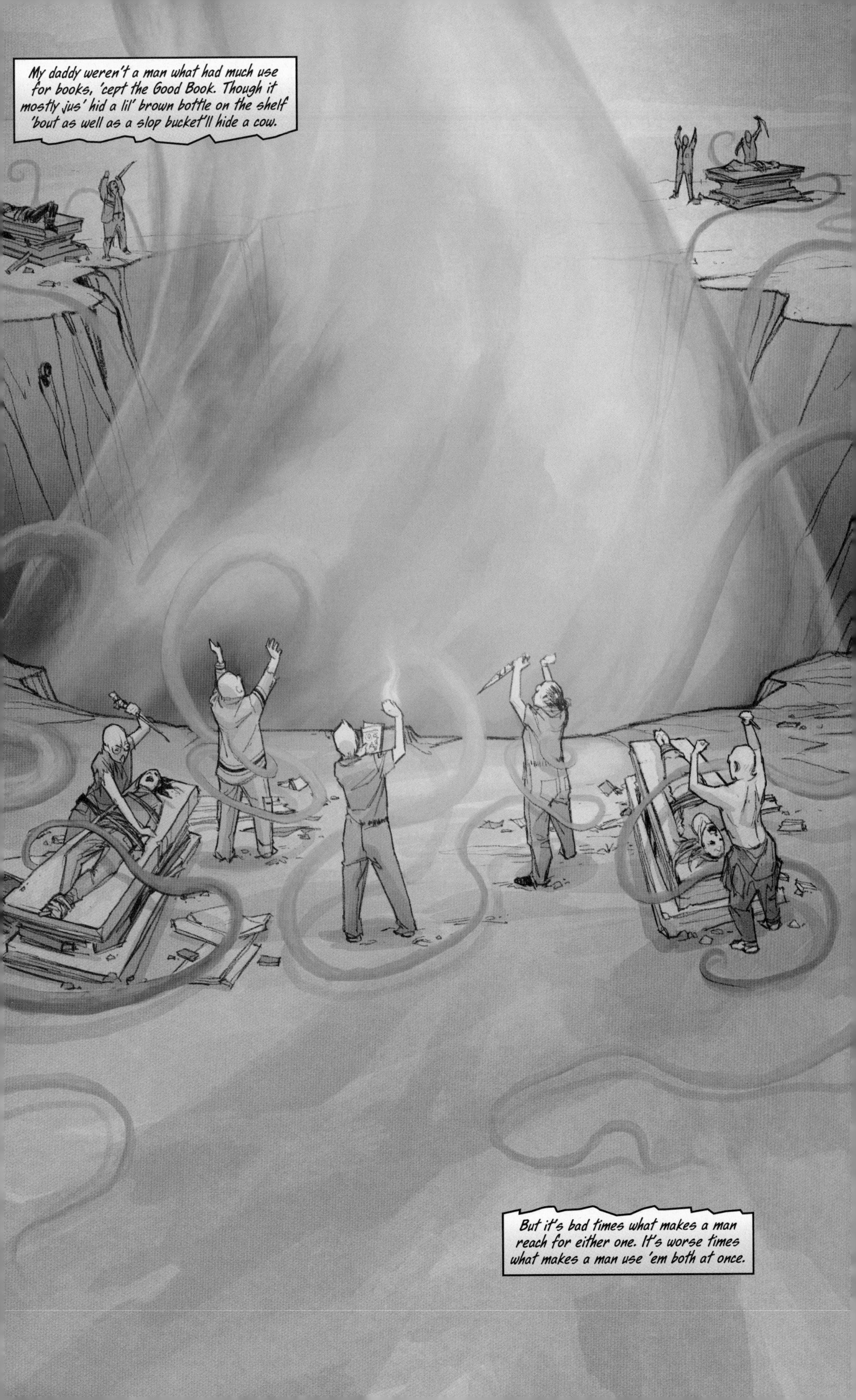
My daddy weren't a man what had much use for books, 'cept the Good Book. Though it mostly jus' hid a lil' brown bottle on the shelf 'bout as well as a slop bucket'll hide a cow.
But it's bad times what makes a man reach for either one. It's worse times what makes a man use 'em both at once.

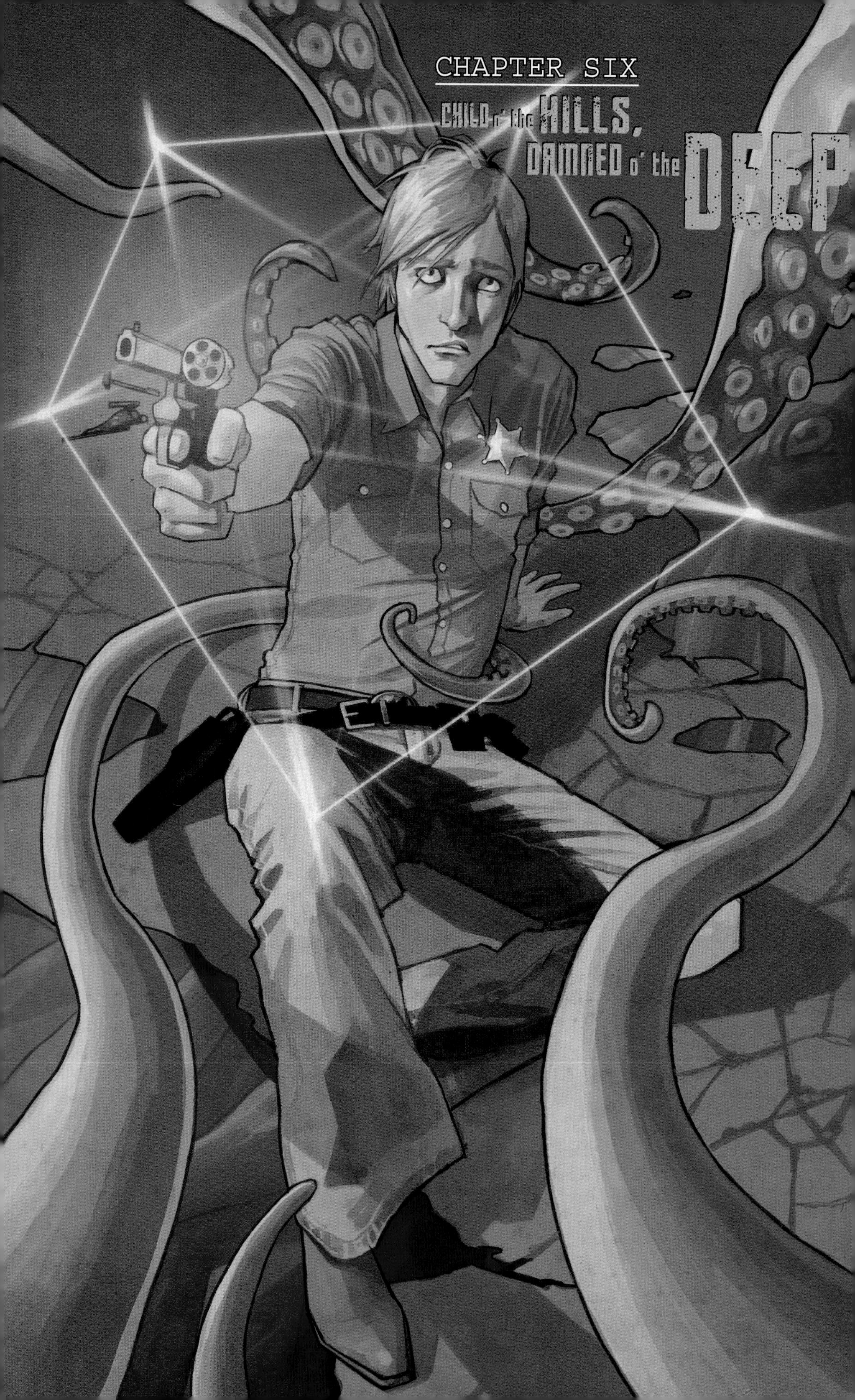
CHAPTER SIX
CHILD o' the HILLS,
DAMNED o' the DEEP

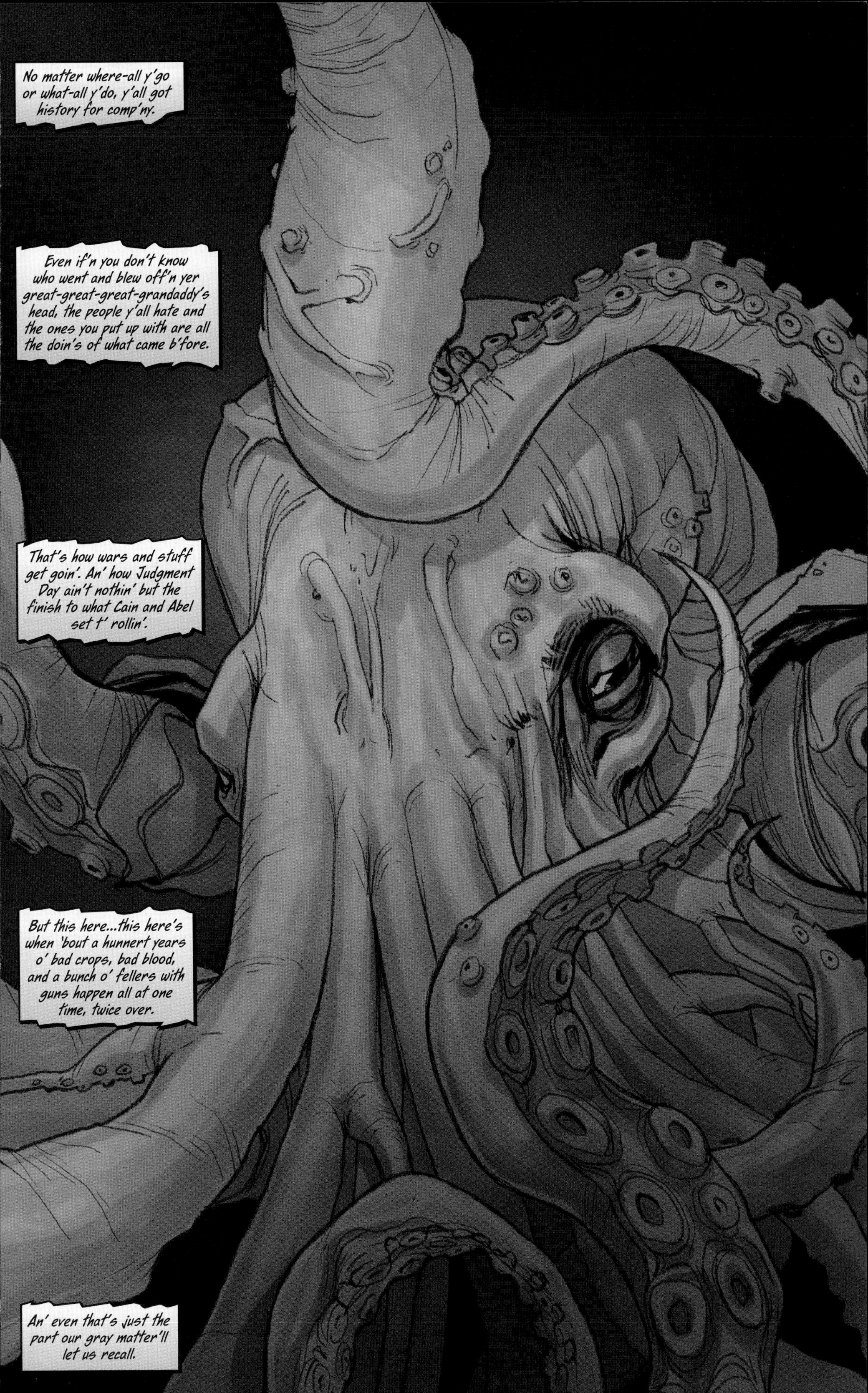
No matter where-all y'go or what-all y'do, y'all got history for comp'ny.
Even if'n you don't know who went and blew off'n yer great-great-great-grandaddy's head, the people y'all hate and the ones you put up with are all the doin's of what came b'fore.
That's how wars and stuff get goin'. An' how Judgment Day ain't nothin' but the finish to what Cain and Abel set t' rollin'.
But this here...this here's when 'bout a hunnert years o' bad crops, bad blood, and a bunch o' fellers with guns happen all at one time, twice over.
An' even that's just the part our gray matter'll let us recall.

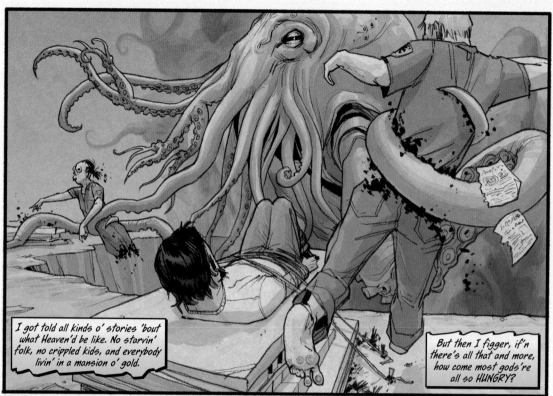

I got told all kinds o' stories 'bout what Heaven'd be like. No starvin' folk, no crippled kids, and everybody livin' in a mansion o' gold.

But then I figger, if'n there's all that and more, how come most gods're all so HUNGRY?

HE STIRS. WE MUST BE READY...

SHAMUS IS DEAD, MA'AM. THEY STRUNG 'IM UP FOR "CONSORTIN' WITH DARK FORCES."

AND WHAT OF OUR BARGAIN, CORPORAL? DO YOU WISH TO BREAK OUR COVENANT?

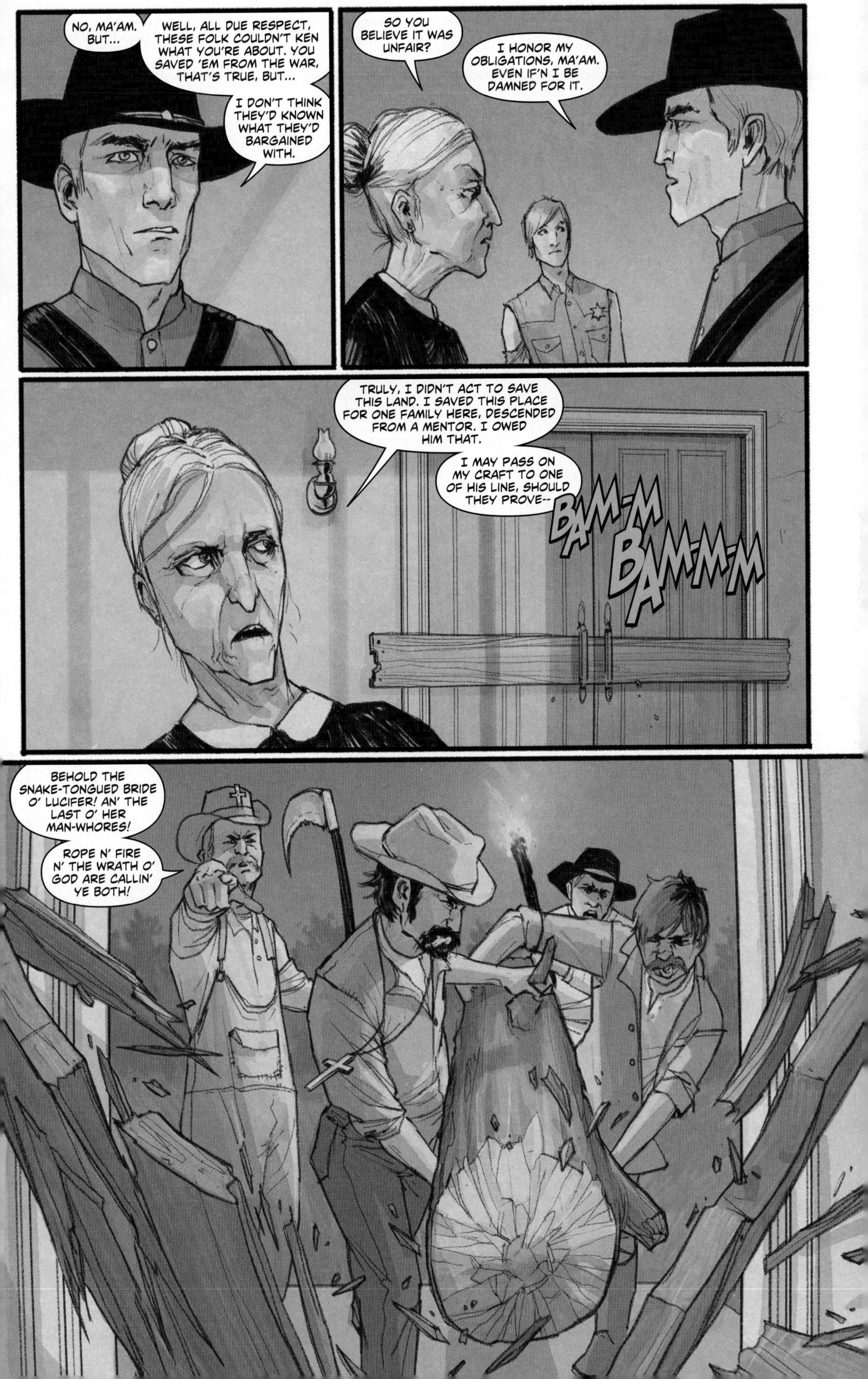
NO, MA'AM. BUT...
WELL, ALL DUE RESPECT, THESE FOLK COULDN'T KEN WHAT YOU'RE ABOUT. YOU SAVED 'EM FROM THE WAR, THAT'S TRUE, BUT...
I DON'T THINK THEY'D KNOWN WHAT THEY'D BARGAINED WITH.
SO YOU BELIEVE IT WAS UNFAIR?
I HONOR MY OBLIGATIONS, MA'AM. EVEN IF'N I BE DAMNED FOR IT.
TRULY, I DIDN'T ACT TO SAVE THIS LAND. I SAVED THIS PLACE FOR ONE FAMILY HERE, DESCENDED FROM A MENTOR. I OWED HIM THAT.
I MAY PASS ON MY CRAFT TO ONE OF HIS LINE, SHOULD THEY PROVE--
BAM-M
BAMM-M-M
BEHOLD THE SNAKE-TONGUED BRIDE O' LUCIFER! AN' THE LAST O' HER MAN-WHORES!
ROPE N' FIRE N' THE WRATH O' GOD ARE CALLIN' YE BOTH!

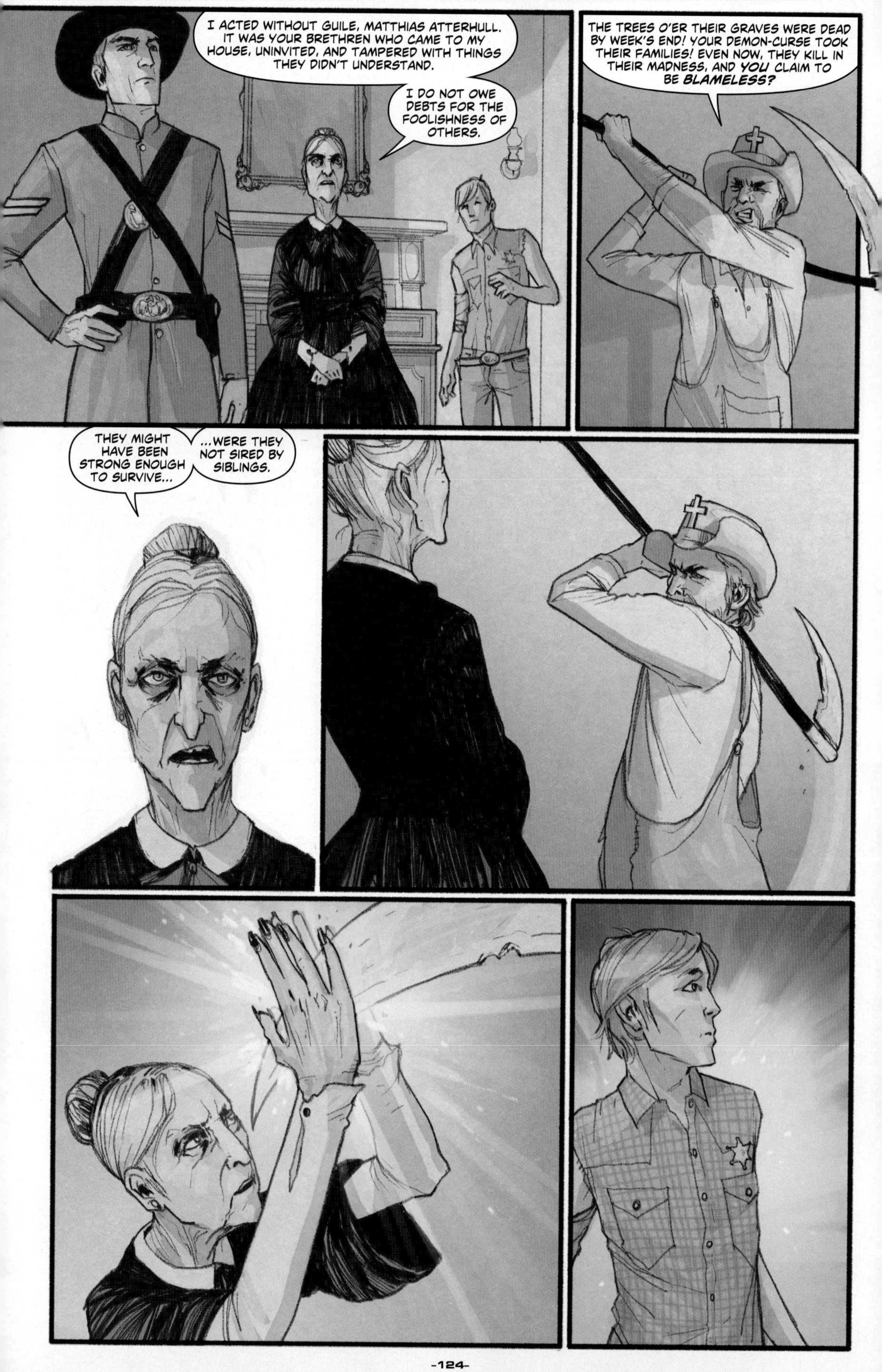

I ACTED WITHOUT GUILE, MATTHIAS ATTERHULL. IT WAS YOUR BRETHREN WHO CAME TO MY HOUSE, UNINVITED, AND TAMPERED WITH THINGS THEY DIDN'T UNDERSTAND.
I DO NOT OWE DEBTS FOR THE FOOLISHNESS OF OTHERS.
THE TREES O'ER THEIR GRAVES WERE DEAD BY WEEK'S END! YOUR DEMON-CURSE TOOK THEIR FAMILIES! EVEN NOW, THEY KILL IN THEIR MADNESS, AND *YOU* CLAIM TO BE ***BLAMELESS?***
THEY MIGHT HAVE BEEN STRONG ENOUGH TO SURVIVE...
...WERE THEY NOT SIRED BY SIBLINGS.

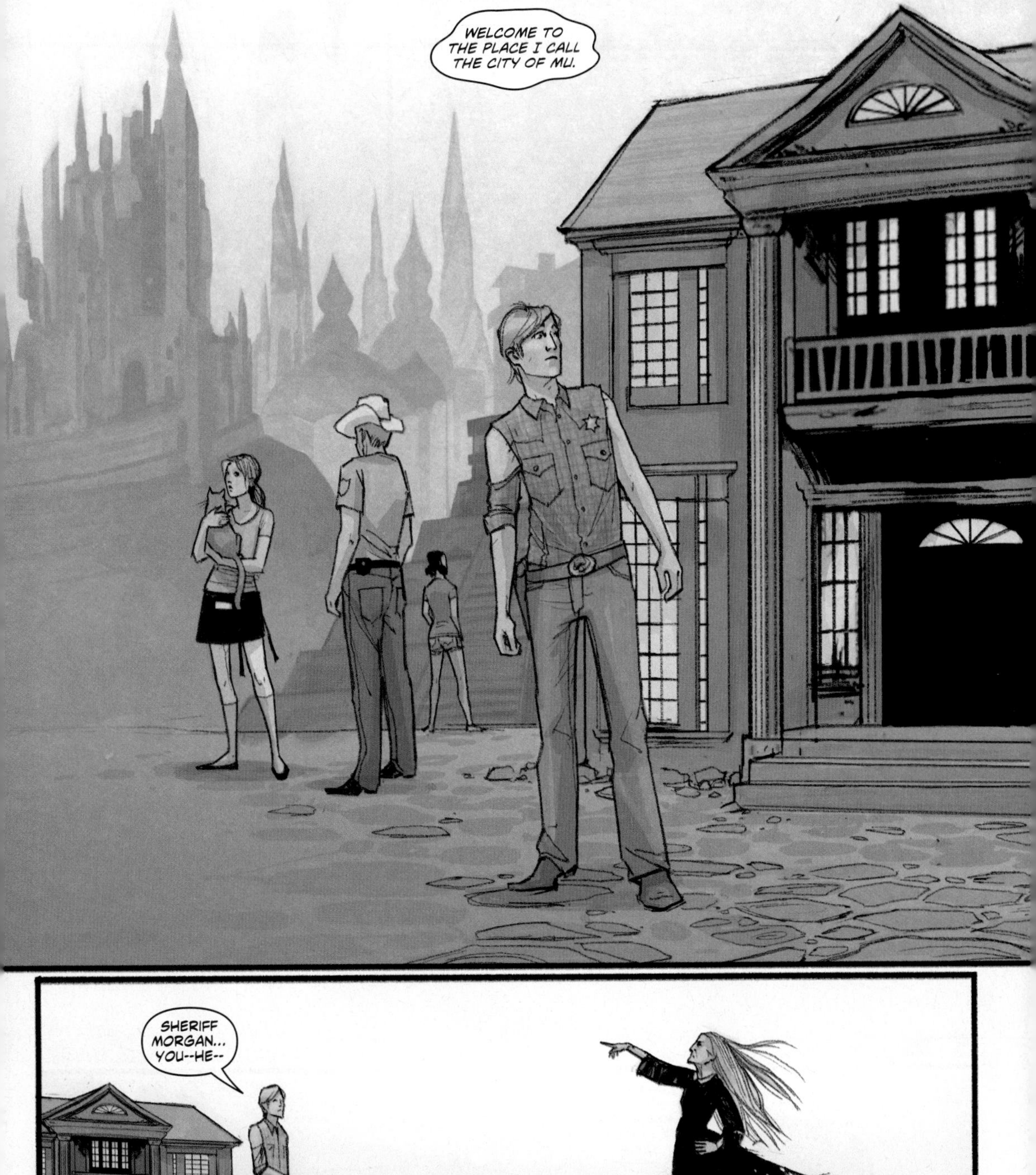
WELCOME TO THE PLACE I CALL THE CITY OF MU.

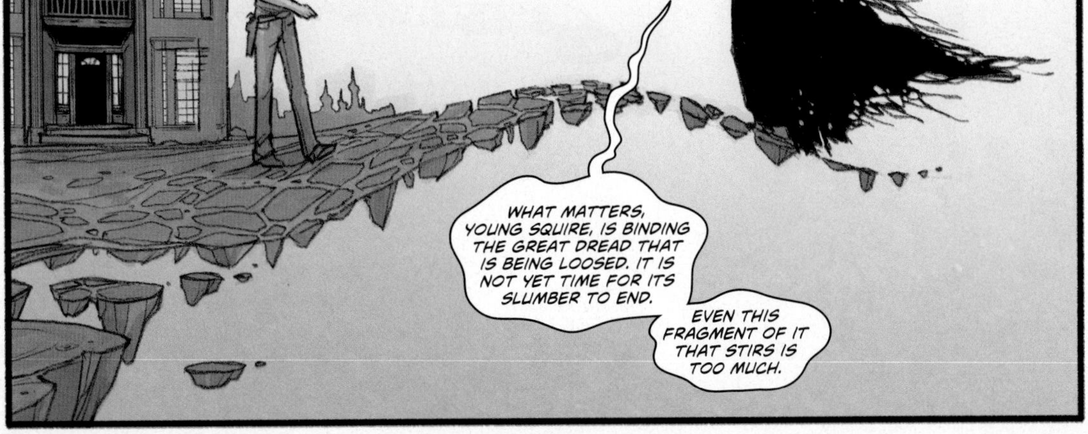
SHERIFF MORGAN... YOU--HE--
WHAT MATTERS, YOUNG SQUIRE, IS BINDING THE GREAT DREAD THAT IS BEING LOOSED. IT IS NOT YET TIME FOR ITS SLUMBER TO END.
EVEN THIS FRAGMENT OF IT THAT STIRS IS TOO MUCH.

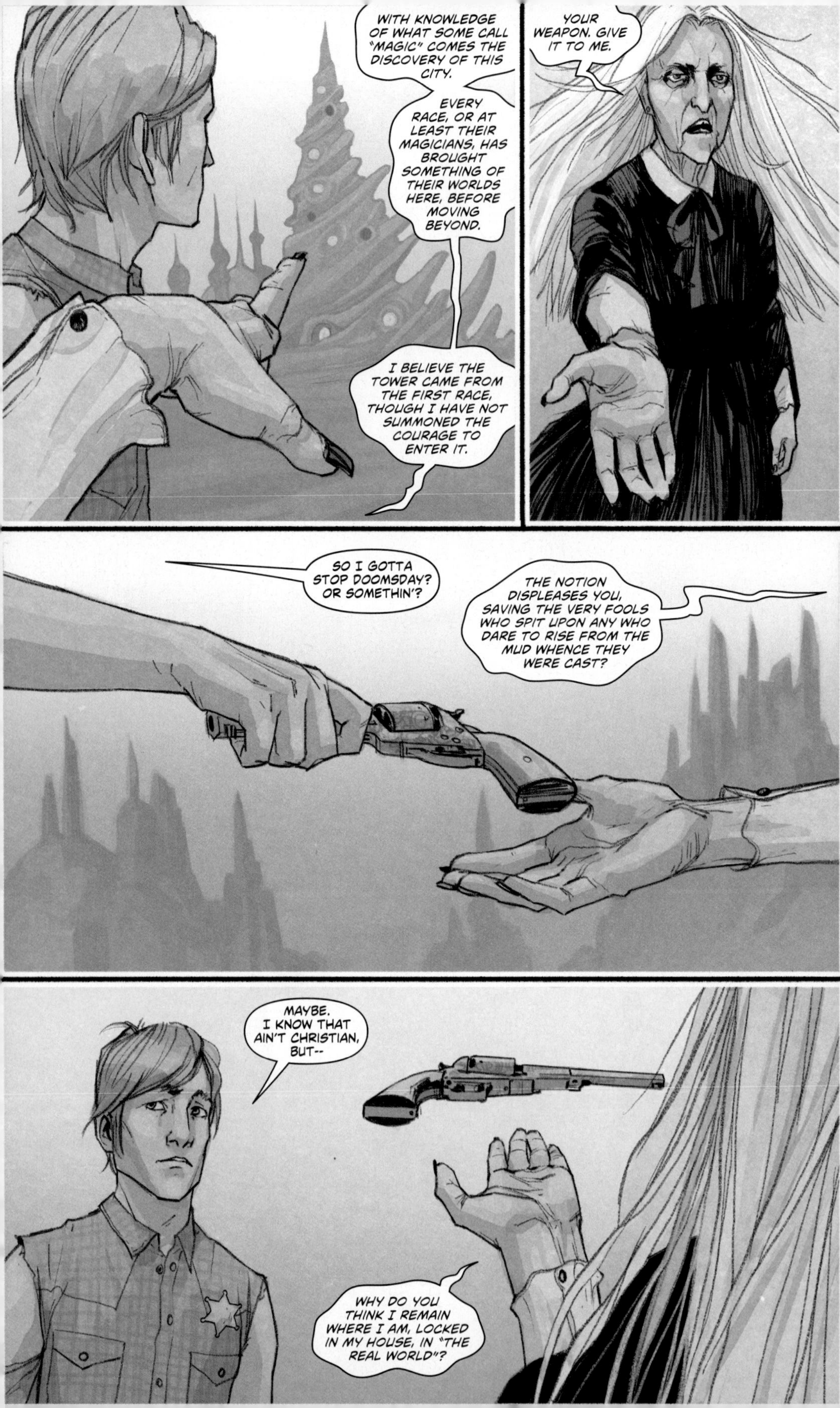
WITH KNOWLEDGE OF WHAT SOME CALL "MAGIC" COMES THE DISCOVERY OF THIS CITY.
EVERY RACE, OR AT LEAST THEIR MAGICIANS, HAS BROUGHT SOMETHING OF THEIR WORLDS HERE, BEFORE MOVING BEYOND.
I BELIEVE THE TOWER CAME FROM THE FIRST RACE, THOUGH I HAVE NOT SUMMONED THE COURAGE TO ENTER IT.
YOUR WEAPON. GIVE IT TO ME.
SO I GOTTA STOP DOOMSDAY? OR SOMETHIN'?
THE NOTION DISPLEASES YOU, SAVING THE VERY FOOLS WHO SPIT UPON ANY WHO DARE TO RISE FROM THE MUD WHENCE THEY WERE CAST?
MAYBE. I KNOW THAT AIN'T CHRISTIAN, BUT--
WHY DO YOU THINK I REMAIN WHERE I AM, LOCKED IN MY HOUSE, IN "THE REAL WORLD"?

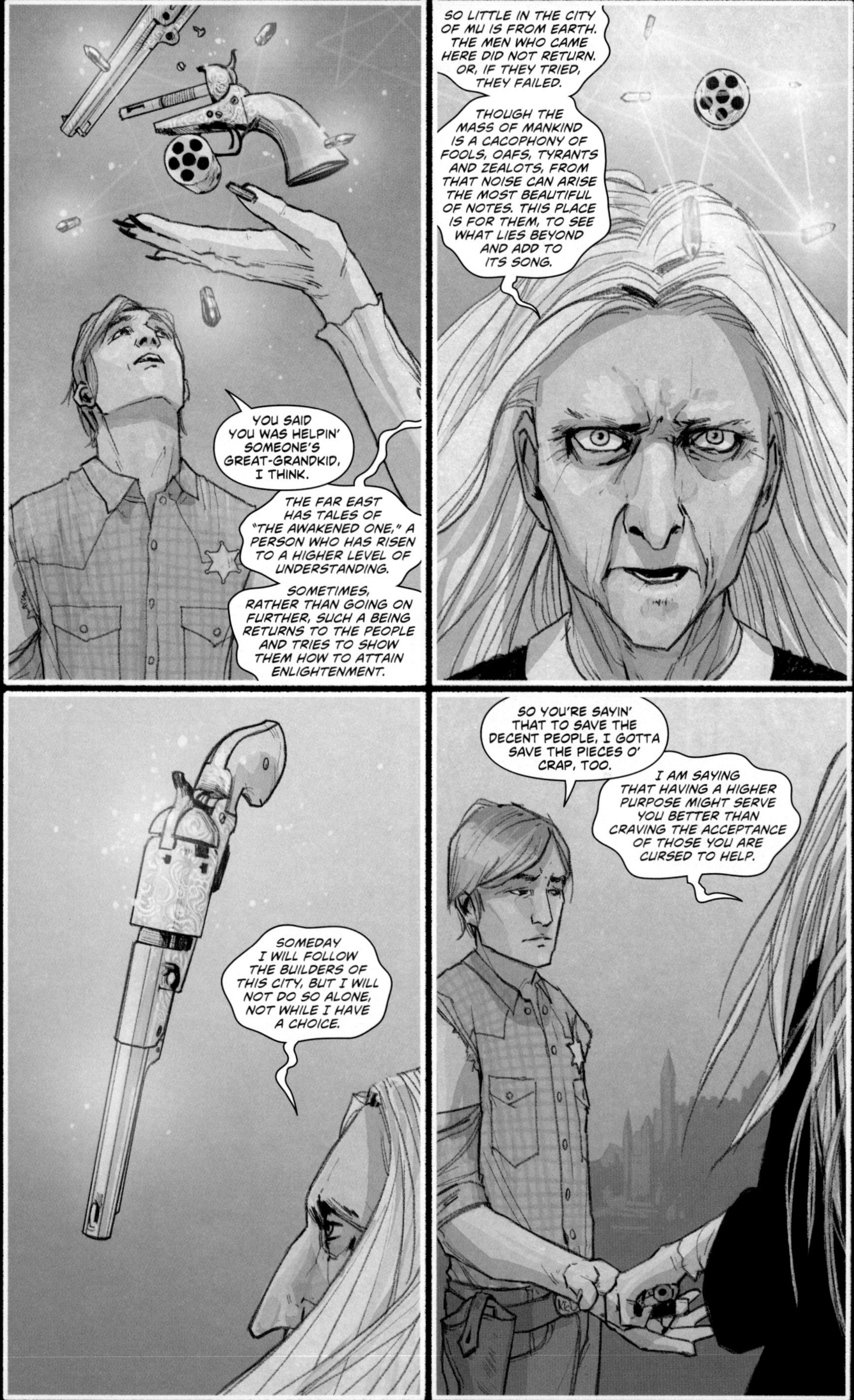
YOU SAID YOU WAS HELPIN' SOMEONE'S GREAT-GRANDKID, I THINK.
THE FAR EAST HAS TALES OF "THE AWAKENED ONE," A PERSON WHO HAS RISEN TO A HIGHER LEVEL OF UNDERSTANDING.
SOMETIMES, RATHER THAN GOING ON FURTHER, SUCH A BEING RETURNS TO THE PEOPLE AND TRIES TO SHOW THEM HOW TO ATTAIN ENLIGHTENMENT.
SO LITTLE IN THE CITY OF MU IS FROM EARTH. THE MEN WHO CAME HERE DID NOT RETURN. OR, IF THEY TRIED, THEY FAILED.
THOUGH THE MASS OF MANKIND IS A CACOPHONY OF FOOLS, OAFS, TYRANTS AND ZEALOTS, FROM THAT NOISE CAN ARISE THE MOST BEAUTIFUL OF NOTES. THIS PLACE IS FOR THEM, TO SEE WHAT LIES BEYOND AND ADD TO ITS SONG.
SOMEDAY I WILL FOLLOW THE BUILDERS OF THIS CITY, BUT I WILL NOT DO SO ALONE, NOT WHILE I HAVE A CHOICE.
SO YOU'RE SAYIN' THAT TO SAVE THE DECENT PEOPLE, I GOTTA SAVE THE PIECES O' CRAP, TOO.
I AM SAYING THAT HAVING A HIGHER PURPOSE MIGHT SERVE YOU BETTER THAN CRAVING THE ACCEPTANCE OF THOSE YOU ARE CURSED TO HELP.

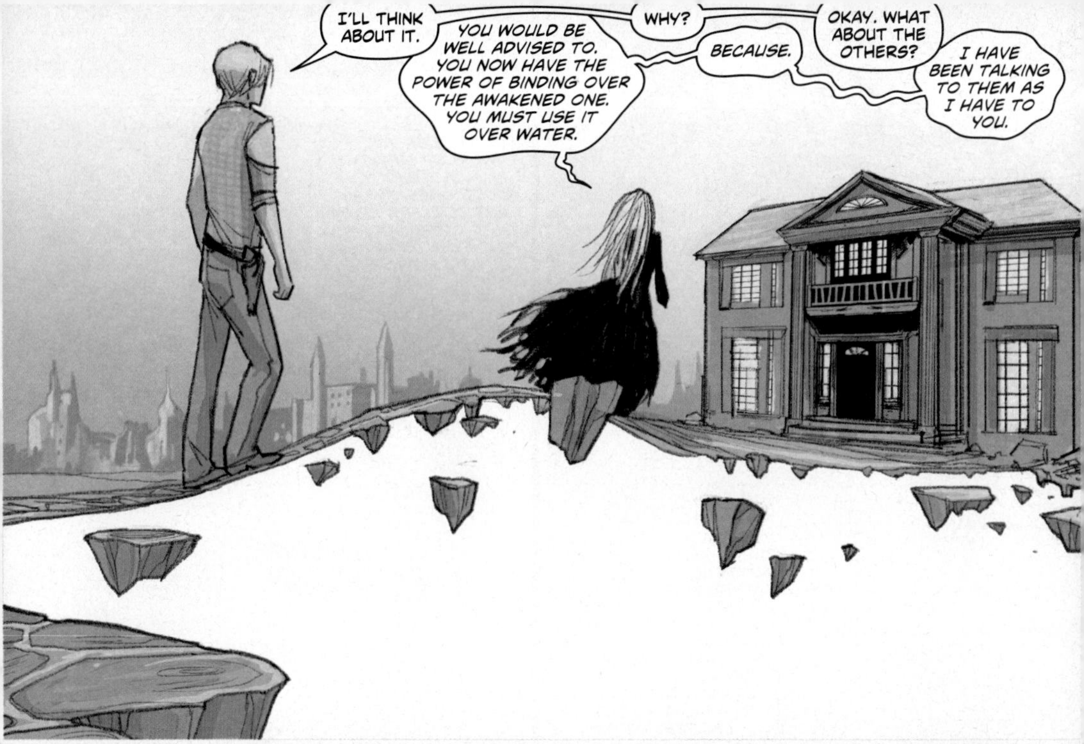
I'LL THINK ABOUT IT.
YOU WOULD BE WELL ADVISED TO. YOU NOW HAVE THE POWER OF BINDING OVER THE AWAKENED ONE. YOU MUST USE IT OVER WATER.
WHY?
BECAUSE.
OKAY. WHAT ABOUT THE OTHERS?
I HAVE BEEN TALKING TO THEM AS I HAVE TO YOU.

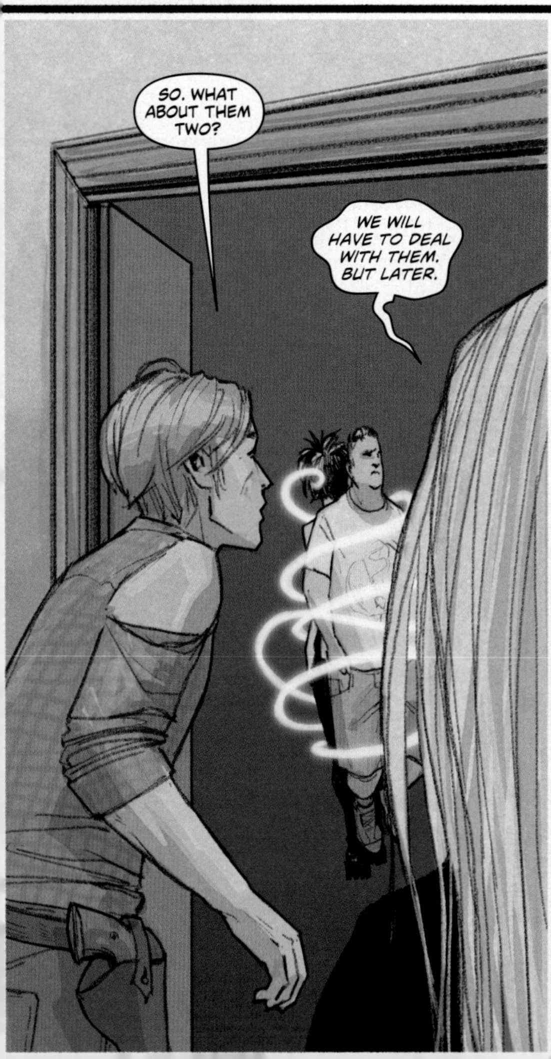
SO. WHAT ABOUT THEM TWO?
WE WILL HAVE TO DEAL WITH THEM. BUT LATER.

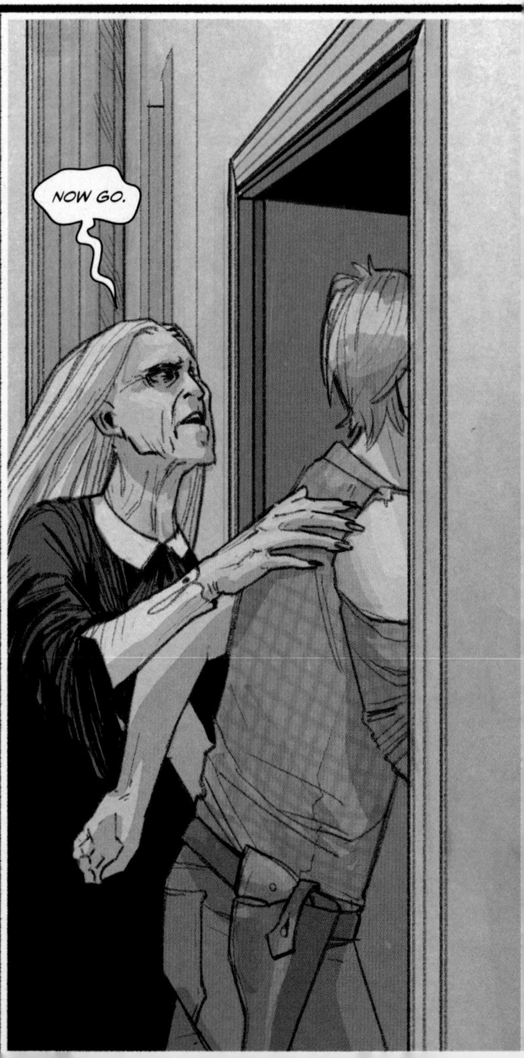
NOW GO.

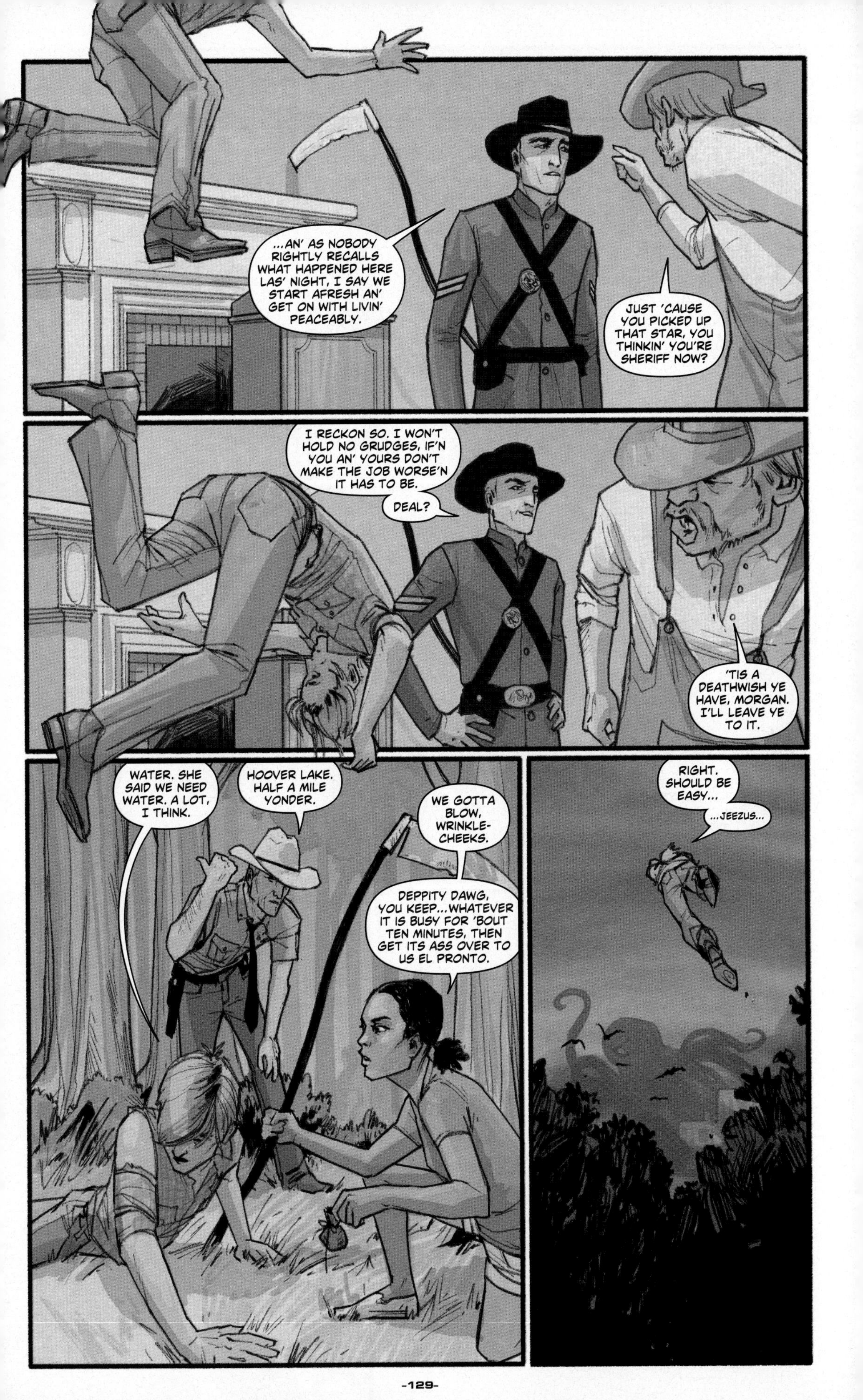
...AN' AS NOBODY RIGHTLY RECALLS WHAT HAPPENED HERE LAS' NIGHT, I SAY WE START AFRESH AN' GET ON WITH LIVIN' PEACEABLY.
JUST 'CAUSE YOU PICKED UP THAT STAR, YOU THINKIN' YOU'RE SHERIFF NOW?
I RECKON SO. I WON'T HOLD NO GRUDGES, IF'N YOU AN' YOURS DON'T MAKE THE JOB WORSE'N IT HAS TO BE.
DEAL?
'TIS A DEATHWISH YE HAVE, MORGAN. I'LL LEAVE YE TO IT.
WATER. SHE SAID WE NEED WATER. A LOT, I THINK.
HOOVER LAKE. HALF A MILE YONDER.
WE GOTTA BLOW, WRINKLE-CHEEKS.
DEPPITY DAWG, YOU KEEP...WHATEVER IT IS BUSY FOR 'BOUT TEN MINUTES, THEN GET ITS ASS OVER TO US EL PRONTO.
RIGHT. SHOULD BE EASY...
...JEEZUS...

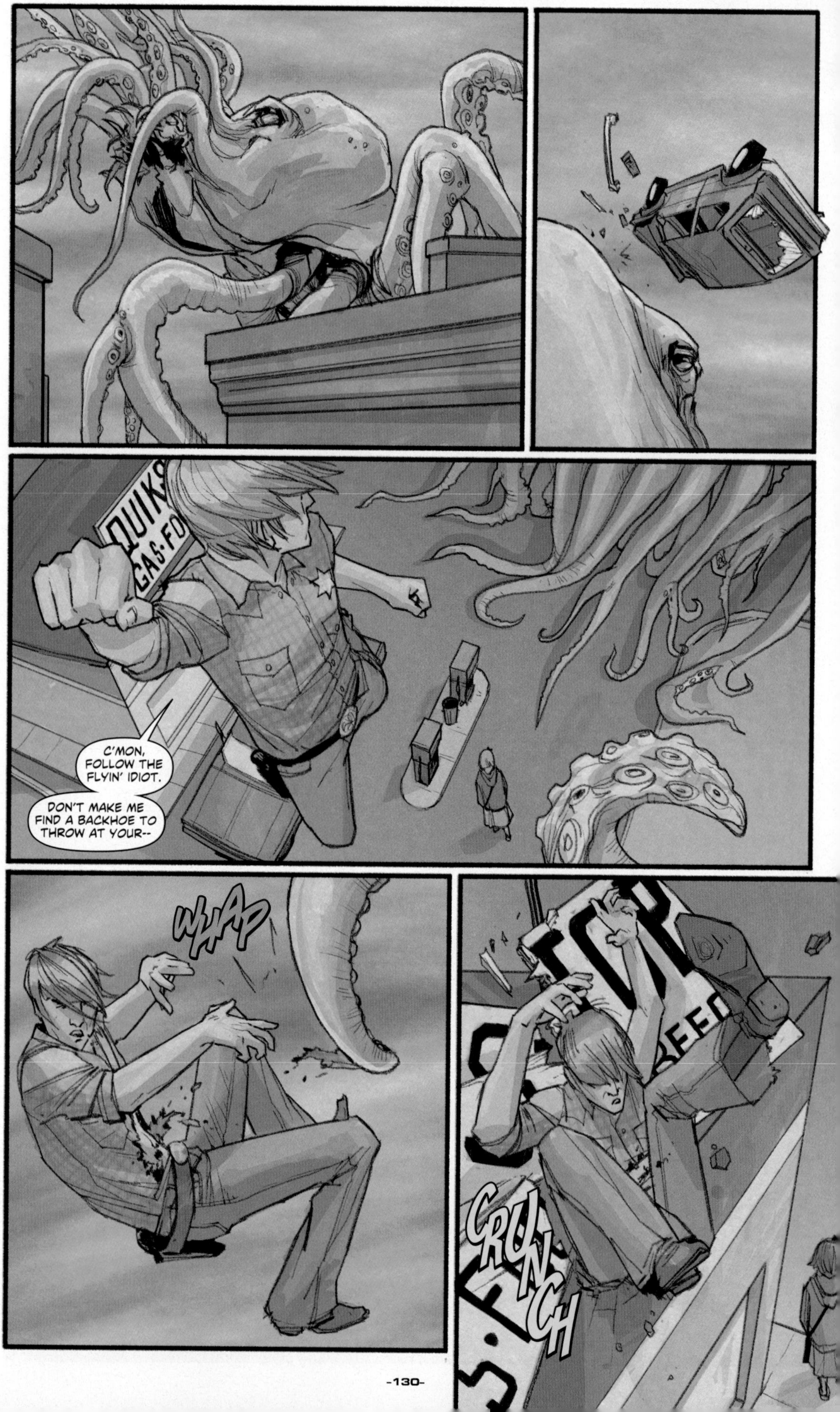
QUIKS
GAS·FO
C'MON, FOLLOW THE FLYIN' IDIOT.
DON'T MAKE ME FIND A BACKHOE TO THROW AT YOUR--
WHAP
CRUNCH

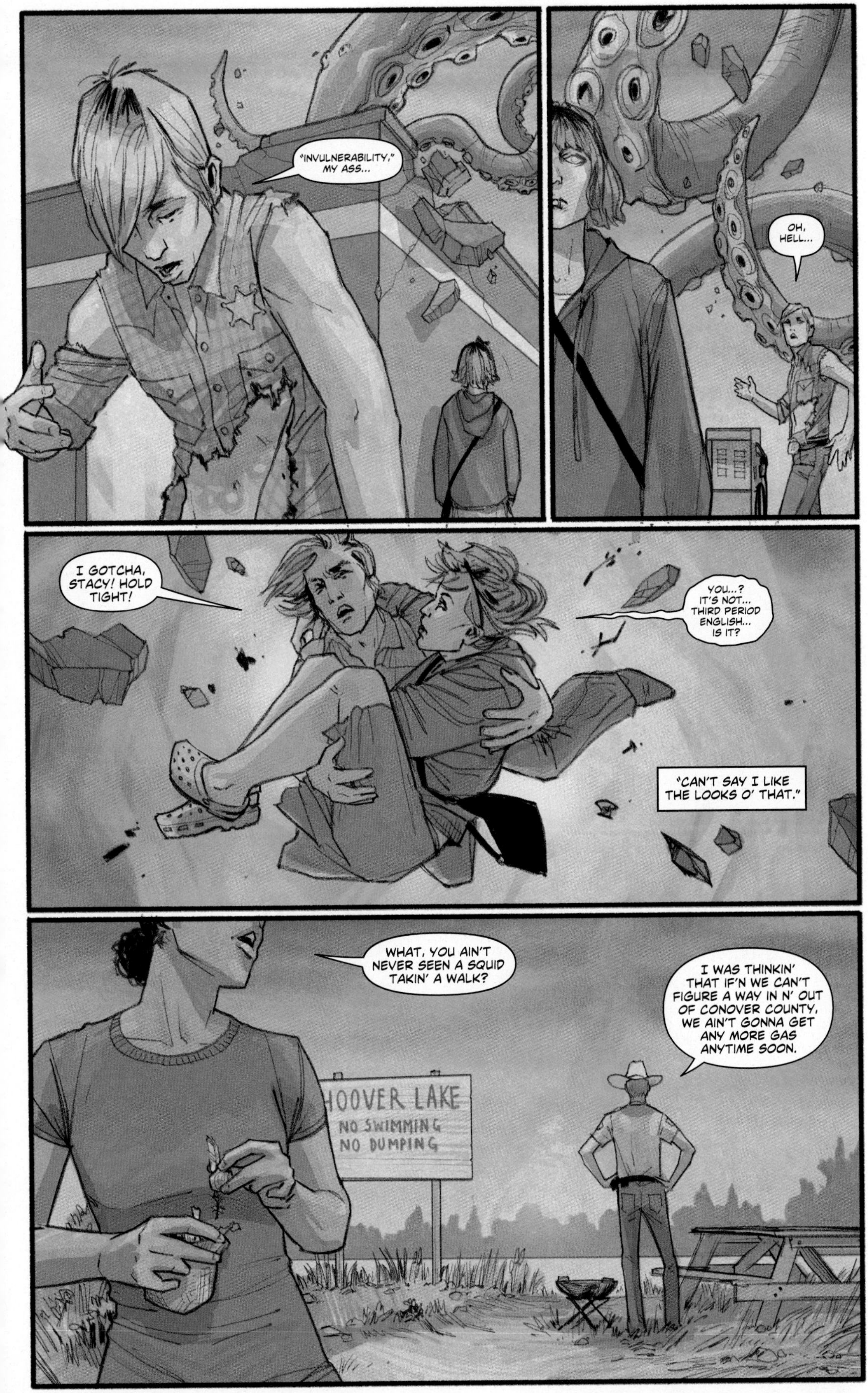
"INVULNERABILITY," MY ASS...
OH, HELL...
I GOTCHA, STACY! HOLD TIGHT!
YOU...? IT'S NOT... THIRD PERIOD ENGLISH... IS IT?
"CAN'T SAY I LIKE THE LOOKS O' THAT."
WHAT, YOU AIN'T NEVER SEEN A SQUID TAKIN' A WALK?
I WAS THINKIN' THAT IF'N WE CAN'T FIGURE A WAY IN N' OUT OF CONOVER COUNTY, WE AIN'T GONNA GET ANY MORE GAS ANYTIME SOON.
HOOVER LAKE
NO SWIMMING
NO DUMPING

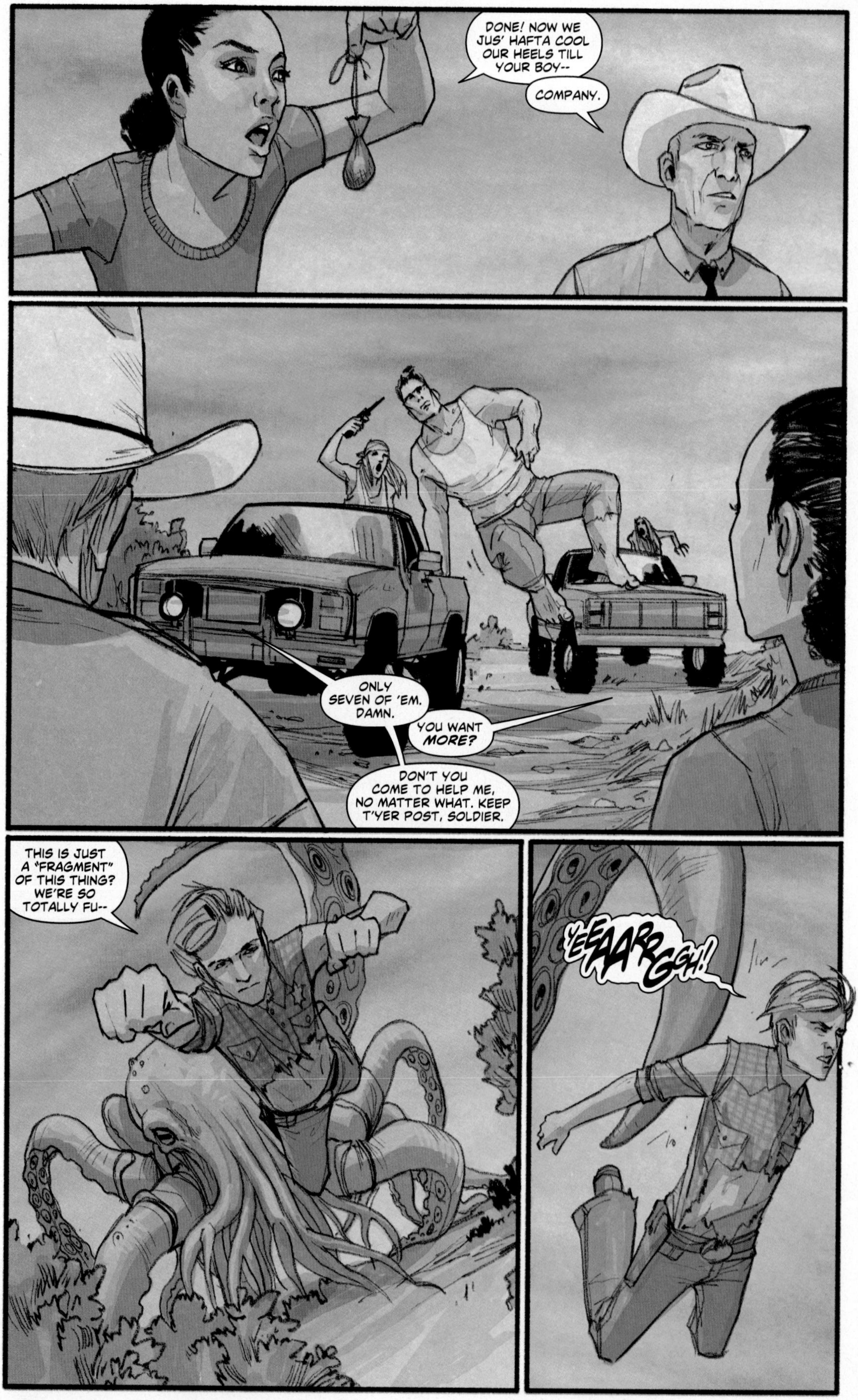
DONE! NOW WE JUS' HAFTA COOL OUR HEELS TILL YOUR BOY--
COMPANY.
ONLY SEVEN OF 'EM. DAMN.
YOU WANT *MORE?*
DON'T YOU COME TO HELP ME, NO MATTER WHAT. KEEP T'YER POST, SOLDIER.
THIS IS JUST A "FRAGMENT" OF THIS THING? WE'RE SO TOTALLY FU--
YEEAAARRGGH!

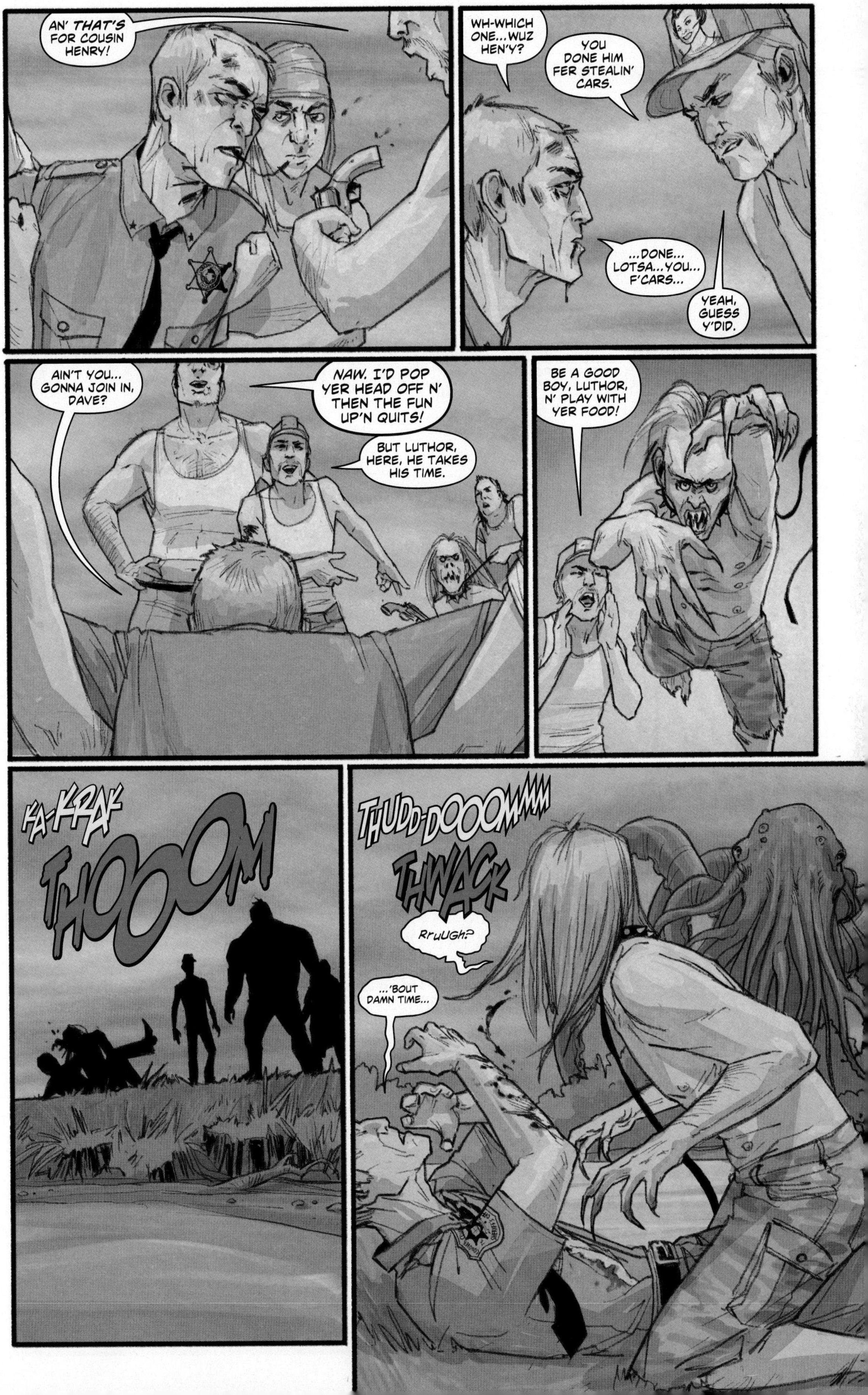

AN' THAT'S FOR COUSIN HENRY!
WH-WHICH ONE...WUZ HEN'Y?
YOU DONE HIM FER STEALIN' CARS.
...DONE... LOTSA...YOU... F'CARS...
YEAH, GUESS Y'DID.
AIN'T YOU... GONNA JOIN IN, DAVE?
NAW. I'D POP YER HEAD OFF N' THEN THE FUN UP'N QUITS!
BUT LUTHOR, HERE, HE TAKES HIS TIME.
BE A GOOD BOY, LUTHOR, N' PLAY WITH YER FOOD!
KA-KRAK
THOOOM
THUDD-DOOOMMM
THWACK
RruUGH?
...'BOUT DAMN TIME...

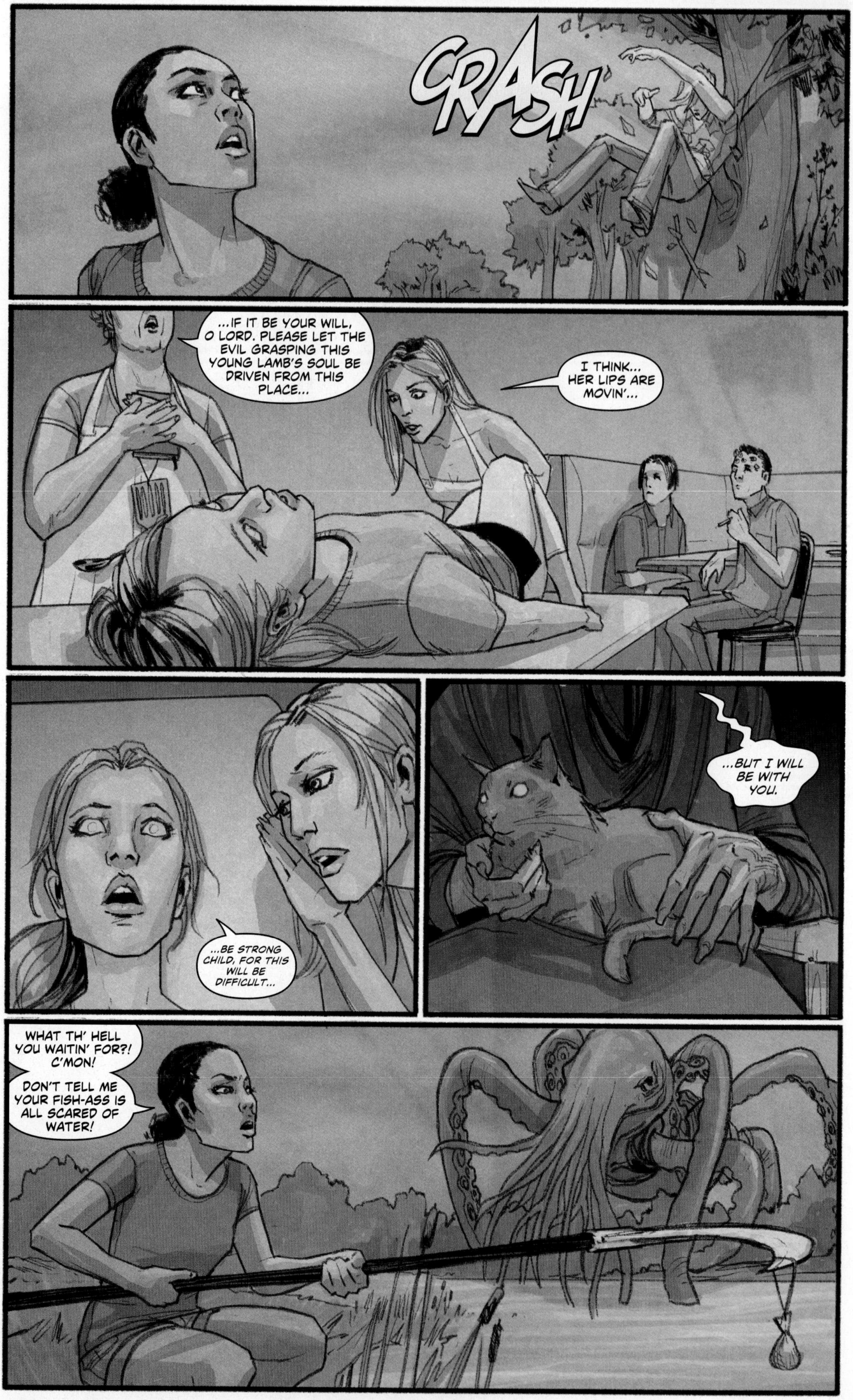
CRASH
...IF IT BE YOUR WILL, O LORD. PLEASE LET THE EVIL GRASPING THIS YOUNG LAMB'S SOUL BE DRIVEN FROM THIS PLACE...
I THINK... HER LIPS ARE MOVIN'...
...BE STRONG CHILD, FOR THIS WILL BE DIFFICULT...
...BUT I WILL BE WITH YOU.
WHAT TH' HELL YOU WAITIN' FOR?! C'MON!
DON'T TELL ME YOUR FISH-ASS IS ALL SCARED OF WATER!

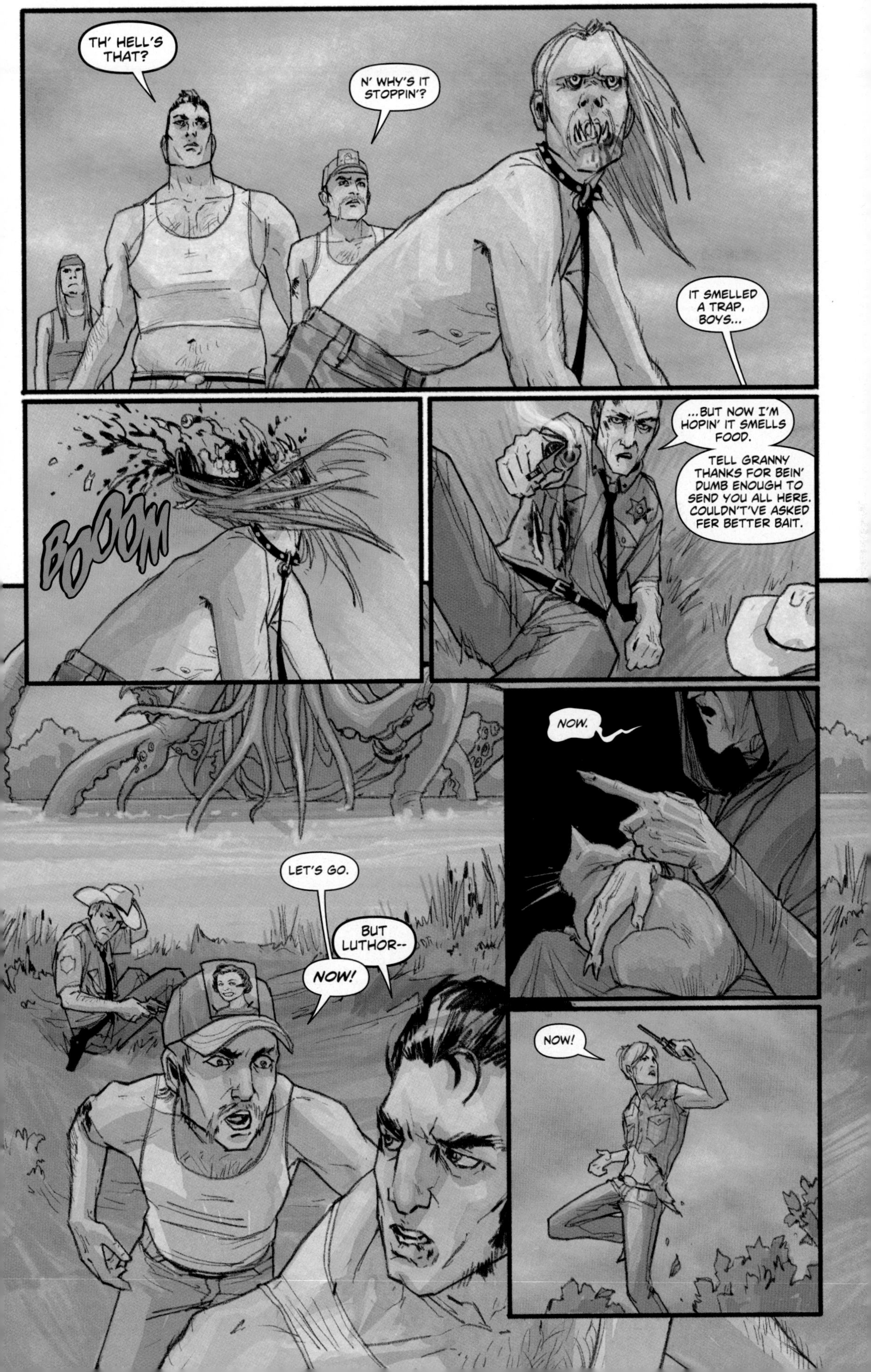
TH' HELL'S THAT?
N' WHY'S IT STOPPIN'?
IT SMELLED A TRAP, BOYS...
BOOOM
...BUT NOW I'M HOPIN' IT SMELLS FOOD.
TELL GRANNY THANKS FOR BEIN' DUMB ENOUGH TO SEND YOU ALL HERE. COULDN'T'VE ASKED FER BETTER BAIT.
NOW.
LET'S GO.
BUT LUTHOR--
NOW!
NOW!

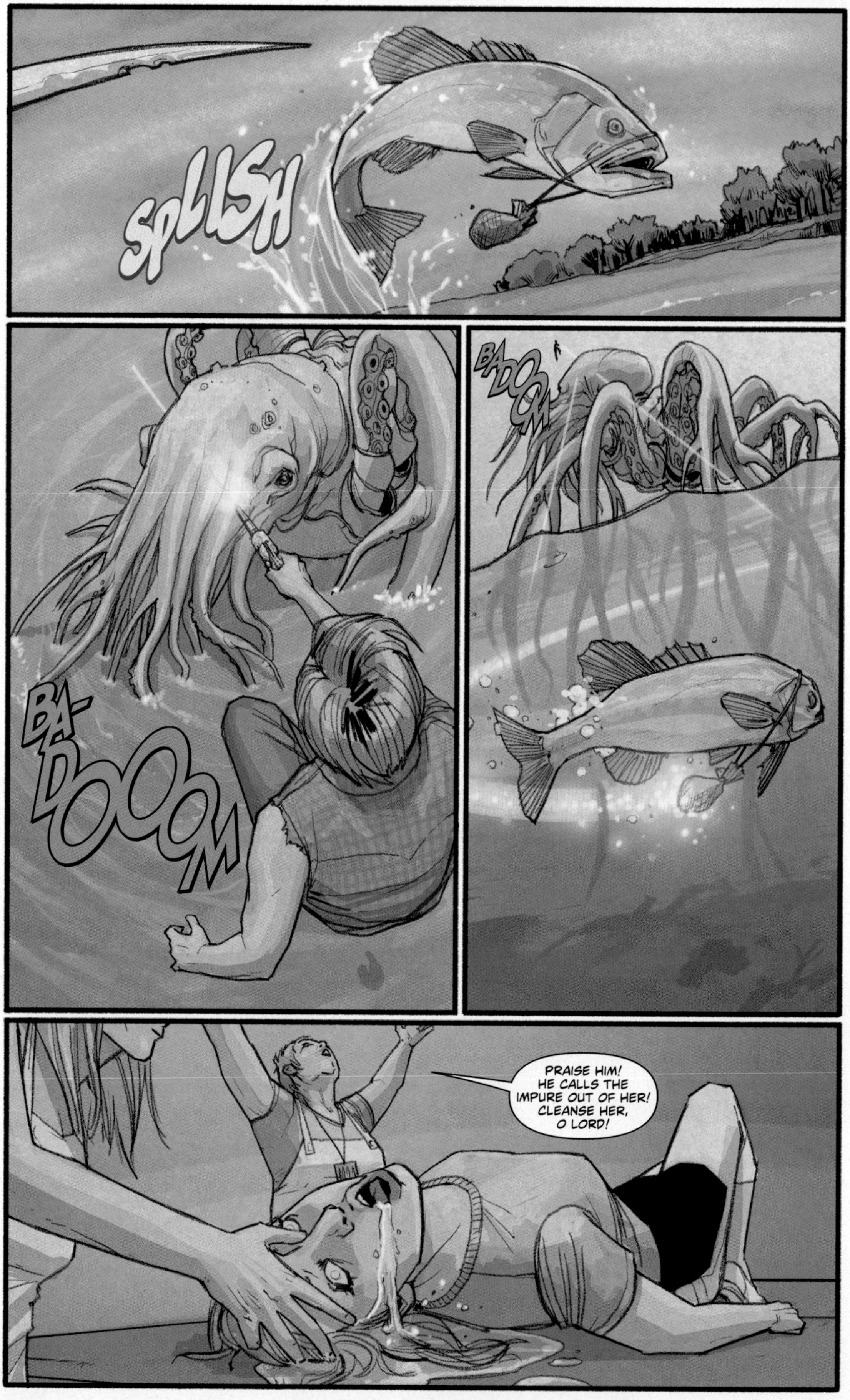
SPLISH
BA-DOOOM
BADOOM
PRAISE HIM! HE CALLS THE IMPURE OUT OF HER! CLEANSE HER, O LORD!

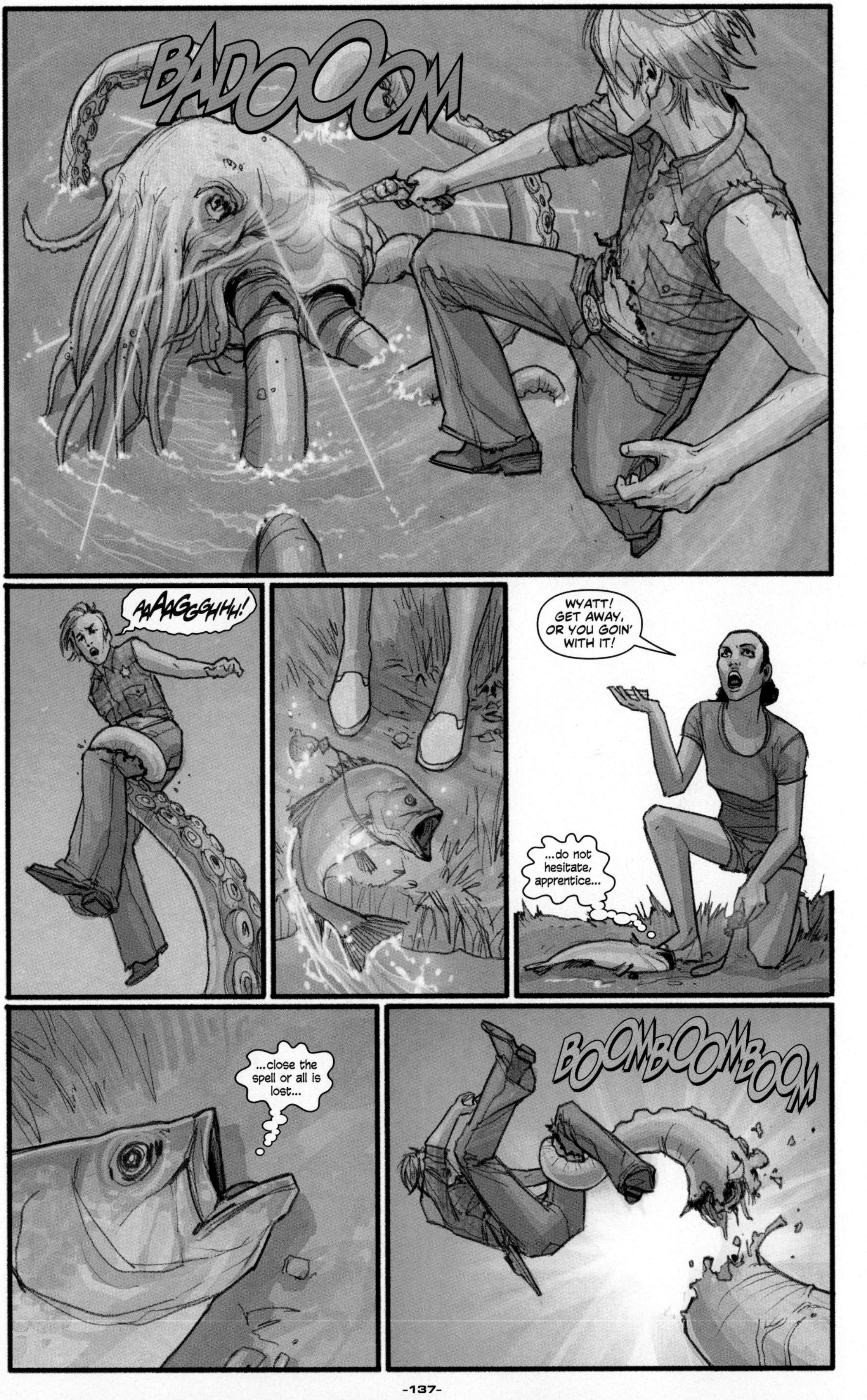
BADOOOOM
AAAAGGGHHH!
WYATT! GET AWAY, OR YOU GOIN' WITH IT!
...do not hesitate, apprentice...
...close the spell or all is lost...
BOOMBOOMBOOM

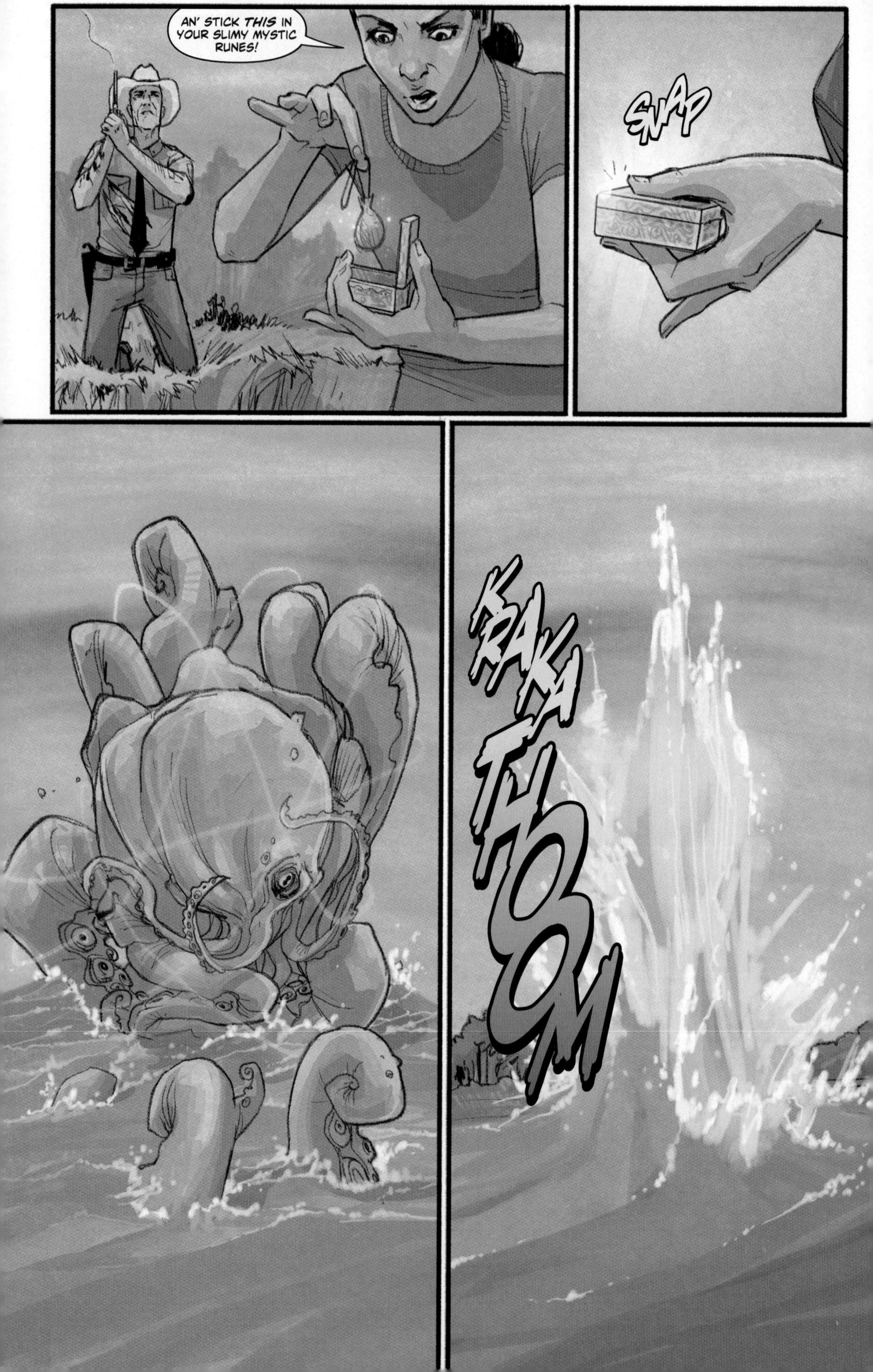
AN' STICK THIS IN YOUR SLIMY MYSTIC RUNES!
SNAP
KRAKA-THOOM

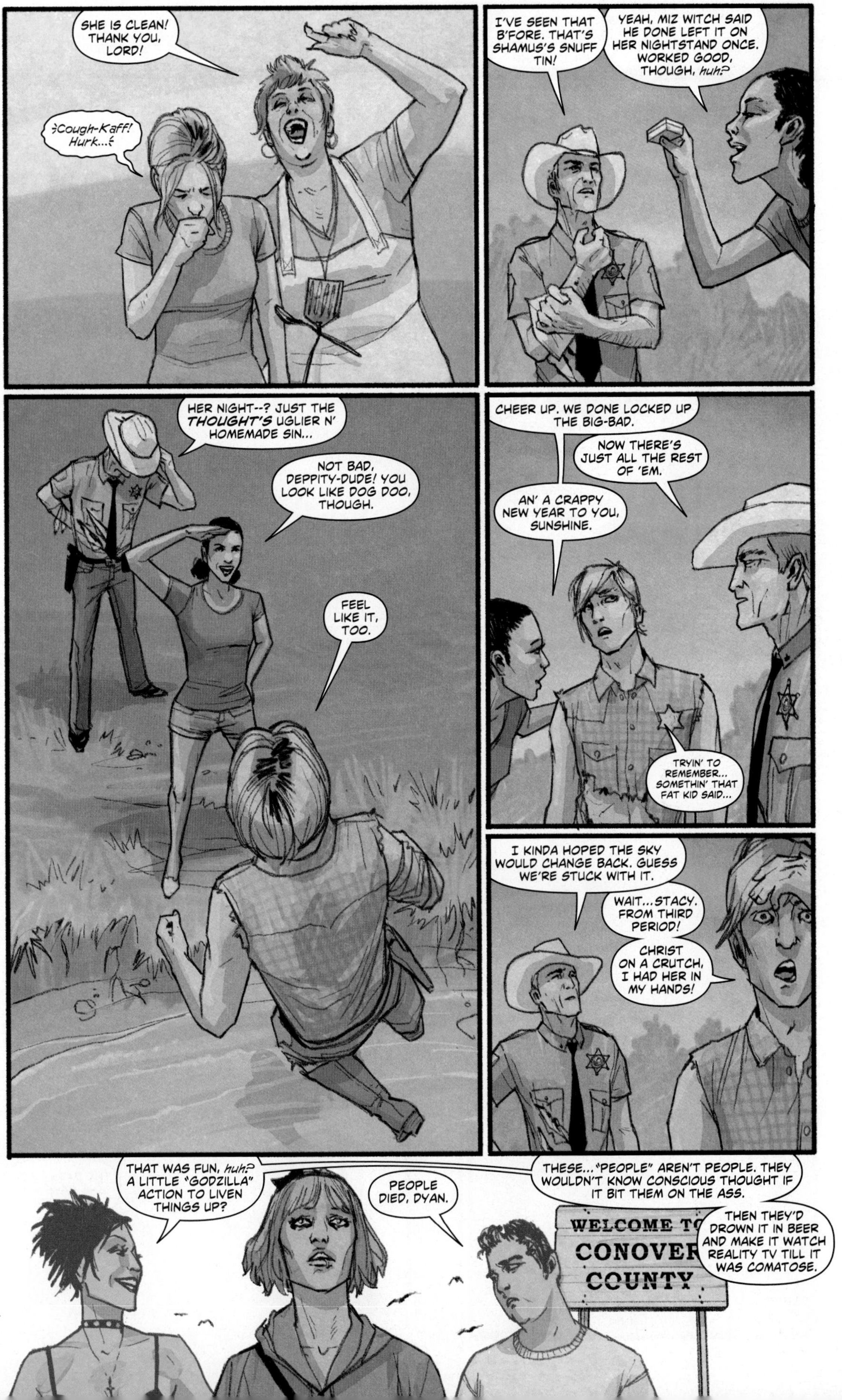
SHE IS CLEAN! THANK YOU, LORD!
Cough-Kaff! Hurk...
I'VE SEEN THAT B'FORE. THAT'S SHAMUS'S SNUFF TIN!
YEAH, MIZ WITCH SAID HE DONE LEFT IT ON HER NIGHTSTAND ONCE. WORKED GOOD, THOUGH, *huh?*
HER NIGHT--? JUST THE ***THOUGHT'S*** UGLIER N' HOMEMADE SIN...
NOT BAD, DEPPITY-DUDE! YOU LOOK LIKE DOG DOO, THOUGH.
FEEL LIKE IT, TOO.
CHEER UP. WE DONE LOCKED UP THE BIG-BAD.
NOW THERE'S JUST ALL THE REST OF 'EM.
AN' A CRAPPY NEW YEAR TO YOU, SUNSHINE.
TRYIN' TO REMEMBER... SOMETHIN' THAT FAT KID SAID...
I KINDA HOPED THE SKY WOULD CHANGE BACK. GUESS WE'RE STUCK WITH IT.
WAIT...STACY. FROM THIRD PERIOD!
CHRIST ON A CRUTCH, I HAD HER IN MY HANDS!
THAT WAS FUN, *huh?* A LITTLE "GODZILLA" ACTION TO LIVEN THINGS UP?
PEOPLE DIED, DYAN.
THESE... "PEOPLE" AREN'T PEOPLE. THEY WOULDN'T KNOW CONSCIOUS THOUGHT IF IT BIT THEM ON THE ASS.
WELCOME TO CONOVER COUNTY
THEN THEY'D DROWN IT IN BEER AND MAKE IT WATCH REALITY TV TILL IT WAS COMATOSE.

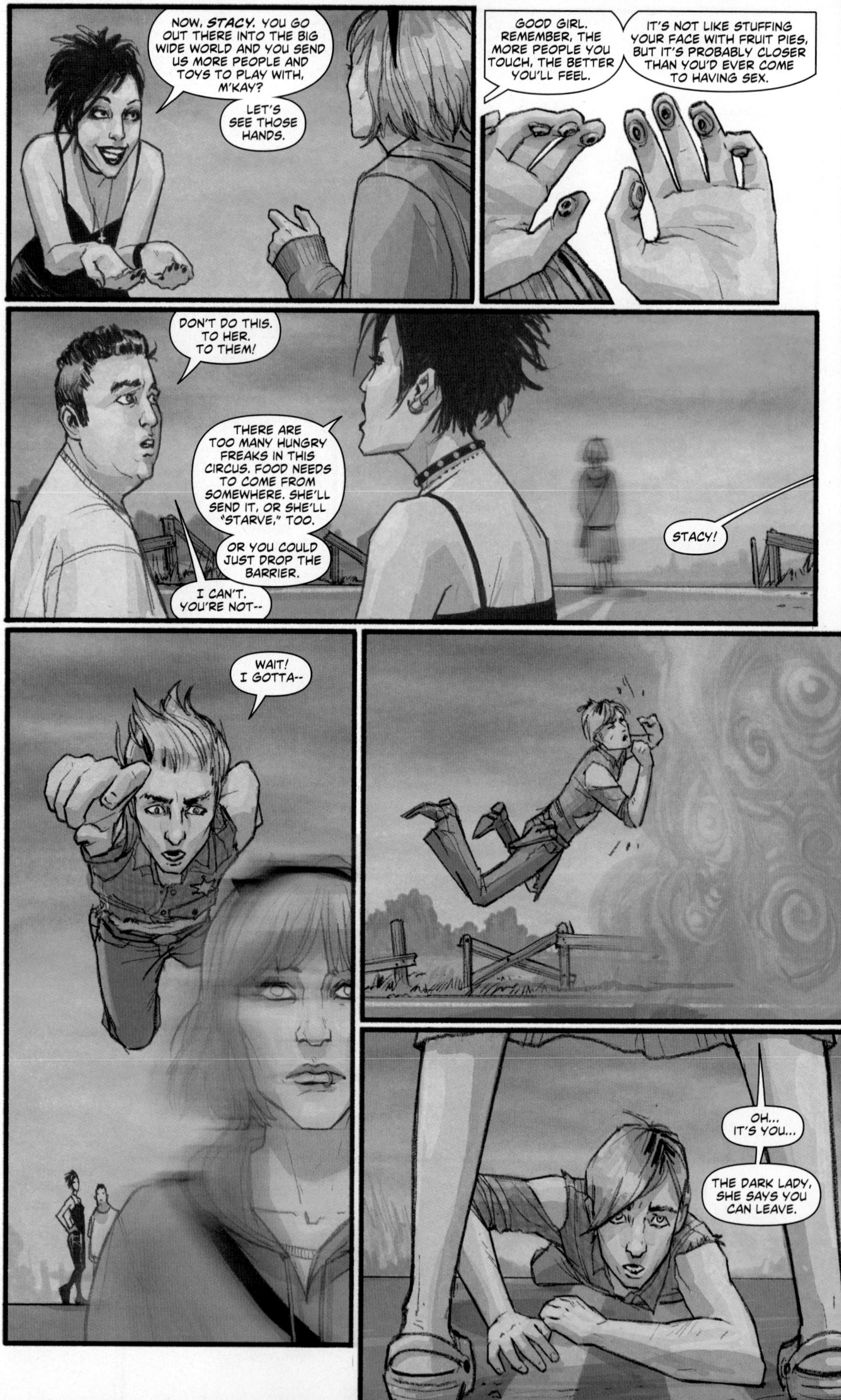
NOW, STACY. YOU GO OUT THERE INTO THE BIG WIDE WORLD AND YOU SEND US MORE PEOPLE AND TOYS TO PLAY WITH, M'KAY?
LET'S SEE THOSE HANDS.
GOOD GIRL. REMEMBER, THE MORE PEOPLE YOU TOUCH, THE BETTER YOU'LL FEEL.
IT'S NOT LIKE STUFFING YOUR FACE WITH FRUIT PIES, BUT IT'S PROBABLY CLOSER THAN YOU'D EVER COME TO HAVING SEX.
DON'T DO THIS. TO HER. TO THEM!
THERE ARE TOO MANY HUNGRY FREAKS IN THIS CIRCUS. FOOD NEEDS TO COME FROM SOMEWHERE. SHE'LL SEND IT, OR SHE'LL "STARVE," TOO.
OR YOU COULD JUST DROP THE BARRIER.
I CAN'T. YOU'RE NOT--
STACY!
WAIT! I GOTTA--
OH... IT'S YOU...
THE DARK LADY, SHE SAYS YOU CAN LEAVE.

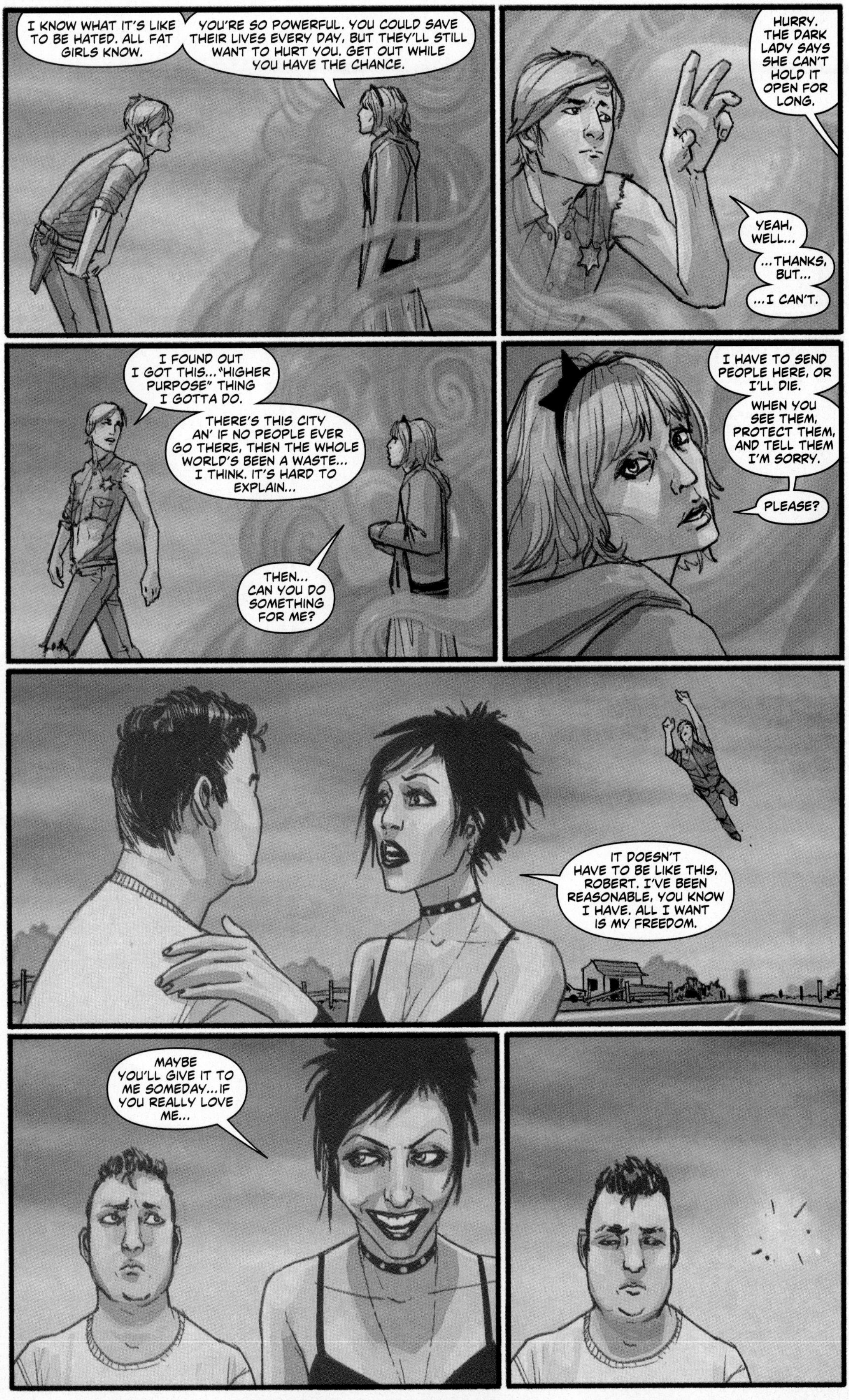
I KNOW WHAT IT'S LIKE TO BE HATED. ALL FAT GIRLS KNOW.
YOU'RE SO POWERFUL. YOU COULD SAVE THEIR LIVES EVERY DAY, BUT THEY'LL STILL WANT TO HURT YOU. GET OUT WHILE YOU HAVE THE CHANCE.
HURRY. THE DARK LADY SAYS SHE CAN'T HOLD IT OPEN FOR LONG.
YEAH, WELL...
...THANKS, BUT...
...I CAN'T.
I FOUND OUT I GOT THIS... "HIGHER PURPOSE" THING I GOTTA DO.
THERE'S THIS CITY AN' IF NO PEOPLE EVER GO THERE, THEN THE WHOLE WORLD'S BEEN A WASTE... I THINK. IT'S HARD TO EXPLAIN...
THEN... CAN YOU DO SOMETHING FOR ME?
I HAVE TO SEND PEOPLE HERE, OR I'LL DIE.
WHEN YOU SEE THEM, PROTECT THEM, AND TELL THEM I'M SORRY.
PLEASE?
IT DOESN'T HAVE TO BE LIKE THIS, ROBERT. I'VE BEEN REASONABLE, YOU KNOW I HAVE. ALL I WANT IS MY FREEDOM.
MAYBE YOU'LL GIVE IT TO ME SOMEDAY...IF YOU REALLY LOVE ME...

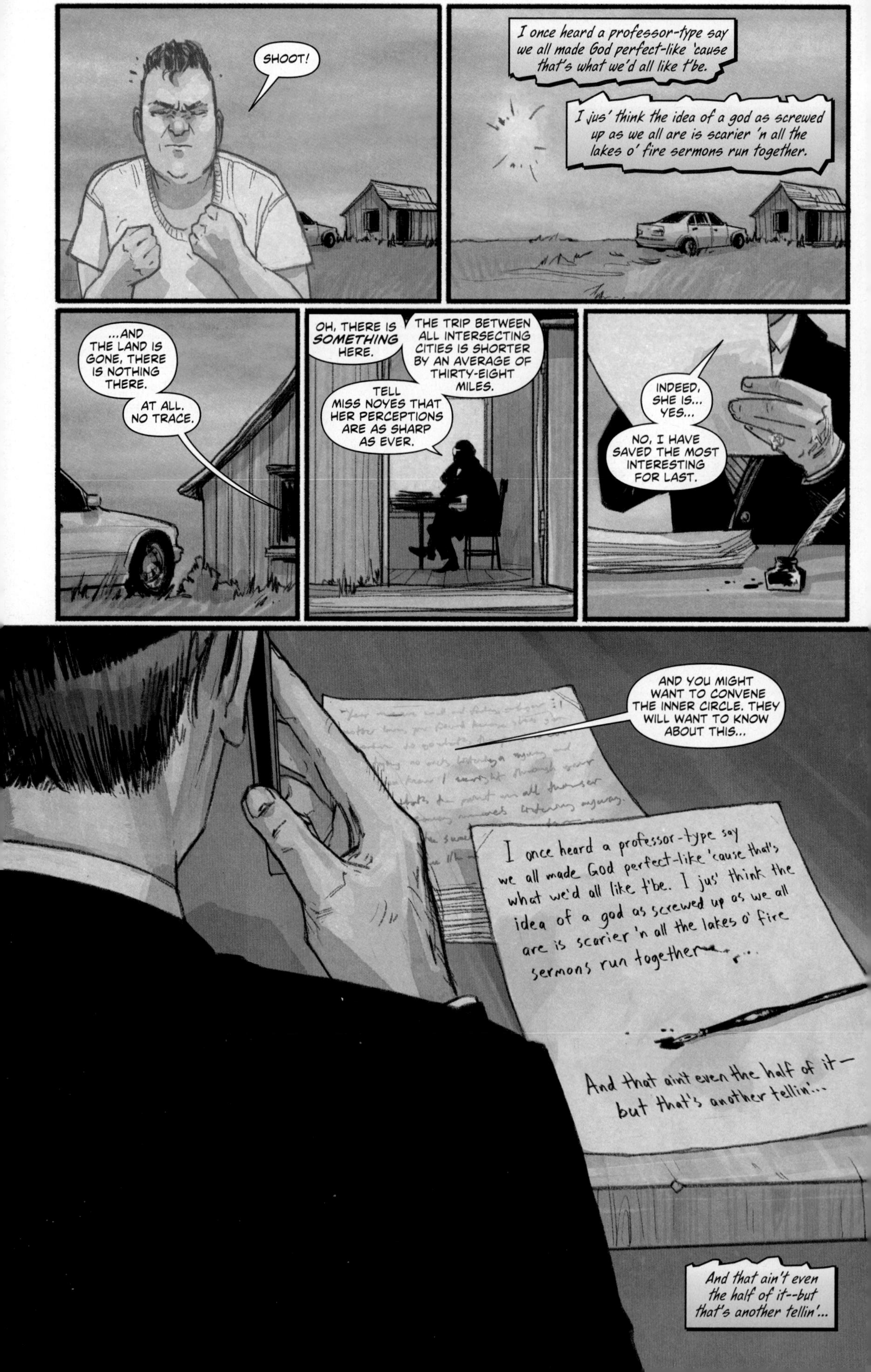
SHOOT!
I once heard a professor-type say we all made God perfect-like 'cause that's what we'd all like t'be.
I jus' think the idea of a god as screwed up as we all are is scarier 'n all the lakes o' fire sermons run together.
...AND THE LAND IS GONE, THERE IS NOTHING THERE.
AT ALL. NO TRACE.
OH, THERE IS *SOMETHING* HERE.
THE TRIP BETWEEN ALL INTERSECTING CITIES IS SHORTER BY AN AVERAGE OF THIRTY-EIGHT MILES.
TELL MISS NOYES THAT HER PERCEPTIONS ARE AS SHARP AS EVER.
INDEED, SHE IS... YES...
NO, I HAVE SAVED THE MOST INTERESTING FOR LAST.
AND YOU MIGHT WANT TO CONVENE THE INNER CIRCLE. THEY WILL WANT TO KNOW ABOUT THIS...
I once heard a professor-type say we all made God perfect-like 'cause that's what we'd all like t'be. I jus' think the idea of a god as screwed up as we all are is scarier 'n all the lakes o' fire sermons run together...
And that ain't even the half of it— but that's another tellin'...
And that ain't even the half of it--but that's another tellin'...

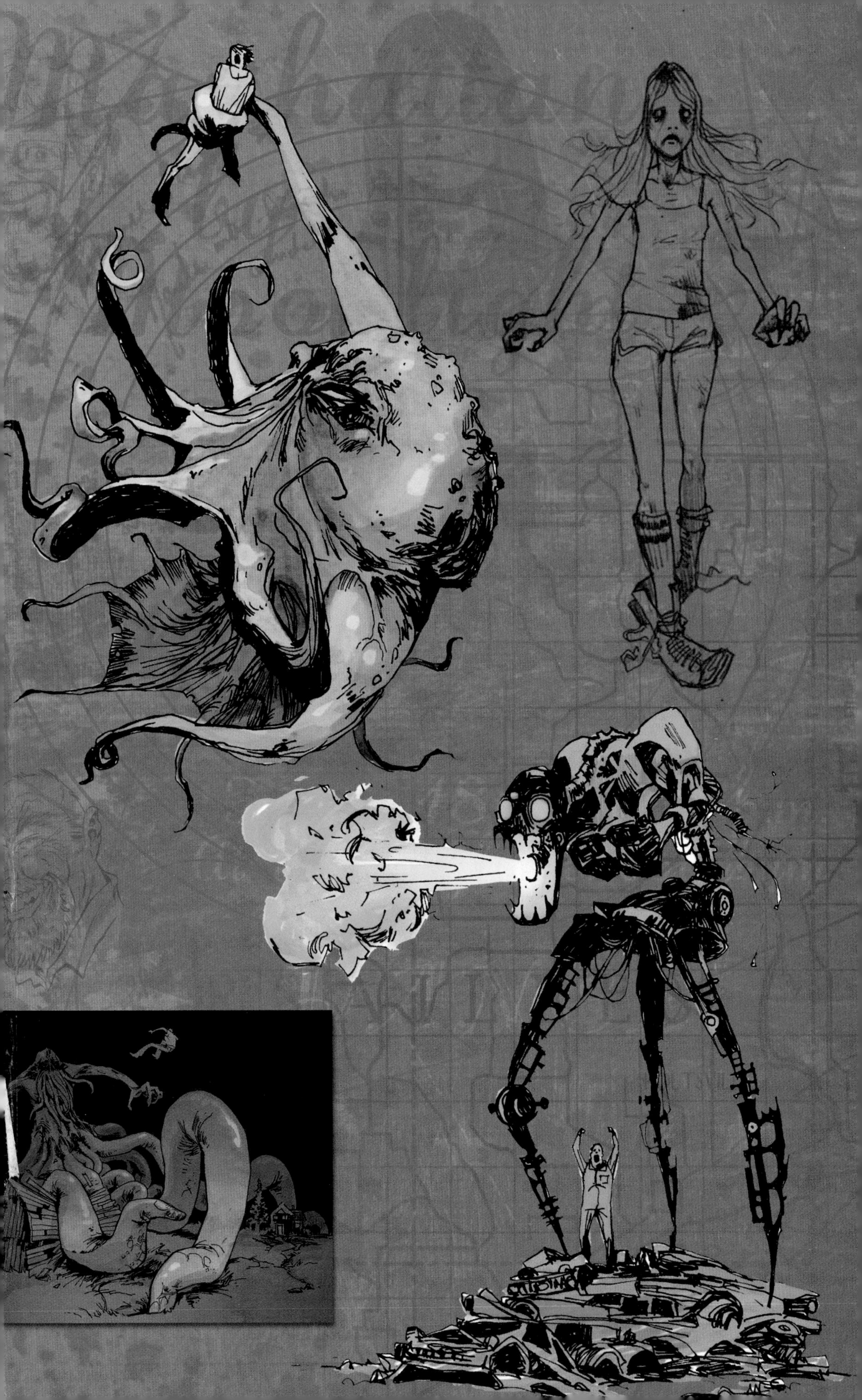

"A sharp-witted gloss on the scientific and sexual obsessions of Victorian society." —TIME

THE LEAGUE OF EXTRAORDINARY GENTLEMEN

Volumes One and Two

Alan Moore and **Kevin O'Neill** present the world's first super-hero team, comprised entirely of characters from classic literature. Thrill to the epic adventures of Captain Nemo, Allan Quatermain, Mina Harker, Dr. Jekyll and Mr. Hyde as they battle evil Asian warlords and invaders from Mars!

More spine-chilling tales...

SUGGESTED FOR MATURE READERS

A GOD SOMEWHERE	MYSTERIUS THE UNFATHOMABLE	SECRET HISTORY OF THE AUTHORITY: HAWKSMOOR

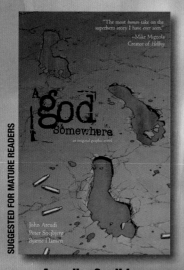

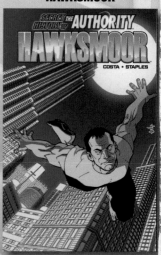

Arcudi • Snejbjerg   **Parker • Fowler**   **Costa • Staples**

SEARCH THE **GRAPHIC NOVELS SECTION** OF
WILDSTORM.COM
FOR ART AND INFORMATION ON ALL OF OUR BOOKS!